STUART SENDALL KING is President Emeritus of Mission Aviation Fellowship Europe. He is a Chartered Aeronautical Engineer and a Fellow of the Royal Aeronautical Society.

After World War II, when he served as an engineer officer in the RAF, he joined the fledgling MAF, flying with MAF's first plane to Africa.

As General Director Stuart saw MAF's work develop across Sudan, Ethiopia, Kenya, Chad and Tanzania. He retired in 1987 and continues to provide consultancy to the mission.

He lives in Folkestone with his wife, Phyllis.

HOPE
HAS WINGS

A story of
Mission Aviation
Fellowship

STUART SENDALL KING

Marshall Pickering
An Imprint of HarperCollinsPublishers

Marshall Pickering is an Imprint of
HarperCollins*Religious*
Part of HarperCollins*Publishers*
77–85 Fulham Palace Road, London W6 8JB

First published in Great Britain
in 1993 by Marshall Pickering

1 3 5 7 9 10 8 6 4 2

A catalogue record for this book is
available from the British Library

ISBN 0551 02551-4

Phototypeset by Intype, London

Printed and bound in Great Britain by
HarperCollinsManufacturing Glasgow

To my wife Phyllis
and our children Rebecca, John and Priscilla
who shared in so many of these experiences.

Also to all our MAF colleagues
who made it possible to reach
countless places with wings of hope.

"Have you not heard? . . .
Those who hope in the Lord . . .
Will soar on wings . . ."

Isaiah 40:28, 31

CONTENTS

PART III

DEVELOPMENT
(1953–1965)

PART IV

PROGRESS AND PAIN
(1965–1980)

PART V

HOPE HAS WINGS
(1980–1993)

ACKNOWLEDGEMENTS

Very many thanks to all those who helped supply information and comments for the contents of this book. Their prompt and enthusiastic assistance has been heartening. Richard Bellamy of MAF produced the excellent maps. I've been grateful to Clive and Elizabeth Langmead for valuable advice from their own experience of writing. I would also like to thank my sister, Joan King, who gladly contributed her editorial expertise throughout the book.

I really don't know how the book would ever have been completed without the teamwork of my wife. She put in months of word processing, discussing, correcting, drafting and redrafting. It's really *our* book, not just mine. I am grateful, too, for the publisher's patience and advice. Finally, I want to express my appreciation for the constant encouragement of the Board and the staff of Mission Aviation Fellowship itself.

PREFACE

All my colleagues in Mission Aviation Fellowship have tremendous stories to tell.

This account is the story of MAF from my own experience. I was privileged to be part of its beginnings and experienced its early challenges and trials. Above all, I've had the encouragement of seeing the results of the work.

To write this story, information covering fifty years has been used: flying logbooks, diaries, personal letters, MAF reports, MAF files and many personal conversations and experiences.

To describe fifty eventful years of MAF in one small book has been a challenge in itself. Because of space what I offer is illustrative, not exhaustive. Many incidents, even some of importance, have had to be omitted. Whole chapters have been thrown away and much of what has been written has had to be cut down to a fraction of the original material. Altogether it's only been possible to tell a tiny percentage of the full story.

I'd liked to have mentioned many more people – people who have contributed very significantly to the work of MAF. However, it's only been possible to refer to a few.

But, I believe that even this contracted story of MAF is an exciting and encouraging one. I trust you will trace in it the things God has done and give Him the glory.

PART I

EARLY HOPES
(1944–1949)

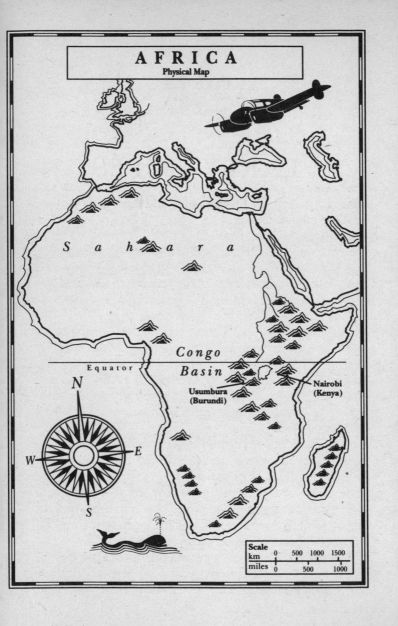

1

Shattered Dreams

The mountains looked beautiful as they rose into the sky around us. Symbols of permanence: awesome, mysterious, dramatic.

We were flying through rising valleys amid the Burundi foothills. Jack Hemmings was beside me at the controls of our sleek little four-seat Gemini aircraft, taking it eastwards from Usumbura towards our headquarters in Nairobi, five hundred miles away. It was Saturday, 10th June 1948, 10.30 a.m.

Six months before, we had left England to make an intensive air and ground survey across a vast tract of central Africa. The last two weeks, in Ruanda and Burundi, had been particularly punishing. Early mornings and late nights, hours on the ground in the tropical heat, constant moving from place to place, had left us dog-tired.

But there was still much to be done and we were determined to press on to Nairobi by nightfall to prepare for the last phase. We were trying to conserve fuel, since to stop for more would involve wasting a night on the ground (our plane was not equipped for night flying). So, rather than gaining height quickly, we were climbing slowly and steadily.

My rather weary eyes scanned the cockpit instrument panel. The altimeter read 7500 feet: all right so far, though we would need still more height to clear

the mountains ahead. The engine tachometers
showed 2500 revolutions per minute, the maximum
for continuous climb. The needle on the rate-of-climb
indicator was recording an ascent of 320 feet per
minute, the most we could achieve at this altitude
with our two small Cirrus engines.

I glanced down at the green slopes of the ascending
valley floor beneath. Patches of broad-leaved banana
trees covered the hills on both sides as we flew. To
anyone on the ground the little silver plane, glinting
in the African sun, must have appeared very small
and fragile against the towering mountain walls.
Looking around, I sensed that frailty. We seemed so
tiny, vulnerable and fleeting, the mountains so
immense and unchangeable.

Jack's eyes were fixed firmly on the horizon in
front. About fifteen miles away loomed a final long
ridge, a thousand feet above us and right across our
flight path. We estimated that, by the time we
reached it, we should be high enough to cross it. A
strong headwind was blowing over the hills towards
us and progress had been rather slow, but much of
the mountainside was now behind us and we
had successfully crossed several transverse
ridges.

As we approached this last and highest of them,
still needing to climb, our engines were running steadily. Suddenly Jack called out, concern, if not alarm,
in his voice:

"What's happening? We're not gaining altitude."
He pushed the throttles fully open. I looked at the
rate-of-climb indicator and didn't believe what I saw.
It was registering zero.

"What's wrong with it?" I demanded.

A moment later the needle had swung down yet further, pointing to a descent of 300 feet a minute. We still couldn't believe it. The engines were straining at full power. How could we be losing height and at such a rate? This was not a situation we'd ever encountered with powerful military aircraft in the war.

"We're in down currents!" Jack sounded tense. The wind was swirling over the final ridge, sweeping down the mountainside and pushing us relentlessly towards the valley floor. Unless we could escape very quickly we'd hit the ground.

"I'm turning out of this." Jack swiftly banked the plane around. "We'd better get back to Usumbura and think again."

Extremely disappointing, but all was not lost.

As we flew down the centre of a valley we realized with horror that we were still losing height. We barely skimmed over a ridge we had crossed with ease on our way up. Suddenly I winced as I felt a brief splintering jerk. The end of the starboard wing had caught and broken off the top of a banana tree, foliage flying in the air. Then I saw that nine inches of the wing tip had disappeared, too. It was a shock, but we'd known many planes limp home with far worse damage during the war. At least we were clear – and still airborne.

"We can still get back to Usumbura and repair that wing," I called. Jack didn't hear. His whole attention was concentrated on avoiding another ridge just ahead. In vain. A cloud of dirt and debris enveloped us as we smashed into it. The Gemini's wooden propellers struck the ground and shattered. The wings twisted and broke. The tail snapped. The plane slewed round and slid down the hillside where it stuck, a silent splintered wreck.

Mercifully the cabin and rear fuselage had remained intact. But, with our fuel tanks still almost full there was an imminent danger of fire. We scrambled out as quickly as we could, bruised and scratched but otherwise unhurt. There was no fire.

We stood staring incredulously at the wreckage of the plane. It was amazing that, by the grace of God, we were still alive.

It had all begun four years earlier with Murray Kendon, a New Zealander who was flying with RAF Coastal Command in World War II. Long hours on patrol over the grey waters of the Atlantic had given him plenty of time to ponder.

He thought about the power and versatility of aircraft; of all the Coastal Command planes on patrol; of bomber, transport, fighter and ground-attack aircraft. Command of the skies had been decisive in the Battle of Britain, the Mediterranean, North Africa, Asia and the more recent invasion of Europe. Man had learned to fly: was such knowledge and experience to be devoted only to conflict?

From childhood, Murray had had the privilege and influence of a Christian family. He'd felt a particular concern for the millions of people who lived, impoverished and fear-ridden, in isolated places – mountains, deserts, jungles or swamps. He was convinced that more should be done to reach them. He believed that planes could be used to bring them help and hope. To show them God's love. To do so in partnership with overseas churches and missions.

But how could it be done? Murray felt strongly that

aviation shouldn't normally be taken on as a sideline by missions, even where it was greatly needed. Such an approach would be neither efficient nor safe. It was a task for specialists.

The Mildmay Movement was an organization based in the Mildmay Park area of Islington, London. It had been founded by Dr Thomas Cochrane (previously a pioneer medical missionary in China), to encourage fresh initiatives in Christian outreach all over the world. Murray knew of its work, so he visited Dr Cochrane, hoping that Mildmay might be interested in developing the use of aircraft.

Dr Cochrane listened closely. He responded to Murray immediately: "What woud be the chance of your coming to start this at once? It will be a full-time job for somebody. Is that somebody you?"

Murray was shaken. The positive response was encouraging, but the immediate challenge threw him. He'd shortly be out of the Air Force and was soon to marry an English girl, expecting to take her home to New Zealand where he planned to continue Christian work. He'd certainly not thought about staying in England. He was not one to sidestep a challenge, but was this challenge really from God?

He struggled and thought and prayed. Eventually it became clear: God had given him not only the vision but also the call to make it a reality.

He obtained permission to be demobilized in England, rather than New Zealand. He moved to the Mildmay Centre with Minnie, now his wife, and began work. He decided to call the new organization

Missionary Aviation Fellowship. It soon became known simply as MAF.

While Murray had been patrolling the Atlantic, Jack Hemmings had been flying with the Air Force in India and I'd been an engineer officer with an RAF fighter squadron in Europe. In those days we were both far too busy to look beyond our immediate tasks.

But neither of us was to remain long untouched by Murray's ideas.

2

RAF and MAF

"We don't want you as a pilot," said the Wing Commander crisply. "We want you as an engineer officer." It was 1941, early in World War II, and I was before an RAF selection board.

I looked at him rather glumly. He explained: "We can train a pilot in six months in wartime – it takes us three years to train an engineer officer."

I'd been a member of the University Air Squadron in Cardiff while studying for a degree in engineering. Having graduated at nineteen, I had volunteered with high hopes of becoming an RAF pilot. But it was wartime; I had to go where I was needed.

By June 1944 I'd been in the RAF for almost three years. Now the D-Day landings had come. The invasion of France was beginning. As the engineer officer for 247 Fighter Squadron I had sailed from Portsmouth with my aircraft servicing unit, part of a convoy of staff and equipment of the Second Tactical Air Force. After landing we were to prepare as quickly as possible for the arrival of our aircraft.

The early morning light was murky with smoke. Through the haze the flat beach at Courseilles-sur-Mer lay ahead of us, drab and hostile, rising into grass-tufted sand dunes beyond. The enemy was there.

Along the smoke-filled coastline lay our own battle-ships, destroyers and frigates. Above them floated hundreds of squat grey barrage balloons, their defensive securing cables tied to the warships below. German aircraft were diving on the ships. Noise was continuous: the roar of aircraft, the bursting of bombs, the crackle of machine guns and the barking "woof" of anti-aircraft fire.

Our small landing craft edged to the shore. Its bows dropped down to form a ramp. We drove our Jeep out over it, followed by our Bedford trucks loaded with men and equipment, and clawed our way up the beach towards the flat fields of Normandy. The fighting raged on around us.

Within an hour we were in a cornfield, near the small village of Coulombs, where a heavy wire-matting aircraft landing strip had already been laid. As we set up our tents and unloaded our supplies, a German Messerschmitt 109, chased by a British Spitfire, roared low above us. Anti-aircraft fire from our surrounding army units blotched the sky with angry black puffs of smoke. Shells from a naval battleship screamed overhead towards the enemy positions a few hundred yards beyond us. One fell short, near our tents. Mercifully it didn't explode.

Our squadron aircraft flew in: formidable, heavy single-seater Hawker Typhoons, their task to knock out enemy transport and tanks. Many of our pilots were lost in dangerous low-level operations, some shot down almost over our heads as they attacked the close front-line targets. For almost two months we remained pinned down in our narrow beachhead, shelled, strafed and occasionally sniped at. Then, sup-

ported by aerial bombardment, the Allied troops
began to break out.

We raced to get our squadron to Holland to support
the ill-fated airborne landings at Arnhem. There we
found the sky thick with RAF transport planes trying
to drop supplies to the beleaguered bridgehead, thick
also with assaulting German fighter aircraft. Our own
Typhoons joined in.

We stayed in Holland some months. As dawn broke
on 1st January 1945 I was already out, seeing to the
early morning preparations of our squadron. Suddenly
some words from the Bible unexpectedly flashed
through my mind. "The angel of the Lord encamps
around those who fear Him, and delivers them." At
the same moment dozens of Focke-Wulf fighters
came diving across our airfield with blazing guns and
roaring cannon. They swept back and forth low above
us raking everything with fire. Our own planes had
no chance of taking off. Together with my flight
sergeant I threw myself to the ground. We lay flat on
our stomachs next to our wooden dispersal hut. A
Focke-Wulf cannon shell splintered through its timbers two feet above my head. Around us the whole
airfield was in chaos, smoke rising, planes full of
holes, transport vehicles ablaze. The smell of burning
oil filled the air. As soon as the attacking planes
disappeared we rushed to get the injured to hospital.
A few of our maintenance staff were among them,
some already dying.

This was the Luftwaffe's last throw. Their fuel supplies exhausted, they were virtually grounded. With
supremacy in the skies the Allies moved northwards
into Germany. Five months later the war in Europe
ended.

Our squadron stayed for a while in northern Germany, but I was allowed a couple of weeks' home leave and spent part of it at a young people's holiday conference at the Lee Abbey Christian Centre in North Devon, thoroughly enjoying myself. Then one day the leader, with cheerful confidence, asked me before the epilogue to tell them all that night what it had meant to me to be a Christian while serving in the RAF.

Help! I thought and looked away. My Christian faith was real, but I didn't feel it had made as much practical difference in my life as it should have done. Ashamed, I looked back at him: "I'm sorry," I mumbled, "I don't think I can."

At the end of the epilogue on the final evening the leader asked, "Will those who want God really to take and control their lives, please stand."

I knew I couldn't live a halfway Christian life any longer. I stood – I had to. That moment at Lee Abbey was a turning point in my life: things were never the same afterwards.

At twenty-five, I had six years of war service behind me. Like many others, I wanted to see a lasting peace. But, even more than that, I wanted to see people find the peace of God in their hearts. I'd been given it. What could be more important and exciting than sharing it?

I was back in Germany when I first heard of MAF. My mother, a close friend of the Cochranes, sent me a copy of *The Mildmay Outlook* with an article by Murray Kendon in it. I was immediately interested and wrote to Mildmay giving them a lot of advice on technical aspects. After all, I'd had a lot of experience in the RAF . . .

Soon after our squadron returned to England I was notified by the Air Ministry that I'd been selected for a permanent commission in the RAF. I was really interested and excited about this. By that time I had become well-adjusted to Air Force life. The modern aircraft, the scope for the future, the opportunities for technical advance, the personnel management involved, were all very challenging to me.

I had also a second, quite different, possibility. Since childhood I'd been fascinated by the design and construction of aeroplanes. I'd read about them avidly and made and flew many models. Now an opportunity came to fulfil my dream of doing post-graduate work in aeronautical engineering and going into aircraft design or research. I had been accepted for these studies at the newly formed Cranfield College of Aeronautics.

At this point I discovered Mildmay were less interested in my advice than in me. Dr Cochrane wrote back asking if I would be prepared to join the new organization. Like Murray Kendon, I hadn't bargained for that: like him, I had other plans and was uncertain about this call. So when I opened the letter from Mildmay suggesting I should join the embryonic MAF, I was far from enthusiastic.

I now had to face three choices instead of just two. Of them all, MAF appeared the most uncertain, the least attractive. "It'll probably mean getting grease up to my elbows in a struggle to maintain old, cheap little aeroplanes in remote, sweaty parts of the world," I said to myself. The prospect was hardly alluring. It didn't seem to offer anything like the technical challenges or fulfilment of the other opportunities. "And besides," my thoughts ran, "MAF is still just a dream. Will it ever materialize?"

I talked the matter over with friends and acquaint-
ances. Most of them were sceptical about MAF. Some
were scathing: "A 'South Sea Bubble' – a wild idea
that will soon burst and vanish." "Just a bunch of
young ex-Air Force men wanting to perpetuate the
flying they've learned in the war." Others encouraged
me towards the alternatives: "Better to go into the
aeronautical profession – you will have good opportunities." "We need Christians in the Air Force, why
don't you stay there?"

After much thought and prayer I concluded that I
should accept the permanent commission in the RAF.
God had provided the opportunity; surely He meant
me to take it.

It was necessary to phone the Air Ministry and
confirm my acceptance. I can still picture the old-
fashioned red phone box near where I was staying at
that time. Stepping into it, I dialled the first digits.
Then I stopped. Something felt wrong. This is stupid,
I thought. I started to dial again but again something
– or Someone – stopped me. After a third try I gave
up.

The strong springs on the phone box door snapped
it shut behind me. And with them closed the door to
the Royal Air Force. Were they the springs of God?
If so, where next? There was still my longed-for opportunity for advanced studies in aeronautical design; a
government grant, available because of my war
service, made it doubly attractive.

Yet I knew what whatever was God's will for my
life was best. And I was scared of missing His best.
Over the next days and months I asked for His direction.

It had been my habit to take time every morning before breakfast to read a passage from the Bible and to pray about it. This had become very important to me. The wisdom, the encouragement, the guidance of the great Book of Books was as vital to my life as aviation fuel to an aircraft's engine.

I had been going through the Epistle to the Hebrews. One morning I reached chapter eleven. It was not a case of trying to pick out some special promise to meet my dilemma. But I read: "By faith Abraham . . . went out . . . not knowing where he was going . . ." In a flash, I knew that that verse was for me. My future was not to be with the known RAF, or with the established aircraft industry. It was to be with something still unknown. I had to step out in faith.

Once again I was in the phone box, this time calling Murray Kendon: "I've made my decision, Murray, I believe I should join MAF."

I found out later that, for several months in the MAF office, they'd been praying hard that I'd know God's will.

3

Planes

As soon as I decided to join MAF, I began to learn to
fly. Like many wartime pilots, I did this in a de Havilland Tiger Moth. The little wood, wire and fabric
biplane was the most famous training aircraft ever
built. Though not easy to fly well, some still consider
it the classic aircraft in which to qualify as a pilot. I
remember the excitement of the open cockpit, the
close-fitting leather helmet, the wartime RAF gog-
gles, the instructor shouting through the Gosport
communication tubes.

The Tiger Moth was fully aerobatic. You always
wore a parachute strapped to you so that it formed
your seat cushion. The plane was quite primitive: no
brakes, no radio, no tailwheel (only a skid), no flaps,
no refinements at all. When you landed you got the
tail down and the skid quickly dragged the plane to
a halt. As you flew, the wind blasted around the
cockpit. If you tried to look out sideways you felt as
though the slipstream would pull the skin off your
cheekbones. In those days one of the first manoeuvres
to learn was the spin, the idea being that, in case of
an accidental spin, the ability to get out of it would
avoid a graveyard spiral to earth.

Whenever we came in to land my instructor would
yell: "Round out at the height of the top of a bus!"
To this day I don't know whether he meant a double-

or a single-decker. Maybe that's why my landings
were somewhat erratic.

I went solo after eleven hours and soon after took
my pilot's licence. In those days, provided you passed
the exams and the flying tests, you could get a licence
with incredibly few flying hours. Mine read "All land-
planes up to 12500 pounds in weight."

I was sometimes to fly as pilot during survey flights
in the early days of MAF. I loved it. But, for me, it
was only a sideline. My usual part was that of radio
operator or navigator. I was to log more than 2000
hours in these various capacities. MAF requires pilots
with full professional licences. I was a professional
engineer but only an amateur pilot.

At the Mildmay Centre an "Operations Room" was
allocated to MAF, and Murray was joined by a few
willing helpers. It was around this time that Jack
Hemmings first appeared on the scene. In India, as a
squadron leader, he'd won the Air Force Cross. A
friend there had lent him a *Mildmay Magazine* containing a brief news item about MAF. Intrigued, he
wrote to learn more but got no reply.

On his return to England for demobilization he
dropped in at Mildmay just to find out what was
happening, only to be told by Murray that they were
all on the point of going away for two weeks. Perhaps
Jack would like to keep an eye on things till they
returned? One thing led to another – there was always
so much to be done. The two weeks grew into
months, the months into years. Jack became an indis-
pensable part of the infant MAF. He was to prove
a staunch friend and colleague in the critical days
ahead.

One of the first tasks to be tackled was to gain interest, prayer and support among churches and individuals in the UK. To that end Murray and Jack wrote articles, took meetings and made all the contacts they could.

But where was a missionary air service to begin? Many places, even as far afield as China, were carefully considered.

"I feel the initial focus of our work should be Africa," Murray told Dr Cochrane eventually.

They all agreed to send an extensive questionnaire to more than a hundred African mission stations, enquiring about travel needs and conditions. The secretary of the Congo Protestant Council, representing forty missions, wrote encouraging MAF to make a survey there and individual missionaries also expressed real interest. Jack, however, detected a note of caution in the responses:

"They want to know if the idea of aviation is a good thing in itself. If it is, they then want to know: 'Is MAF a good thing?' "

On large maps of Africa he plotted hundreds of mission stations in Kenya, Uganda, Tanganyika, Congo, Ruanda and Burundi and what was then French Equatorial Africa, with other areas as well. It was a mammoth, eye-straining task. Word soon got round that MAF had detailed maps showing mission work in Africa; mission leaders and researchers were eager to study them. But while excellent maps soon covered the walls, the MAF office floorboards remained bare, the equipment limited to two tables, an old typewriter and a filing cabinet. The little money they had was kept for essentials. Good discipline for the future.

Murray and Jack meant business. They wanted specific and exact information from the missions. Were there real travel needs? How much could a plane help? What about the terrain? What were the weather patterns? Would it be feasible to make airstrips? Was aviation fuel available? Would the local governments allow the use of planes? If so, would there be restrictions or special requirements?

Answers to such questions were understandably slow in coming. Only three or four replies came. Every day seemed to confirm that the only way to get the necessary information would be an on-the-spot survey. In view of the vast areas and the isolation of so many places, a plane would be essential for this.

At an early stage Mildmay had formed a temporary Advisory Council for MAF, consisting of twenty well-known Christian leaders and mission heads, together with half a dozen Christian pilots from the services. Its first meeting was chaired by Mr John Laing, founder of the internationally known Laing construction company. He had a deep and far-sighted interest in Murray's proposals and was a great support in those early days. The idea of an exploratory trip to Africa using an aircraft was unanimously agreed. A suitable plane would cost some £5000, half of which was promised on the spot by various Council members.

Support for the MAF concept came from other sources too. In South Africa and Australia, young men were receiving a call similar to Murray's and the Mildmay Movement had been in touch with the Christian Airmen's Missionary Fellowship (CAMF) in America who were already putting a plane into Mexico.

In the summer of 1946, Murray was invited by CAMF to attend a conference in the USA. He found they shared both his vision and his desire to see it worked out in a professional and practical way. A deep bond was established from the beginning. CAMF changed its name to the one Murray had chosen: Missionary Aviation Fellowship. The Americans agreed that for the present they'd concentrate on Central and South America while MAF from the UK would start in Africa.

Back in London, a ten-month air and ground survey was planned. For days Jack and Murray explored possible types of plane. It was difficult. Neither of them had any first-hand knowledge of Africa and the areas to be visited held so many unknowns. Clearly the plane must be small and able to land on tiny rough airstrips hacked out of jungles, grasslands or hillsides. But should they choose from older, well-proved types or from later designs with promising new features? Specifications were studied, planes were test-flown.

In the end they decided on the Miles Gemini. It was new in design, clean in its lines and relatively simple in construction. The two small engines, neatly cowled, were installed on either wing and gave a cruising speed of 120 mph. The four-seat cabin was enclosed in a pleasing perspex canopy allowing an excellent all-round view. The electrically operated retractable undercarriage facilitated streamlined flight. The large wingflaps, when lowered, enabled the plane to land slowly and safely on quite short airstrips. Altogether a beautiful little aircraft.

The order for the Gemini was placed in September 1946. The remaining money needed for its purchase took eighteen months to come in, right up to the delivery date. MAF supporters were still few, for it was a new organization and Britain's economy had been severely battered by the war. When the time came to pay, funds still fell short. The Mildmay Movement managed to find the balance.

When I myself began working full time at Mildmay in August 1947, I soon got to know and appreciate Murray and Jack and the others who worked there. Jack was twenty-six, six months older than I was. Murray, our senior at thirty, was the driving force in everything that went on. We were all enthusiastic, but even so, there were days when the slowness of detailed preparations got us down. Dr Cochrane came into our office on one such day.

"Don't worry," he said with a wave of his hand. "Everything will work out. I can foresee the day when there won't be just one aircraft in Africa, but twenty!"

We blinked. Two or three planes, perhaps – but twenty? We didn't believe it.

Tom Banham also arrived that summer. He had been a Fleet Air Arm navigator, having served in the navy since before the war. A little older than any of us and a steady married man, he was a sort of father figure, giving balance to the survey team. He was also ideally qualified to be our navigator.

So, it seemed settled. With Tom as navigator, Jack would be the pilot and I would be co-pilot and engineer. We would be flying for about seven months, some of the time in the most remote and underdeveloped regions of Africa, areas where there were few land-marks and no servicing facilities for our aircraft. It seemed all three of us would be essential.

In August 1947 we brought the Gemini to Brox-bourne airport in Hertfordshire. On 6th September there was quite a crowd at the dedication service. The plane was named the *Mildmay Pathfinder*. One of the RAF's principal chaplains, Group Captain Marsh, gave the prayer of dedication.

Murray, Jack, Tom and I, with others from Mildmay, then took the plane on a nationwide tour, visiting more than thirty centres to speak and to demonstrate the aircraft. Interested supporters were offered a flight. I still hear of people who say, "I flew in that first MAF plane," and who have faithfully backed us ever since.

We had two purposes in making the tour. One was to tell Christians about MAF and gain further prayer and support: twenty thousand heard of our plans first-hand. Equally important was the need to get to know the plane thoroughly before we left for Africa.

Detailed plans were made for the whole survey. A new and still more comprehensive questionnaire was prepared for us to complete at each of the hundred mission stations we were to visit. We hoped it would provide sufficient data for us to decide where any future service should be started. We had to get visas and permissions from many different embassies, identify fuel supplies all across Africa and where necessary adjust our routes to take advantage of them.

I ordered the spare parts essential to ensure that we should never be grounded for lack of some vital part. Getting a suitable radio was a real problem. We needed a small lightweight, long-range, high fre-

quency transmitter and receiver. Finally Grady Parrott, who headed MAF in America, sent us an ex-
military Command set. We gratefully installed it and
calculated its weight. Then we also weighed what we
would need in spares, maps and supplies, together
with ourselves and a full load of fuel.

We had a shock. We were a hundred pounds over
the legal safety limit. Something or someone had to
go. We certainly couldn't dispense with the supplies
or spares or the load of fuel. We couldn't do without
the pilot. The plane could well become stranded with
no engineer. A navigator would minimize our chances
of getting lost in a vast unknown continent. But the
agonizing decision was made. We would have to
manage without our full-time navigator, relying
instead on Jack's extensive Air Force experience and
my amateur assistance. He and I would go alone.

This seemed to leave Tom out in the cold, but he
and his wife, Dorothy, remained quietly confident
that, if it was God's will for them to remain with
MAF, He would work it out. He did. A vital new role
opened up for Tom almost at once. Our long and
complicated survey needed a full-time coordinator.

We wanted someone in Africa to maintain contact
with those we were to visit, to keep them informed
and handle any changes in plan. Tom was a good
administrator, meticulous and careful. Nairobi, the
capital of Kenya, then a well-developed British colony,
seemed the obvious place for him and the best communications centre for our survey. We all decided he
should be there ahead of us, though it meant him
sailing from Tilbury on Christmas Day 1947. It was
a hard parting for Tom and his wife, but they accepted
it wholeheartedly.

Jack and I were left to make the final preparations. Since our twin-engined aircraft bore the name Gemini — the constellation of Castor and Pollux, otherwise known as the Twins — it was perhaps inevitable that the two of us were soon nicknamed the heavenly twins.

4

The First Long Journey

Tuesday, 13th January 1948 could hardly have been less promising. It was cold with icy rain and gale-force winds buffeting the Croydon control tower. Many famous pioneering flights in the pre-war years of aviation departed from Croydon, so it was an honour for us to set out from there on the first flight of MAF.

A last-minute fault on our radio delayed us until afternoon, but finally at two o'clock, in the still stinging downpour, Jack and I clambered into the plane and buckled up our safety belts. Our friends were shrouded in tightly buttoned raincoats, wet hair blowing around their heads as we waved our farewells. We taxied the Pathfinder to the take-off point and turned into the strong headwind. The control tower radioed final clearance. Jack opened the throttles, released the brakes and eased the control stick slightly forward. We didn't need to gather much speed in the gale before the tail came up; we were airborne almost at once. A squall of rain quickly blotted the airport from sight and we scudded low over the drenched Kent countryside under heavy black clouds.

Jack flipped the undercarriage switch to retract the wheels. After a moment two green lights came on, showing they were up and locked. He eased the flaps up and the plane gained speed. Soon the tossing waves

of the Channel were beneath us, ahead the 4000-mile
journey to Africa. There was little time to consider
the historic nature of our mission. We were busy just
surviving.

Half an hour later we crossed the dark coastline of
France near Dieppe and headed inland for Paris. The
Gemini's short range was going to mean more than
twenty refuelling stops between Croydon and Nairobi. In those days even the major airlines made
several night stops between London and Africa.

We carried only £250 for the whole ferry flight, the
maximum allowed under the tight exchange control
regulations after the war. We had a credit card for
fuel, but all our other needs and expenses, known
and unknown, would have to be met from the £250
cash.

By the time we reached Paris there wasn't much
daylight left and we stayed the night in a little hotel.
Jack and I hungrily scanned the appetizing French
menu. The prices seemed exorbitant. Ravenous
though we were we dared not buy what we would
have really liked, settling instead for a meagre supper
of soup and bread. We weren't going to get fat on this
trip.

The next day there were still very strong winds
and the French controller refused to give us take-off
clearance until the afternoon, by which time heavy
rain had again set in. The cloud base was only 300
feet above the ground as, in violent and bumpy winds,
we headed south for Lyon and another night stop.
This time, in another small hotel, we sat in our bed-
room and ate some emergency rations from the plane.

The first part of our flight from Lyon continued the
saga of bad weather, ice on our windscreen making

it difficult to see. Things improved later and when we reached Marseilles it was dry and comparatively warm. We felt a bit like RAF fighter pilots as we put on our Mae West life jackets and pressed straight on across the Mediterranean towards our third night stop in Corsica.

From there we flew on south. The calm of the long steady flight over the sea felt like peace after storm. Then, far ahead, we made out a distant yellow shoreline – our first ever glimpse of Africa. What would the unknown continent hold for us?

With a jolt I noticed something was wrong: "Every so often the port engine is missing a beat," I shouted to Jack above the engine noise.

"I've heard it," he observed drily, looking at the water below us. "It makes my heart miss a beat too."

Still complaining, the engine kept going and forty minutes later we were over land, losing height in the warm skies above Tunis airport. Our excitement on our first landing in Africa was tempered by the urgent need to get the plane's engines running properly. As soon as we had changed into tropical kit, I donned some overalls, removed the engine cowlings, pulled out the sparking plugs and checked the magneto and distributor. The plugs were bad: their points were too close. That was easily rectified. The regapped plugs were replaced and the engine ran sweetly.

We left Tunis next morning. Two full days and five refuelling stops later, we reached Almaza airport, Cairo.

The hot Arab market felt foreign and hostile. Stall upon stall crowded together, piled with clothes, food and a jumble of Middle Eastern goods. We felt danger-

"GEMINI" FLIGHT TO AFRICA IN 1948

Croydon
Paris
Marseille
Corsica
Tunis

LIBYA
S a h a r a
EGYPT
Cairo
Saudi Arabia
FRENCH WEST AFRICA
Wadi Halfa
Atbara
Asmara
Khartoum
ERITREA
ANGLO-EGYPTIAN SU'DAN
Malakal
Addis Ababa
Juba
ETHIOPIA
GOLD COAST
NIGERIA
FRENCH EQUATORIAL AFRICA
KENYA
Nairobi
BELGIAN CONGO
TANGANYIKA
N
ANGOLA
RHODESIA
W   E
MOZAMBIQUE
MADAGASCAR
S
UNION OF SOUTH AFRICA

Scale	0	500	1000	1500
km				
miles	0	500		1000

ously conspicuous: white foreigners amidst the jostling Arab crowds, repeatedly obliged to shake ourselves free from the eager traders who grabbed our arms.

At Almaza airport we had been told that, contrary to previous information, our Command transmitter lacked the right frequency for radio communication in the Sudan. None of the correct radio crystals were available in Cairo. We'd made friends, however, with a British Airways foreman based there.

"Many military planes with Command transmitters came down in the desert during the war," he told us. "The area is littered with wrecks, bits and pieces of all kinds." The Egyptians had salvaged them. So he suggested that we should try the big Muski Bazaar on the edge of the city.

We eyed each stall carefully until at last we spotted what looked like an untidy military museum: tables loaded with amazing piles of old wartime equipment.

Sure enough we discovered some old aircraft radios among the debris. Under the hopeful gaze of the Egyptian stall-holder we examined them carefully. Here was just what we wanted: a Command transmitter with the frequency we required to get permission to fly on from Cairo to the Sudan. The price soared as the stall-holder noted our interest. He demanded £2, a fortune to us when we had so little money. But in the end we paid less than £1. Even a pound was worth a lot in those days.

After much swapping of parts between our original transmitter and the one from the bazaar, and with help from our BA friend, we eventually got a strong signal on the right frequency. The following morning, after five days in Cairo, we continued our journey southwards. As we crossed the border into Sudan and landed at Wadi Halfa, the heat struck us with blistering intensity.

> The land that God laughed at when He made it. A land of scorching desert and scorpions.

> The poor Sudan! The wretched, dry Sudan ... overhead the pitiless furnace of the sun, under foot the never-easing treadmill of the sand, dust in the throat ... searing flame in the eye. The Sudan is a God-accursed wilderness, an empty limbo of torment for ever and ever.

So writers at the turn of the nineteenth century had described the largest country in Africa. As we flew on to Atbara, I was at the controls, Jack navigating. Below us were miles upon miles of flat sand. While we'd been over Egypt we'd watched the ribbon of the Nile. Now it wandered off out of sight, 200 miles to the west of our course. We had no navigational aids, our map showed nothing. We knew that if we got lost over this vast desert we would be lost indeed.

"A sheet of sandpaper would make as accurate a map as those charts you're holding!" I observed to Jack.

He nodded but had some good news: "I can see the railway line below us now."

There was the faint but important landmark, to be followed religiously, a tiny, thin thread of railway, originally built by Kitchener's army during the 1896

Sudan campaign against the Dervishes. It ran for more than 500 miles across the northern deserts of the Sudan to Khartoum.

From AD 540 this previously pagan area had formed part of a widespread Christian kingdom which flourished for over a thousand years. But Christianity probably came there even earlier through the conversion of the chief treasurer of Queen Candace, mentioned in the Acts of the Apostles. Her palace once stood by the Nile near where we were flying. Islam, now dominant in northern Sudan, did not arrive there until one thousand five hundred years later.

Jack flew the final leg from Atbara to Khartoum. The sun was low as we saw the sandy outskirts of the Sudan capital with their many clusters of mud houses. Beneath us flowed the White Nile coming up from the distant south. We could also see the Blue Nile which rises in the far mountains of Ethiopia to the east. The two rivers met and mingled just north of the city. To our right was the large sprawling Arab town of Omdurman. In front of us now were the white-painted, flat-roofed houses and buildings of Khartoum itself, its mosques and minarets casting long shadows across the dry landscape in the setting sun. On the dusty streets below us, people, cars, carts and donkeys bustled together in the welcome cool of the evening.

Our survey was beginning.

"Here's where we would like an air service," explained Howard Borlase, the field leader of the Sudan Interior Mission.

We sat on the verandah of his headquarters in Khartoum, our maps of the Sudan spread on the table before us. As we leaned over them, he indicated an area about half the size of the UK, its centre some 400 miles south of Khartoum. It was quite flat, lying between the Nile and the high mountains of Ethiopia.

"We have mission stations here," he went on, moving his finger over the map. "A hard, rough, three-day drive will get you to them in the dry season. The rains last for six months and the earth roads can be too wet to drive on for up to nine."

We looked up at him. "In that case how do your people get in and out during that period?" we asked.

"They can't," he replied, "except on foot, or by mule or donkey where there's less swamp."

"So an air service could help you?'

"Yes, but the government won't allow it. They feel the Sudan is a very difficult country for navigation. They don't want any unsuitable private planes operating over it."

He told us that the government had asked the RAF, who had a base at Khartoum, to fly over the mission area and give an opinion on it. He'd gone with them, but they couldn't find even one of the stations. The landscape was too featureless.

There was obviously a need here, but one that had to be borne in mind for the future. Our immediate target was 1200 miles further south, in East and Central Africa.

"I am sure our mission in Ethiopia would be interested," said Howard, still hopeful. "Why don't you route yourselves through Addis Ababa on your way to Nairobi and talk to them?"

That seemed feasible. It wasn't that much further

and it would give us an opportunity to get a glimpse of Ethiopia and the need there.

But we had a great deal to learn. Operating in Europe or flying aircraft with supercharged engines in the RAF was one thing. Flying a plane with normally aspirated engines was quite another. In the tropics the lower density of the air robs a light plane of both power and lift. Height and heat spell danger.

We headed for Addis Ababa, first flying eastwards from Khartoum up to the highlands of Eritrea where we landed at Asmara to refuel. The airfield was nearly 8000 feet above sea level, and only fifteen degrees north of the equator: that meant it was both high and hot. Our little Gemini didn't like it. We took off again with our maximum permitted weight and full fuel tanks for the long journey ahead. Jack opened up the throttles, we accelerated rapidly and got airborne. But the plane was reluctant to climb. We were unable to rise more than twenty feet above the long runway. As we passed the end of it a ring of encircling hills loomed before us.

"We'll never make it over those," called Jack, "I'm going to have to put the plane down."

Ahead of us was a small grassy patch and after that a rough ox-ploughed field. Hard sunbaked furrows ran right across our flight path. If we hit them we could be flipped on to our back.

Jack snapped the throttles closed, pulled the emergency undercarriage release, lifted the machine's nose up into a stall and dropped it in a three-point landing on to the grass. We didn't stop in time and our wheels struck the furrows. He hauled back hard on the control column to keep the tail down. The whole plane shuddered, but mercifully didn't nose over. We came to an abrupt stop. Jack turned off the fuel and ignition. There was a momentary stunned silence. We jumped out.

We were about half a mile from the airfield. I checked the plane for signs of damage but none were immediately obvious and a later investigation showed that, amazingly, all was well. It was a tough little machine. An airfield control officer rushed out and told us we had been lucky: "You've chosen the only flat spot anywhere near Asmara."

A crowd of spectators quickly gathered and helped us to manhandle the plane across fields, over a ditch and through a hole cut in the airfield fence. Back on the parking apron we offloaded as much weight, spares and supplies as we could, sending them by a commercial flight back to Khartoum. We gave up the idea of trying to get to Addis Ababa. The next day, with slightly heavy spirits but a considerably light-ened plane, we headed back to Khartoum to continue our journey south through Sudan. This time the take-off gave no problems at all.

The little town of Malakal on the banks of the Nile lay below us. To Jack and me the flat countryside seemed utterly desolate. Having piloted the plane from Khartoum I now took it in for landing; we stopped at the parking apron near the tiny square control tower and pushed open the hinged perspex canopies above our heads. Sweaty and uncomfortable, we looked at each other's perspiring faces.

"Hot!" said Jack. "This is about the last place on earth I'd like to live." I agreed, with no inkling that one day I would call it home.

Jack took off on the next leg, about 330 miles, to

Juba. As we climbed we bobbed up and down in the bumpy air rising from the scorching ground below.

South of Malakal the Nile again takes an enormous bend to the west. To have followed it would have led us too far off our direct track to Juba. Our maps showed various little rivers and villages that should offer landmarks to guide us safely on our way. We kept a sharp lookout for them, but it was the dry season and many of the lesser river tributaries were hard to spot and often impossible to identify. The villages were not to be seen at all. The grasslands were frequently burnt into large black patches of irregular shapes and sizes, an enormously effective camouflage which further disguised the arid land-scape. All we could do was keep our compass course and press on in the hot and hazy skies.

After about two hours we began to get anxious. According to our maps, the Nile should be coming into sight on our right as it swung back towards us north of Juba. But there was no sign of it.

The swift sunset would come at six p.m. and it was already past five. We could get no radio contact. The fuel gauges were creeping down. A plane could just disappear in this vast featureless area. A forced land-ing would almost inevitably write it off. And what about us? The whole countryside seemed deserted: no villages, no signs of life.

Why hadn't we yet seen the Nile? Had strong head-winds been holding us back? If so, by holding to our present course, we should eventually reach Juba. But what if a strong tailwind had already swept us beyond, there? Or might a wind from the west have been blowing us towards Ethiopia? This seemed the most likely explanation.

Jack took a decision: "I'm going to alter course forty-five degrees to westward. The Nile must be over there somewhere. We've got to find it. It's the only reliable landmark." He swung the plane round to head southwest. The sun was now very orange, approaching the horizon, and visibility was dwindling. There was still no sign of anything and the needles in the fuel gauges had dropped perilously near to empty.

Suddenly I caught sight of an orange reflection just below the horizon. The Nile! The setting sun glinted across the barely discernible ribbon of the distant river. But where would we intersect it? Had we still enough fuel to reach Juba? At last we got close enough to identify our position.

"The wind must have blown us about thirty miles off track," reasoned Jack.

His decision had been the right one; we had arrived just north of Juba. We slid down through the twilight to the welcome sight of the small airfield and the tiny, primitive capital of south Sudan.

We'd learnt another lesson. The vast distances, featureless country and lack of radio aids in parts of Africa could make the sky a very lonely place. MAF work was going to need the best navigational skills and techniques available. It would be vital to develop and use these with utmost care. Though our small radio had gained us permission to fly into the Sudan, it seemed to work only within a few miles of a major airport. It couldn't cope with long distances.

The next day saw a striking change in the landscape beneath us. As we flew yet further south, the scorched, flat and lonely vastness of the little-developed Sudan gave way to the green hills of Uganda. Well-defined roads ran between small towns and farmsteads. It was a civilized rural scene.

For the last stage of our long flight out we went up to 11000 feet, skirting Mount Elgon on the Kenyan border. Two hours later, Jack called out triumphantly: "There's Nairobi!" The city was clearly visible ahead. After twenty-seven eventful days, we'd arrived at last.

5

Breaking New Ground

When Jack and I arrived in Nairobi, Tom Banham greeted us with tragic news. A light plane, flown by an outstanding young missionary who'd recently qualified as a private pilot, had just crashed on take-off. He and his passengers had been killed. It was discovered that the plane's engine had failed.

The accident shocked the mission community. People in Nairobi and beyond had been asking Tom how MAF intended to ensure its planes were kept airworthy. He told them that we had a qualified engineer flying with the Gemini and emphasized that high professional standards, both in flying and maintenance, were integral to all our plans.

Tom had secured a very basic little upstairs office in the town, at minimal rent. There was just room for the essentials: a kettle, of course, a desk, Tom himself and Wangi, the Kenyan helper, who made tea, kept the place clean and ran errands. For the first twenty-four hours it seemed that Jack, Tom and I talked nonstop – there was so much to tell and to plan. We gave the Gemini a very thorough checkover; changing oil, curing some oil leaks, adjusting flying controls and brakes.

Tom had our programme well organized. We faced over six months of intensive flying. Countries and places which had been mere names on maps in our London office were now to become very real to us. So were their varied peoples, living conditions and travel needs. Our first and longest journey, which lasted a month, took us in a great loop of 3000 miles, from Nairobi in East Africa across the huge expanse of the Belgian Congo (now Zaire) to Leopoldville, the modern Kinshasa, in the extreme west, then back by a more northerly route.

After that we flew initially into the more isolated parts of Kenya and northwest to Arua in Uganda. From there we made a detailed exploration of northeast Congo before flying a further 500 miles to French Equatorial Africa where we visited some of the remotest places in the continent.

Finally we went south into Ruanda and Burundi, planning to return to Nairobi before we tackled the last phase: a survey of Tanganyika.

During each visit we faithfully worked through our set questionnaires. Apart from that, we saw, as we travelled, the dramatic differences in landscape and climate. We began to realize some of the problems of operating in the bush and, incidentally, also discovered how inadequate and unreliable were many of the maps then available.

The responses of missionaries to our ideas were extremely varied: some enthusiastic, some cautious, some quite dismissive. The reactions of Africans to the plane varied too, especially where they'd never seen one before.

MY AIRSTRIP IS READY BUT A LITTLE SOFT. COME AT YOUR OWN DISCRETION. The telegram was from a mission doctor who'd just cleared a strip in a remote region

of southern Congo. Two-thirds of the way across
Africa on our long survey trip to Leopoldville, we
were being asked to try it out. Dr Mark Poole and his
wife had suffered from sleeping sickness as a result
of frequent long journeys through tetse-fly areas. A
plane could have spared them that. To make their
airstrip at Bulapé, the doctor and his helpers had
cleared six thousand trees, filled the holes left by
them and levelled and rolled the surface.

Knowing about all that effort, we were eager to
land at Bulapé. If, on arrival, we felt the strip was
unsafe, we'd just have to fly off again.

Dense, green tropical forests stretched like a sea in
every direction beneath us, unbroken except for one
spot. There the small sandy-coloured clearing, hacked
out from the tall trees around, stood out clearly. As
we circled directly above it we were startled to see
movement along a few narrow paths leading towards
it.

Hundreds of people were running as fast as they
could, in spite of the scorching midday heat, converg-
ing on the clearing like a mass of swarming ants.

"Any moment that airstrip's going to be covered
with people," observed Jack. If that happened landing
would be impossible. Then we realized that everyone
had stopped dead at the edge of the forest. No one
ventured even a step on to the strip.

We descended to about 400 feet, trying to size up
the situation.

"We'll go down and take a look," Jack concluded.
He lowered the wheels, then the flaps and, keeping a
fair amount of engine power, made a cautious
approach to the clearing.

"I'm making a dummy run first," he called across

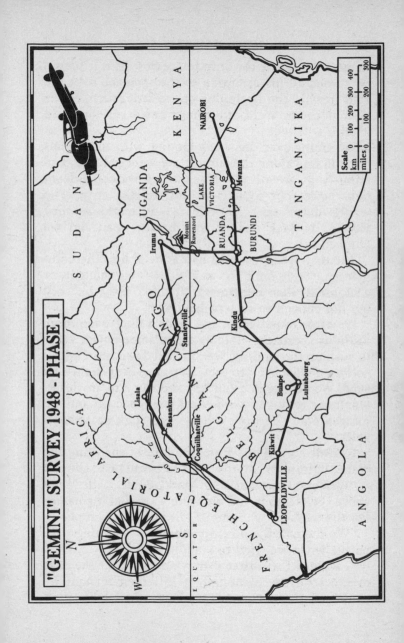

to me. "We'll test the strip to see how firm it feels."
He turned all his attention to the approach over the
high trees at the beginning of the strip; then, as we
cleared them, we both concentrated on the strip
itself.

Skimming over the sandy ground, with the wheels
just running along the surface, we were only subcon-
sciously aware of the black faces watching from
either side; our focus was still on the strip. The
wheels didn't sink in or leave any marks as they
touched it. Jack pushed the throttle open and we
climbed away.

"At that speed we still had a lot of lift," he commented. "So it's not too good a test." He thought for
a moment, then continued: "I think it's a bit soft,
but not enough to stop us landing."

We came round again and made a final, even more
cautious approach. Holding on to some power again
to cushion the landing, we touched down, the control
column pulled back to prevent a nose-over in the soft
sand. We decelerated quickly and came to an abrupt
stop after only 120 yards. Jack switched off and we
jumped out. The little wheels had sunk up to their
axles.

Crowds surged out from the forests engulfing the
plane. In front of them were a tall American couple.

"Welcome! welcome!" Mark Poole called out
above the clamour and we were soon shaking hands.
For the moment we ignored our bogged-down plane.

"We thought the airstrip would be swarming with
people when we tried to land!" I said.

"I warned them that if they stepped over the edge
of the strip the plane might kill them instantly,"
explained the doctor. "They have their own ques-

tion," he added. "They want to know how you found their village when you've never come here before."

We'd known that this small place in the forest might be hard to find so had taken special pains with our navigation, checking our map and course carefully all the way. So the Bulapé villagers had seen the plane in the distance coming straight towards them and arriving directly overhead. That had really impressed them.

"They are asking how many wives you have," the doctor interpreted further. "Important people in this area have lots of wives." They were shocked to learn that we had none. One chief present had thirty. It was our turn to be shocked. We noticed another chief had lost many front teeth. The doctor explained this to us as well:

"Whenever there's a special occasion in their lives, a tooth is removed. He's had a number of special occasions, as you can see."

I winced, wondering whether our landing would demand yet another tooth extraction.

Over that weekend three thousand people came from all around, walking up to thirty miles through the bush to see the aeroplane. As usual on these visits, Jack and I were asked to preach at the Sunday services. We did it through interpreters (sometimes being interpreted into more than one tribal language). On this occasion the church was crowded with people who wanted to hear what these strange "flying men" had to say.

Throughout the weekend Jack and I were wondering how we'd get the plane out. The newly cleared strip was very soft. We'd landed without damage, but our plane might now be unable to leave. A lesson for

the future: never land on a new untried strip until
you've gone in by road or trail to check it personally,
however difficult that may be. We had to lighten
the plane by taking out all the removable spares and
equipment and let Jack fly off on his own. Dr Poole
drove with me over ninety miles of unimaginably
rough roads to the nearest official airstrip where Jack
was waiting.

At Leopoldville the Congo Protestant Council gave
us a very encouraging welcome, unanimously requesting further MAF surveys of their areas. During our
ten days in the city we visited various government
departments. The Belgian director of Civil Aviation
was courteous, but reminded us that the Congo was
a large country, still very young in its development.
Warning us not to expect too much, he gave us a map
showing all the landing grounds, with emergency
landing places too.

Returning eastward we flew up the Congo river,
the longest in Africa after the Nile. From Leopoldville
it curves in an enormous arc across the whole
country, draining thousands of square miles of equatorial lowland. We visited four mission stations along
its course and dropped a bag of mail to a fifth. When
we occasionally left the line of the river to take a
more direct line to our next destination, we found
that the continuous carpet of dense, tangled trees and
creepers beneath us offered no navigational pinpoints
at all.

Nearing Irumu, on the northeastern border of
Congo, the seemingly unending forests abruptly gave
way to open grassland. We almost gasped. The change
was dramatic. This was where Stanley, after three
terrible years of trekking through jungle from the

west coast to find Livingstone, had at last come out into open country. We could understand why he sat down and wept.

During the third phase of our survey we went to French Equatorial Africa, flying first to Bangassou where every European in the town came out to give us a terrific welcome. From there we flew eastwards along the southern edge of the country to some of the loneliest mission stations we had seen. The area was called in French *Le coin perdu*, the lost corner. We listened as one elderly missionary couple just sat and talked and talked and talked. It had been so long since they had someone they could speak to in their own language. They were incredibly grateful that I was able to repair their electrical generators.

During our surveys we twice flew south from Irumu past the steep sides of the Ruwenzori mountains. The first time the 16000-foot peaks were heavily shrouded in forbidding clouds. They looked as awesome to us as Mount Sinai must have appeared to the children of Israel when Moses went up to meet with God on the summit. We carefully skirted the precipitous slopes, keeping in the clear under the heavy cloud base.

By then we were learning that dangerous tropical storms could rapidly spring out of the sky apparently from nowhere. Dark, brooding walls of cloud could build up quickly to heights of 20000 feet, hemming us in. Before we knew it, we could be totally encircled and trapped, sometimes with no way out and nothing but thick forest or steep hills below. That's why we adopted the saying within MAF: "For every one look forward, take two looks back." We had to make sure we always had a way out.

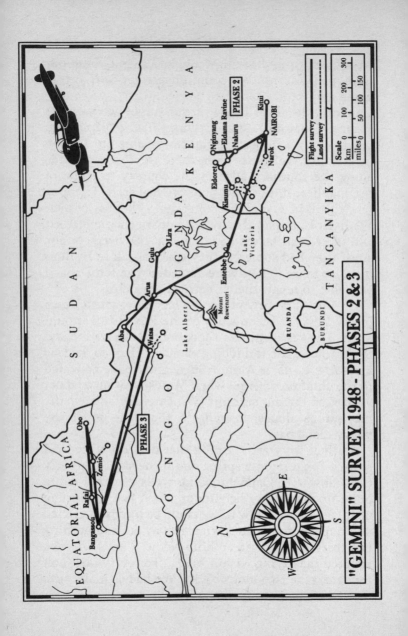

"GEMINI" SURVEY 1948 - PHASES 2 & 3

But it was 200 miles further south that destruction came to our plane. The danger came out of a clear sky, with none of the visible drama of cloud and storm. Just the silent, inexorable pressure of the wind driving us relentlessly downwards into that sunlit tropical valley in the Burundi mountains.

6

Learning the Lessons

As we stood on the Burundi mountainside, looking at the wrecked Gemini, we felt totally dazed, our minds reeling. Why hadn't we foreseen the danger of down currents in the lee of the mountain ridge? Why hadn't we gained more height before we attempted to cross the mountains? We'd have then escaped the marauding winds.

The war had accustomed us to crashes, disasters and the unexpected. But this was different. This wrecked plane was not one of thousands of military aircraft. It was the only one we had. Its broken remains symbolized our own shattered hopes.

For two years we'd worked and prepared for this survey. For two years we'd prayed and waited for the funds to buy our plane. For six gruelling months we'd flown and landed, talked and listened across the width of Africa. Had it all been for nothing?

A dirt track followed a ridge in the mountains above us. After half an hour two Belgian agricultural officers came bumping along it in a Peugeot car. They spotted us and the wrecked plane and scrambled down to where we were. We explained our unhappy situation as best we could in French. After listening to us they headed off to Usumbura to inform the airport officials. As we waited in the sun, we were glad to

be able to salvage and drink the water we'd brought
with us.

Several hours later, two airport officials arrived and
made out a full report. Then they took us to an American mission station a few miles down the mountainside. Unexpected as we were, the missionaries were
generous in their hospitality. Their sympathy was
a real comfort and encouragement. But the whole
incident had left us shocked and dispirited. We tried
to sleep through the customary afternoon siesta, but
our thoughts and our discussions were too disturbing.
In our unwise attempt to save time we had brought
the survey to a halt.

Tom Banham in Nairobi received our telegram from
Usumbura informing him of the crash. He wrote to
Murray in London:

"To have been enabled to do so successful a survey
and then at the very end to meet with such a disaster
is a considerable shock spiritually as well as physically. We shall all need God's guidance about our
future decisions."

He also wrote to the missionaries and local friends
with whom we'd been in contact. Would they retain
any confidence in us as an aviation organization?

"We quite understand that the accident may cause
you to have second thoughts as to the desirability of
air travel. Before we can decide on action for the
future, we need to know your reactions. Above all
we would especially value your prayers."

Our roundabout journey back to Nairobi took nine
days. We travelled by lake steamer, by slow train and
by a series of local lorries which often had to be
repaired, pushed or abandoned. In all we covered

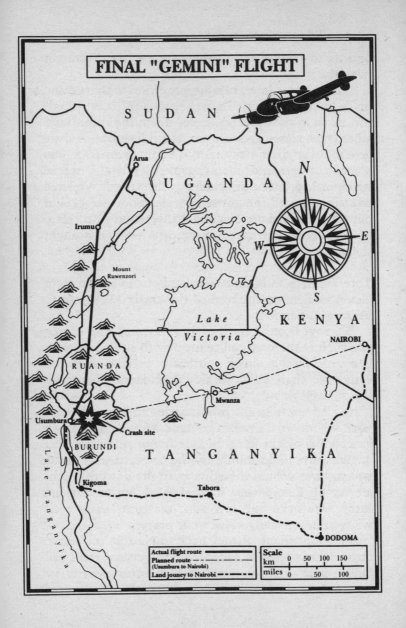

FINAL "GEMINI" FLIGHT

S U D A N

Arua

U G A N D A

Irumu

Mount
Ruwenzori

Lake
Victoria

K E N Y A

NAIROBI

R U A N D A

Mwanza

Usumbura

Crash site

BURUNDI

T A N G A N Y I K A

Lake Tanganyika

Kigoma

Tabora

DODOMA

N
W — E
S

Actual flight route ——————
Planned route – – –
(Usumbura to Nairobi)
Land jouney to Nairobi –·–·–

Scale
km   0   50   100   150
miles 0   50   100

more than a thousand miles – twice the distance it would have been by air.

"At least we're learning more about surface travel in Africa," I remarked dolefully.

On our way we found plenty of time to think more about air travel too, as we painfully analysed the events of the past months. The little Gemini had been underpowered for its task. We had struggled with its various limitations: poor take-off at high altitudes and in high temperatures; slow rate of climb; difficulty in clearing tall trees at the end of short airstrips; tendency of the small wheels to sink into soft soil on landing. Finally, lack of power had aggravated our problems in the mountains. Special techniques for flying in tropical valleys were later developed by MAF. But at that time we were still learning by trial and error – plenty of both.

Back in Nairobi, it was a relief to talk and pray with Tom about what had happened and what to do next.

"You must get back into an aeroplane immediately," he stressed, "in case you lose your nerve for flying." This was in line with RAF practice following a crash during the war. But we didn't want to waste time and money hiring a plane. Though Jack and I had lost some of what Tom used to call our "irrepressible spirits", neither of us felt in any danger of losing our nerve. So he arranged instead for us to have a few days' holiday on the Kenya coast. Much better.

As soon as we got back we started an intensive analysis of all the data we'd collected at the eighty mission stations visited so far. We wanted to get a report out to missions, not only on the accident (that was comparatively brief) but also on the findings of the survey to date. We worked hard for two weeks, analysing nine hundred pages of information. Our finished report covered eleven pages, plus four pages of statistics. It included all the comparisons of surface and air travel emerging from the five months of research.

We were surprised by what we found. The relative merits of travel by car or plane seemed very evenly balanced. In countries like the Congo the roads were very carefully maintained by the Belgian colonial authorities.

"Why should I need the help of a plane?" one missionary there had asked us. "I can drive my pick-up truck in any direction at seventy miles an hour along a good road. When I reach my destination I've my vehicle conveniently for local use."

His comments were typical of a number of people we met. In more isolated areas, on the other hand, missionaries like Mark Poole at Bulapé were understandably enthusiastic about an air service. But, looking at the area we had surveyed as a whole, we had to admit that the case for MAF was not as clear and obvious as we had assumed.

We had another concern. Would our accident have now put missionaries completely off the whole idea of MAF? We were soon relieved to find that our fears on this score were groundless. Many missionaries were reassured to find our report so objective and thorough and had actually gained confidence in what we were trying to do. Certainly our accident had stimulated interest and prayer rather than the contrary. We were asked to go ahead with the survey of a small part of northern Tanganyika which had been postponed after the crash. This we did, in a second-hand station wagon. There were some needs there but, at that time, the case for an air service was no stronger than we had found elsewhere.

Though our survey report was received with encouraging warmth by the missions in Africa, it precipitated a major and unforeseen crisis at our headquarters in London.

We had sent Murray Kendon a copy of our preliminary findings, together with some additional comments. We pointed out that many missionaries preferred travel in their own cars or trucks; that the man hours required to run an air service would equal the missionary hours it saved; that where roads were good and easy on vehicles, costs by air could be a lot higher than costs by road. Conversely, in difficult mountain areas, where air travel was most needed, the question mark over safety now loomed largest.

Jack, Tom and I had, of course, been digesting these issues for some weeks. But they had descended on Murray suddenly and *en masse*. Our previous letters to the London office had concentrated mainly on the interesting and exciting events of our survey. Now he was faced with the cold analysis of statistical and technical data. He was deeply shocked. In his eyes our report undermined the very *raison d'être* of MAF.

He felt we could not have assessed the overall picture correctly.

"Where are the examples of an aeroplane saving immense time as compared to slow journeys by mule or canoe?" he asked. "How do the missionaries get to distant medical centres?"

We had to reply that those we had met were not making slow, long journeys by mule or canoe and that, generally, they seemed to have reasonable road access to medical centres.

It was a pity Murray had not been out in Africa with us to see the facts and problems on the spot. It is more than likely that if he had, his visionary enthusiasm would have enabled him to see more possibilities than we or the missions could then imagine. God had truly given him a vision though we had to wait for its fulfilment.

In spite of all these differences of opinion there remained one country where we had sensed an indisputable need for MAF. The Sudan continued to haunt us.

On our initial journey to Nairobi we'd made some contacts in the Sudan, though it hadn't been part of our main survey. We had inevitably been impressed by its great distances and minimal communications. There were vast areas where there were no real roads at all and what tracks existed were impassable for months at a time. We'd learned of places where missionaries and their children were out of range of medical help and had died for lack of it. We'd listened to descriptions of those long, slow journeys by boats, canoes, donkeys or mules that Murray had pictured.

We asked Mildmay to allow us to make a thorough survey of the Sudan on our way back to England. But the idea had to be abandoned for lack of time, for the insurance company was questioning our claim for the crashed Gemini. Jack and I were urgently needed in London to put the facts before them personally. In November 1948, we flew by the Scandinavian Mission Flights "Ansgar" plane to Switzerland and travelled by train to London.

*

Just before we had left England on our survey, an enterprising MAF supporter had thrust a small movie camera into my hands urging me to bring back our story on film. Equipped with a book on amateur movie-making, I had done my best to comply. On our return Jack and I were kept busy showing the film in churches and sharing the excitement of flying in little-known areas. But, after a while, we began to feel we couldn't continue indefinitely stimulating interest if nothing else was happening – and if MAF was unlikely to be involved in flying again soon.

This was only one of a series of crises. The insurance company eventually paid out on the loss of the Gemini, but by then the Mildmay Movement was running into financial difficulties. It was hard for them to contemplate using the insurance money to buy another plane. So we couldn't plan any further surveys or attempt to set up an air service anywhere, even if we wanted to.

Also, although we had sent fuller reports to all the missions whose stations we'd surveyed and maintained active discussions with them, nothing had emerged to trigger the start of a specific service. If we'd had the experience we have now, we would have initiated something ourselves. We'd have known that, at least in some of the areas surveyed, once a plane was available it would soon be in active use. As it was, because nothing was happening, Jack and I felt we were in limbo. We became increasingly uneasy.

A further crisis arose when the Mildmay Movement sent Murray to his native New Zealand to stir up interest in MAF and at the same time conduct an evangelistic campaign there. He left in October 1949 full of enthusiasm, intending to return six months later. But in the meanwhile Jack and I were left to carry on without him. It turned out to be a time of crucial decisions.

Shortly after his departure an urgent request came from Dr Don McClure, a pioneer missionary in south Sudan, appealing to us to set up an air service in the remote region where he was working. The call was strong and specific. But we still had no plane and Mildmay had little money. Should we face the fact that, apart from the Sudan, there appeared to be less scope for using planes in Africa than was originally imagined? Should we give MAF a decent burial?

We had a special day of prayer in our office. At the end we felt more clearly than ever that God was calling us to trust Him and go to the Sudan. But when we approached Dr Cochrane he was doubtful. He called a meeting of the Mildmay Council.

"Your survey in Africa was hardly a total success, was it?"

The council of the Mildmay Movement was in session. The table in the council room was long and narrow. The chairman, Mr Lindsay Glegg, was at one end, Dr Cochrane at the other, the remaining council members along both sides. Jack and I had been asked to join them. The light from the windows illuminated quite a number of white and grey heads, a venerable group of well-respected people. And they were sceptical about our going to the Sudan.

One of the members had just said so. He emphasized it further.

"If we let you go out to the Sudan I can see you

coming back within the year with your tails between your legs again!"

"Why not go to South America?" a lady member suggested. "There are needs and opportunities there. We have requests for an air service in that area. You should take a plane there."

We explained: "American MAF are already working in South America and we feel that is the natural area for them, not for us. We don't want to duplicate their work."

There was still no enthusiasm for the Sudan idea. Dr Cochrane was obviously unsure. Only Jack and I were quite clear that we had only two alternatives: to go to the Sudan – or to disband MAF.

Lindsay Glegg was a man of genial face and gracious manner. A successful businessman, he was also a man of vision whom God had greatly used to promote Christian outreach in England. Suddenly he spoke up.

"I think if these two young men feel God is calling them to go to the Sudan, then we should let them do so."

That's all he said. But Jack and I sensed God was fully in control. The council members absorbed his words. They weren't yes men or yes women. Yet, somehow, there was hardly any discussion after that. His proposal was passed. God had intervened. We were allowed to plan to get a plane and go.

After the council's decision we contacted the Sudan Government. They would not permit us to operate any small, single-engined aircraft over the desolate countryside within their borders, reminding us that they'd already had incredibly expensive experiences searching for lost planes. Having been seriously lost ourselves in the Sudan, we could understand this.

There weren't too many twin-engined planes we could afford without spending more than the insurance settlement from the Gemini. The only one of reasonable size and price was the veteran de Havilland Rapide.

Rapides had first been designed and built in the 1930s, twin-engined biplanes with space for eight passengers and a crew of two. Made of wood, fabric and metal, their slender, pointed, dragonfly-like wings were braced with innumerable struts and wires. Thousands had been made and flown all over the world. Their performance was adequate for the relatively flat, low-lying regions of the Sudan. And they were acceptable to the Sudan Government.

Having been used for training RAF radio operators during the war, the Rapide we bought already had a heavy military Marconi receiver and transmitter. It had also been used for navigation training and had a special drift-sight which would be invaluable for our own navigation.

Plans went ahead for our departure to the Sudan. Jack was now married and Helen, his wife, was to come with us. The target date for leaving was early March 1950. At this point a final crisis occurred. Dr Cochrane appeared in our office with the treasurer of the Mildmay Movement.

"I've got bad news," he said. "Our finances are in a difficult state. I'm afraid we're going to have to sell the Rapide."

This really was a blow, especially when Lindsay Glegg's move to let us go to the Sudan had previously been accepted by the council. Amazingly, Jack and I felt quite calm. We were sure God had already made the situation clear to us:

"Dr Cochrane," we told him, "if that is what has to be, so be it. In that case we must wind up MAF too."

"All right, I'll let you go," said Dr Cochrane without even a sideways glance at his startled treasurer, "but we may have to sell the plane at any time."

It was on that basis that we headed out to the Sudan. I can tell you now – that plane was never sold.

PART II

❧

THE FIRST AIR
SERVICE
(1949–1953)

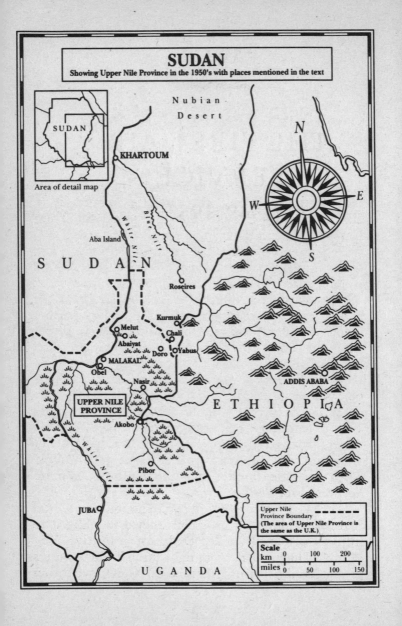

SUDAN
Showing Upper Nile Province in the 1950's with places mentioned in the text

SUDAN

Area of detail map

N u b i a n   D e s e r t

KHARTOUM

Aba Island

S U D A N

Roseires

Kurmuk

Melut
Abaiyat
Doro
Chali
Yabus
MALAKAL

Obel

Nasir

UPPER NILE PROVINCE

Akobo

Pibor

JUBA

E T H I O P I A

ADDIS ABABA

U G A N D A

N
W   E
S

Upper Nile
Province Boundary — — — —
(The area of Upper Nile Province is
the same as the U.K.)

Scale
km 0   100   200
miles 0   50   100   150

Land Beyond the Nile

"We've got to get Betty out of here."

Betty Guth had been desperately ill with a high fever for two weeks. Sam Burns, the missionary in charge at Yabus in south Sudan, was talking to her husband, Chuck. She was getting worse, they suspected sleeping sickness and knew she could die without medical help. But none was available in this isolated place. They had to get her to hospital.

Hospital was five hundred miles away in Khartoum and at Yabus it was the middle of the rainy season. Chuck and Betty had been able to drive there before the rains set in, together with a year's supplies and their three-month-old baby, Carol. But it would be impossible to drive out now. The trails were swamped and would remain so for some months yet. They dared not wait. Betty could not walk. They would have to carry both her and little Carol.

Betty viewed the prospect with dread. "It's not about myself I'm most worried," she told Chuck. Then her voice broke: "It's about Carol . . . I'm so frightened for her!"

She had good reason for fear. The journey would take many days during which they'd be obliged to mix Carol's milk under the most primitive conditions. They'd have to go right through the swamps of the Dinka plains where they knew two other

missionary children had already died. Betty couldn't
escape the terrible picture of leaving her own baby
in a tiny, lonely grave somewhere out in the vast
marshlands.

Sam sent a runner from the local tribe to the government post at Kurmuk, seventy miles away, with a
telegraph message. It informed their mission headquarters in Khartoum what they were planning. They
made a rough stretcher for Betty and the baby. A
frame over it supported a mosquito net to protect
them from the malaria-carrying insects that swarmed
in the swamps; a piece of canvas on top acted as a
shield against the sun. Local carriers were found and
they set out.

The initial journey stretched a hundred and eighty
miles ahead over boggy trails, westward towards the
Nile. They could expect burning sun and torrential
rain overhead, snakes and scorpions underfoot, and
no guarantee of shelter if they got stuck on the way.

The first hard day took them thirty-four miles, to
Doro, the nearest mission station. Since this was in
the territory of the Mabaan people the carriers from
Yabus refused to venture further. George Morrow, an
Australian missionary at Doro, organized a fresh relay
of Mabaan carriers for the stretcher, brought out his
own mule and hired some donkeys from a Sudanese
police outpost nearby. In addition, Christine Scott, a
nurse at the mission station, volunteered to travel
with them; a most welcome companion.

The going got no easier. Sometimes they were
chest-deep in water. They rode the animals until they
could no longer bear to ride, then they walked until
they could no longer bear to walk, then they rode
again, on and on.

They slept in Mabaan villages. Making up milk for Carol's bottles was the expected nightmare. Sometimes the only water available came from mud puddles. They boiled it for a long, long time on a Primus stove. When they added the milk powder and shook it the mud made it look like chocolate milk. They watched Carol anxiously as, in happy ignorance, she trustingly guzzled it down. But it was well sterilized mud; she seemed none the worse.

As they moved on into the Dinka marshlands it became harder and harder to find carriers. They had hoped to catch a paddlewheel steamer to Khartoum when they reached the Nile, but after six days, still a day short of their goal, the carriers refused to go any further. The missionaries' morning prayers became very urgent.

"I believe we shall meet a truck," said Nurse Christine, right out of the blue. The men looked at her incredulously. A truck in that swampy plain?

One answer to their prayers came at once, however, as four of the tall Dinkas announced they had changed their minds: they would carry the bed after all. So they plodded on through the rising heat and humidity, the tall swamp grass often right above their heads. Suddenly Chuck stopped:

"Do you hear that? What is it?" It was the sound of a truck engine, distant but unmistakable.

They pushed their way as fast as they could through the long grass in the direction of the sound. They reached the truck in twenty minutes. To their amazement they recognized it, as well as the tall figure of Stan McMillan, a missionary from the station on the Nile at Melut which they were trying so hard to reach. Their message to Khartoum had been relayed to him and he had set out to look for them. Prevented by swamp from getting any further, he'd waited a day and a half to see if they appeared, running the engine at intervals to keep it in starting order. He interrupted the excited explanations:

"The postboat comes today. We could miss it if we don't hurry."

The twenty-five-mile dash to Melut was the worst Betty and Chuck had ever experienced. Bumping over high tufts of grass and swerving around pools of water, Stan drove as fast as he dared. Mercifully their pith helmets saved them from injury as their heads kept bumping the cab roof. They arrived at Melut completely exhausted, dirty and unkempt, with just time for a wash and a meal before a distant horn blast signalled the arrival of the steamer.

Aboard it they could rest at last. It was dry, there was food, there was a place to sleep. Two days on the river brought them to Kosti, the railhead, 180 miles south of Khartoum. A further hot day's journey by train brought them at last to the capital. From Yabus to Khartoum had taken ten days.

Betty recovered completely. But it was six months before they were able to return to Yabus and take up their work again.

Such stories were only too common, some of then ending in tragedy. They made missions, as well as the Sudan Government, reluctant to allow people to work in such remote situations. A better means of getting in and out was essential.

I felt a great peace at last when we returned to the Sudan. Here there was no question about the need for MAF. The previous two years had not been just a blind alley. They'd been a preparation.

Getting an air service started in the Sudan took us months. First, government permission had to be obtained from the Civil Aviation Department. The British, who ran it, kept a tight control. They needed to in a country ten times the size of Britain, only sparsely dotted with officials.

We were given permission promptly enough for an initial survey, but we were warned that any subsequent permit for regular operations would depend on the outcome of it and also that such a permit would require approval on a stricter basis. We were to report back after our survey.

One of our first tasks was to find suitable airstrip sites. South Sudan is very flat; that helped, but the swamps did not. At each mission station we had to seek an area slightly higher or drier than the surrounding waterlogged country, preferably with soil a little better than the pure clay "cotton soil" covering most of the region and which was rock hard in the dry season and treacherously soft in the rains.

The first of our journeys was to the very area in which Yabus lay. We flew in the Rapidé to Roseires, a remote trading town 350 miles southeast of Khartoum, landing in a temperature of forty degrees Celsius. The small government airstrip was surrounded by tall, tinder-dry grass. It would be easy for a bushfire to start and our wood-and-fabric Rapide was highly flammable, so we parked it as far from the grass as possible and left a Sudanese policeman to guard it.

From there we travelled by truck and car with Dr Malcolm Forsberg, who'd come with us. He was the

Sudan Interior Mission local field leader, known to
his friends as Mal. The dry season trails, though
rough, would be passable. This was the "good" time
to travel. With our food, water bottles and bedrolls
we crossed the Blue Nile on a local barge. On the far
side we boarded a battered traders' truck carrying
sacks of onions to an outpost called Kurmuk, a
hundred miles further south. Kurmuk was on the
edge of a far-reaching, desolate area of southeast
Sudan which Mal had christened evocatively The
Land Beyond the Nile.

George Morrow arrived in Kurmuk from Doro to
pick us up. His Ford truck bumped us through grassland and thorn trees for a couple of hours to the first
of the mission stations we were to visit. This was
Chali-el-fil, amongst the Uduk tribe.

"Jo Li! Jo Li!" The short, very black Uduk people
were running to welcome Mal. The men were carrying spears and bows and arrows. The women came
with their babies on their backs, supported there by
a strip of wood.

These friendly people had been classified by Western anthropologists as some of the most primitive in
Africa. They clasped the middle finger of Malcolm's
hand between the thumb and fingers of their own
which they clicked as they drew them away. It was
their distinctive tribal greeting. Their cry of "Jo Li",
however, was not their tribal "hello" but the name
they had given to Mal. His eldest child was a boy
called Leigh. According to Uduk custom a parent
took the name of his first son. So Mal was the father
of Leigh – in Uduk, Jo Li.

Mal, an American of Swedish parentage, with his

wife, Enid, had pioneered missionary work amongst them. When they came to Chali they learned the Uduk language and started on translation. Things had been far from easy at the beginning. Living conditions had been hard; Leigh had become ill and almost died. The people had been unresponsive and ridden with superstition (one of their customs had been to kill any twin babies). But the Forsbergs had seen the first Uduks become Christians and the radical changes that resulted, including the beginnings of a Uduk church. This work was now being led by two very capable ladies, Mary Beam and Betty Cridland, and was some of the most promising in the area.

Unlike most other places in south Sudan, Chali had a fair amount of red soil giving a better all-weather surface than the usual cotton soil. Frequent grass fires ensured there were no very tall trees. So we fairly easily found an area long enough for an adequate airstrip and marked some of the larger thorn trees at each end to show the correct alignment into the prevailing winds. Mary and Betty undertook to get the strip cleared.

We found another good site for a strip at Yabus, two hours further south. We also stopped at Doro and another station to look for more possibilities, getting back to Roseires a few days later.

When we reached the Rapide again the Sudanese policeman was still diligently guarding it. In fact he was cooking his food on a fire he'd lit in the shade under the wing right next to the fuel tanks. Fortunately the plane was unscathed.

A year later Betty Guth had to be evacuated again when her second baby was due. Instead of a dangerous ten-day overland journey we flew her to hospital in Khartoum in only four hours.

Having completed our survey of the Sudan Interior Mission stations along the Ethiopian border, we flew into the area further south where Don McClure worked. It was he who had written to us previously, at that critical point in London, with urgent appeals for a plane in south Sudan. It was he who had been the catalyst which finally brought us back to Africa to start MAF operations there. Now we were to see very vividly the reasons for his appeals, to experience at first hand more of the problems of surface travel, and, of course, to spend time with the man himself.

8

Better by Air

Don McClure lost his balance and fell. He'd been standing on the top of his pulpit at Akobo – a four-foot high wooden box – and his back hit it as he slipped. His head cracked down on the cement floor. He lay there unconscious.

He'd been using the pulpit to conduct physical exercises for the Anuak schoolboys inside the mission church because it had started to pour with rain outside. His vigorous demonstrations had tipped the box forward. When he recovered consciousness he was in agony, thinking he'd broken his back. It took his wife, Lyda, and two other missionaries four days to get him to hospital at Malakal.

The local rivers had been blocked by grass. The mission launch was tied up ten miles away, only accessible through swamp and forest. Don was carried to it on a stretcher slung high on the shoulders of eight Anuaks. Every step was excruciating. They started along the river in the launch but after only a mile it struck a large matted block of waterweed infested with crocodiles and snakes. They struggled through the night to clear it until, in the morning, local villagers helped them get free. Two miles later the process was repeated. Having lost a day and a half, they eventually arrived at Malakal.

From hospital Don wrote again: "Never did we
need a plane more."

Red-headed, Rash and Religious was the title of a
book about Don and his work as a missionary. So far
as it went the description was spot on, but there was
a lot more to Don than that.

In 1950, when we first met him, he and Lyda were
working among the Anuak tribe who lived partly in
the Upper Nile Province of the Sudan and partly over
the border in Ethiopia.

An experienced missionary, Don had initiated an
imaginative outreach plan called the Anuak Project.
The aim was to establish a self-supporting, self-propa-
gating Anuak church within fifteen years. The Anuak
language had to be reduced to writing, then the Bible
translated and the people taught to read it. Evangelists and pastors had to be trained. To cope with the
famines that regularly swept through the country,
agricultural development had been started and
schools and dispensaries were already functioning.
Ultimately the Anuak themselves should be able to
take over and the missionaries could move on, pioneering new areas.

Akobo, a remote government outpost, boasted an
airstrip though it was only a stretch of cleared and
levelled cotton soil. Jack and I, informed that the
landing ground was serviceable, flew there dodging
heavy rainstorms. We located it and landed safely.

We were immediately attracted to Don. Life around
him was never dull and we learned much during our
two weeks at Akobo. We were struck by the houses
all the missionaries lived in. They were of similar
materials and construction to the grass-roofed circu-
lar *tukls* of the Anuaks. Each house was made of

three wood-and-mud *tukls* joined by thatched verandas. Culturally, environmentally and financially
these struck us as better than the foreign type of
house usually erected by missions.

We saw quite a wide area during our visit. The
rainy season had barely begun and trails were still
passable, though only just. We travelled with Don
and Lyda in an unforgettable introduction to work in
south Sudan.

We were stranded by the roadside with the old mission Jeep, eighty miles from Akobo. It was the latest
of several mishaps since we'd left the mission station.
After only half a mile we'd had to stop to deal with
water in the carburettor, a common problem in that
humid atmosphere. Ten miles after that we'd had the
first puncture. The tyres were very vulnerable to the
many big thorns along the track. Tubeless tyres
weren't then available in Sudan and good tyres were
in short supply. Ours were very bad.

A temporary lack of puncture repair materials
hadn't worried Don much: he'd cheerfully resorted
to the method used by the Arab traders. Cutting a
patch from an old spare inner tube, he held it with a
pair of pliers over the flame of our Primus stove.
When it was half-melted he zapped it swiftly over
the hole, pressed it with his foot for a couple of
minutes and lo! it stuck. This was repeated almost
every half hour after that as new punctures appeared
or old patches failed.

All night we had slithered and stopped along the
muddy trails, bleary from lack of sleep. With dawn
we'd found that the wall of one of the tyres had itself
split wide open and the tube was bulging out. Don

was undaunted by this further challenge. He used a
piece of zebra skin to make a gaiter inside the tyre,
by no means the first time he had been obliged to
resort to such an expedient.

That got us to our next stop, Pibor, where we were
glad of a sleep in the government rest house. The
simple little grass thatched building had been provided for the use of the local British district commissioner. His task was to administer and travel,
often on horseback, an area the size of Wales.

The government had already agreed to a mission
station here and a site for it had been chosen. It was
vital to know whether an airstrip could be provided
to give better access than was possible overland. So
we were glad to find a sandy patch which would make
a reasonable all-weather landing ground. Another outpost could be established. On our way back to Akobo
we inspected several further areas.

Another journey, another government outpost and
mission station, another tribe. We were making for
Nasir, amongst the Nuers. Don had been unable to
come with us; Lyda was our guide and I was driving.
This time we were using the McClures' big but well-
worn Ford station wagon. We'd been travelling all
day along the side of the winding Sobat river.

En route we'd had trouble with the car overheating
and repaired a burst radiator hose with a roll of
adhesive bandage. When darkness fell we were only
halfway to our destination, so we pressed on, our
headlights swinging up and down on the uneven surface and reflecting off the walls of tall grass on either
side of the trail. It was very dark and the eyes of wild
animals glinted occasionally as we disturbed their

prowls. Otherwise we could see nothing ahead beyond the limited range of our lights.

"What's that?" I exclaimed suddenly. Just in front of us the earth road rose sharply. Then we saw it was built into a ramp to lead up to a bridge. But there was no bridge – only a yawning gap – and beyond that the river.

I braked hard, then realized the brakes were not working – we discovered later they'd been fractured by scraping over the rough roads. Unable to stop, I instinctively swerved, turning the station wagon sharply to the right. We bumped off the track just short of the dark river ahead. But I had swung the wheel the wrong way. A great hole yawned before us, some twenty feet across and eight feet deep. We lurched right into it. The car rolled over and lay on its side. Shaken but unhurt, we were able to get out. We looked at the hole and saw it had been made when soil was dug out to build the ramp.

"This is what happens in Sudan," said Lyda philosophically. "You've seen it for yourselves. That's why we want a plane!"

The station wagon was too heavy to move, so we decided to wait for daylight to seek help. We lay down in the grass and went to sleep. Yes, we did sleep, though I remember hearing lions roaring in the night. Many wild animals roamed these areas. We were all badly bitten – by mosquitoes.

Early next morning, twenty Nuer tribesmen came walking along the trail, spears in hand. They helped us push the car out of the hole. The engine started and we piled in hopefully, but the car didn't budge. I found the drive key on the rear axle had sheared. We managed to find a six-inch nail amongst some building materials in the car and I was able to file a rough replacement. It eventually got us to Nasir by mid-afternoon.

The mission at Nasir was different from the others we had visited. It wasn't a new location, having been there for thirty-seven years, dedicated to the service of the Nuer. It had a dispensary, two nurses, a doctor, an agriculturist, separate boys' and girls' schools and a church.

The Nuer were an intelligent, independent, warlike and semi-nomadic people. Black as ebony, they were generally very tall and slim. I have a photo of Jack and Helen Hemmings next to some Nuer men. Jack himself was a full six foot but in the picture Helen, sitting on his shoulders, had her head only just level with that of one of the Nuers.

Life for the Nuers revolved around their cattle. Cows were needed to buy a wife. The number of cows owned was the measure of a man's wealth. They drank their milk, the men mixed cattle dung with ashes to plaster down their hair, bleaching and straightening it. The dung was also used in finishing and firing their clay pots and was an essential ingredient in house construction. It strengthened the mud and made it more durable.

Fascinating as we found all this, we soon learned that the Nuer lifestyle had some dark undertones: taboos and totems, constant fear of malevolent curses, sacrifices to ward off evil spirits and the evil eye. Theirs wasn't the happy and carefree existence it seemed at first sight.

Like other outposts, Nasir was very cut off and the missionaries were keen to find an airstrip site. With Chuck Jordan, the mission agriculturist, we tramped

around the outskirts of the village and identified the
driest area in the generally swampy countryside. Here
was another situation in the Upper Nile Province
where it was going to be better to travel by air.

After our survey of the Nasir and Akobo areas we
flew back westward to Malakal. The town was not
much to look at. We'd been totally unimpressed
when we'd called there two years earlier on our first
trip out from London to Nairobi. But small and insig-
nificant though it might appear, it was the focal point
of the Upper Nile Province, the centre of its administration and headquarters of the Provincial Government.

The Sudan is the largest country in Africa. The
Upper Nile Province alone was the size of the UK.
(It's been divided into two since then.) Imagine a
single small, sleepy, very primitive town at the centre
of Britain. In terms of scale that would represent
Malakal. Imagine, too, every British hill flattened,
leaving nothing but a vast, monotonous expanse of
grassland, hot and dry for half the year, swamped by
rain for the other half: that will give an idea of its
surroundings.

Malakal stands on the bank of the Nile, which
flows through the whole length of the Sudan. It is
exactly halfway along the course of the river from its
distant source in Uganda to its delta mouth in Egypt:
2000 miles in each direction.

The Nile is the main artery of communication in
the south and Malakal is one of the principal stopping
places for its slow postboats. In those days these
wood-fired paddle steamers carried most of the mail,
supplies and passengers to and from Khartoum and

northern Sudan. They had passenger cabins on top
and pushed a barge in front, with another at either
side to give extra carrying capacity and stability. The
Province also had two steamers – smaller versions of
the postboats – for more local use along some of the
Nile tributaries in the region.

As Jack, Helen and I flew back into Malakal, we
were again dodging heavy storms. Torrential rain and
wind-driven cumulo-nimbus clouds had only just
moved away from the town itself and the runway of
the little airfield was still glinting with water. As we
circled over the town and river, Jack, peering through
the wet windscreen, suddenly tightened his grip on
the control column.

"Look at the river – one of the steamers has turned
over!"

I looked and was horrified. The steamer's barges
had broken away and were scattered in the water.
The steamer itself had completely overturned and
was floating upside down, the cabins underneath the
water.

As soon as we landed we heard the tragic news:
the wife of a British official and her daughter had
drowned. So had a police officer who'd tried to save
them.

Travel by air had its dangers, but other travel
methods could be dangerous too, even the safe-seem-
ing steamers on the peaceful Nile. The river never
seemed quite as innocent to me after that.

In Malakal we visited the Provincial Governor, John
Winder, a British official of the Sudan Civil Service.
He was interested to hear details of our survey and
issued authority for the immediate clearing of air-

strips at the places we'd explored with the McClures.

We had one final area to visit before returning to Khartoum. It lay at Obel, just south of Malakal. There we sat on the shady veranda of the home of an English couple, Alan and Phyllis Webb, whilst Phyllis poured welcome cups of tea from a large teapot. We drank it thirstily after coming in from the glare and heat outside.

Obel was a secluded spot in the bush where the river Sobat joins the Nile. Alan was headmaster of a teacher training school there. As the senior education-alist in his mission, he particularly wanted to visit similar schools among the Nuers at Nasir and the Anuak at Akobo. We were discussing how we could help him.

Drinking tea with us was another Englishman, Mr Meadows, the government education officer for the province. He was listening enviously to the plans being made.

"I want to see the government let us officials fly by MAF too," he said.

"Where would you want to go?" we asked.

"I'd like to get into Doro and see the schools in that area."

"That should be possible," we said. "It's less than an hour and a half's flying from Malakal."

"Do you realize," said Meadows, "that if I wanted to go to Doro now, while the rains are on and the roads closed, I'd have to go via Khartoum and Rosei-res? That would be a thousand-mile surface trip com-pared with your one and a half hours by air!"

Here were comparisons that would more than satisfy Murray Kendon's vision!

Our survey had been very positive: the needs very clear, the contrasts between land and air travel dramatic. There was none of the ambivalence revealed by the earlier Gemini survey. Missionaries were already pressing for bookings on the plane in every direction. The Provincial governor and his officials wanted to use it too.

But . . . would the Sudan Government let us operate in this difficult region? Would they lay down so many restrictions that it would be impracticable?

In spite of everything, would we have to return to London again, unable to establish an air service, even in an obviously needy region? Would we, as had been predicted at the Mildmay council meeting, once more "come back with our tails between our legs"?

We had to return to Khartoum and await the government's answer.

9

Patience

A big ceiling fan rotated slowly above us with a
steady, rhythmic creak. It was May 1950, and it was
hot in Khartoum. The fan stirred the warm air in the
large bare office where we sat. Faded green louvred
shutters were closed over the large open windows,
allowing air to enter but excluding the glaring sun-
light and searing heat. At one end of the office stood
a big brown wooden desk with big brown wooden In-
and Out-trays.

At the desk opposite us, dressed in tropical khaki,
sat Squadron Leader McCall, the Sudan Government
Civil Secretary for Air, reading a document we had
given him. Behind him hung a portrait of King George
VI, while the wall facing the windows displayed a
large detailed map of the Sudan. Jack and I had
brought in our survey report and, with it, our request
to start an air service for missions in the south. We
were awaiting his reactions and praying silently.

McCall looked up: "I see Governor John Winder of
the Upper Nile Province has been helpful and positive
regarding your survey this past month," he commented. This seemed a promising start, especially as
he went on: "I see no great problems in your proposals."

But then came the bombshell: "One major requirement will be that you always fly with a qualified and

licensed wireless telegraphy operator, able to trans-
mit and receive messages in Morse code. It's essential
that you keep in touch with our air traffic control
system so that we can always know your take-offs,
your position and your landings."

One of our crew would have to obtain a WT operator's licence, for which a speed of twenty words a
minute would be required. If issued to us, it would
be the first flight WT radio operator's licence ever
given by the Sudan Government. At that time there
was no long-range radio telephone (RT) for voice communication in air traffic reporting in Sudan. It all had
to be done in Morse code.

My Morse speed at that stage (learned in the Cardiff
University Air Squadron ten years before) was about
eight words a minute, far short of the international
standard. We were surprised and shaken by this new
demand. It would take me some months to reach the
speed required, a serious delay in starting any regular
flying. But it couldn't be avoided.

McCall was speaking again: "The other thing is
that your whole proposal for an air operation in the
south will need to be considered and agreed by the
Political Department. This will take time."

That was the beginning of a new series of challenges.
To meet the first I immediately started to study
Morse to reach the standard demanded. My father
had been one of the first members of the newly
formed Royal Corps of Signals in World War I. He
could read Morse at high speed – even automatic
Morse. Always a keen radio enthusiast, he picked up
messages from all over the world. As a child I had
watched him do this with fascinated admiration. He

told me of amazing operators who could send out Morse messages at high speed while receiving and writing down equally rapid incoming messages at the same time. That legendary ideal I never attained.

Learning Morse in the heat of Sudan proved demanding. For part of the time I was helped by a Sudanese official from the Khartoum Post and Tele- graph offices. Effendi Youssef Banyouti, an Egyptian, would come and give me an hour's instruction each afternoon, after which I had to put in a lot of hard and hot practice on my own.

I shared a room at the headquarters of the Sudan Interior Mission in Khartoum with two other men, Bill Rogers and Dr Lionel Gurney. At that point, each of us had a different task. Mine was to learn Morse as quickly as I could. Bill's was to learn Arabic. Dr Lionel's was to discover whether God wanted him to set up Christian medical work along the Red Sea coast.

There were days when all three of us were working away in the room together. In one corner I would be making a buzzer sing out Morse messages in a continuous rhythm. In another corner Bill would be poring over his books, muttering away in Arabic. In the centre Dr Lionel would be kneeling beside one of the iron bedsteads, lost in silent prayer.

In later years Dr Lionel founded the Red Sea Mis- sion team; Bill pioneered work in south Sudan and later went to Nigeria. I became involved in a life- time's work with MAF.

Whilst I was concentrating on meeting one challenge, others were building up.

"We are seriously in debt," wrote a worried Dr

Cochrane to us in Khartoum. "We already have an overdraft of £3000 with the bank."

Then came another blow: Jack and Helen had to return to the UK. Although an experienced and professional RAF pilot, Jack had been unable to obtain a civil commercial pilot's licence because of a very slight defect in his sight. Our policy in MAF was to operate only to full commercial standards, in both flying and maintenance, even though we were not going to be flying for profit. The lack of a commercial licence ruled Jack out as a longer-term pilot with MAF.

Dr Cochrane had made it clear that, with a rapidly increasing bank overdraft, Mildmay could not pay Jack and Helen's passage home; nor could they pay a pilot to replace him. Nor, worst of all, had they even the funds to support the ongoing work of MAF in the Sudan.

We believed the problems would be overcome. Jack was prepared to pay for the passages home himself. As for the costs of continuing to stay in the Sudan, we were still sure God had called us there and convinced He would provide for us.

Our position on financing future operations was based on three main principles. First, the cost of providing the plane had already been covered and we'd continue to subsidize the operating overheads (such as insurance, operating fees and administration) as far as we could. Second, we would make a minimum charge for running costs, including fuel and spares. Third, we would each find our own living expenses and personal financial support.

This was similar to the policy followed by MAF USA. It meant that MAF services had a basic financial viability. Any new funds could be used to purchase further aircraft and subsidize or expand the work. We felt that this was a wise, God-given policy. It certainly proved effective through many subsequent years.

I was more than sorry to part with Jack and Helen when, late in July, they went home, leaving me very much on my own. We knew a replacement pilot would soon be available, but didn't know when he'd be able to arrive.

The last crisis of this series was yet to come. Mildmay sent word that they were unable to pay Murray Kendon's return passage to England. He decided to stay in New Zealand so was no longer available to represent MAF in the UK.

I had hoped that Jack Hemmings, with all his experience and ability, would stay in the work, but that was not to be. Another ex-RAF man, Bill Knights, who had come in to administer the office while Jack, Murray and I were away, was able to continue for a further couple of years. Mildmay certainly could not afford anyone extra, so Jack returned to his prewar profession of accounting.

I was left to negotiate with the Sudan Government our proposals for an air service for missions. Further stories of missionaries' travel needs and hardships continued to reach me. While I was still waiting for the government's response, requests for the plane kept coming in.

Humanly speaking, things were hardly hopeful. Jack had gone, we were short of funds and I hadn't yet attained the necessary speed in Morse. Strangely, I don't remember being discouraged. God promises to provide all our needs and there was friendship, encouragement and fellowship at the mission head-quarters there in Khartoum. God must have given me the necessary measure of faith (looking back, I'm amazed at how much He must have given!). I continued to see the real need and purpose of MAF in the Sudan. If God was with us, who could be against us?

"Stuart, I've some good news for you!" It was the SIM treasurer in her little Khartoum office. "I've been given the money to pay the customs duty on the spares that have arrived for the Rapide." She was not allowed to tell me who had provided it.

That was just one of many encouragements. Two other gifts came from SIM missionaries, this at a time when they were not receiving even their own very small salaries in full. There were some other anonymous gifts. The love and practical help that came from the very people we were seeking to serve was heartening. God was good; God was faithful.

Then came even greater encouragement. The new MAF pilot was ready. He was Steve Stevens, an officer in the South African Air Force, who'd won the DFC flying twin-engined Beaufighters over the Balkans in World War II. Later he'd flown many transport flights, ferrying military staff from Cairo to South Africa. He knew Africa well. Khartoum had been one of his staging posts. Posted there for a short time in 1947 as an Air Force liaison officer, he'd made contact with the SIM and learned of the great isolation of their southern stations and the need for a mission plane. He realized then why he'd been brought to Khartoum: God was preparing him to fly that plane.

Soon after this, Steve heard of MAF and wrote to

the office at Mildmay. His letter came at the time of our preparations for the Central Africa Gemini survey. Murray Kendon had promptly replied, telling him of the plans, telling him, too, that Sudan would be considered in the future. Now that future had arrived and Steve got ready to leave the Air Force and come to Sudan. He wrote saying that he would be able to support himself and his family from his Air Force savings, at least until other support could be generated from Christian friends in South Africa.

A little over a month after Jack and Helen had left, I was called in to see the Political Secretary. Mal Forsberg came with me. The meeting was at Gordon's Palace, built on the site where General Gordon died in 1885 while defending Khartoum against the attacking Dervishes. We had come to the heart of the Sudan Government.

The political secretary had before him the file from the Civil Aviation Department containing our survey reports and application.

"This is the first time we've had anything like this!" was his opening remark. He added: "There's a great deal involved in trying to grant such a permission. Are we going to put you under the classification of 'traders'? You are going to be working in districts in the south that we classify as 'closed areas'. We will need to think about granting you special permits for entry to these areas. Then we've got to ask ourselves: what effect will granting you a charter licence have in the future? It will set a precedent. We are going to have to consider all these things very carefully."

He went on to ask us how we were supported. I

don't remember how I answered him on that, but somehow he seemed satisfied. God was on our side.

"It will be three weeks before we can let you know our final decision," he warned as we left. It was with some surprise that, only six days later, I received a letter from him. It said, "Your project has been approved."

Steve had said he could come up in mid-September. I now wired saying, "Come". On 14th September he arrived from Johannesburg, leaving his wife, Kay, and their three daughters (with Coleen just one month old) to follow later. In God's grace he only had to pay half-fare and was given a double baggage allowance. I was glad to see him. After all the years of preparation, after all the setbacks, our regular operations were about to begin.

◆◆◆◆◆

10

Starting the Service

Herbert Major was used to wide open country. He came from the little town of Dorance in the USA in the middle of the immense Kansas wheatfields where fast, straight roads took him anywhere he needed to go.

However, Herb wasn't at Dorance, Kansas, but at Doro in the Sudan – the same station as George Morrow. He had ridden in there on muleback from Roseires, 125 slow miles through boggy rain-soaked bush. His family, left in Khartoum, would have to wait five months for the dry season before they could join him. Even then they would have a long, hard journey.

Was there an alternative? Could he get an airstrip cleared at Doro? A few months earlier those Englishmen from this new Aviation Fellowship had been to Doro with Mal Forsberg. They'd considered an airstrip feasible. Someone would have to provide one soon. Why wait?

The work needed was daunting. The good news was that the length of ground near the mission station was not pure cotton soil: it was part sand and silt. The bad news was that this particular spot, unlike much of the surrounding grasslands, was covered by thick undergrowth and trees. There were many palms and, worse, some baobabs, up to sixty feet high and thirty feet in diameter. An axe stuck in their pulpy trunks if anybody attempted to cut them down. They would have to be burned. For good measure there were numerous termite hills, hard, solid and nine feet tall.

How could the job be tackled? The mission had few tools and the local Mabaan would need persuading to help. It wasn't work they took to naturally and it would be long and hard. Moreover, now in the rainy season they'd be busy with their crops and money wouldn't tempt them.

Herb and George consulted Mal Forsberg, who encouraged them to go ahead. Mal wrote his own account of what happened.*

They decided that they would have to get the people excited enough about the coming of the plane to work on the airstrip.

They called the chiefs together. "One of those things that flies overhead is going to land here," they explained. "It needs a long clear place for sitting down."

It was hard to explain why the little speck on the horizon needed a long space in which to sit down. "It has wheels. It comes down fast and can't stop quickly . . ." The Mabaans had seen wheels on cars and trucks. They had cleared the roads of grass each year to allow vehicles to travel during the dry season. But the thing in the sky didn't need a road. And besides, when birds landed, they didn't need much room. They could land on the branch of a tree.

*Malcolm Forsberg Last Days on the Nile pp. 135–6, J. B. Lippin-cott Company, Philadelphia and New York, 1966

The conversation went back and forth.

"Where is the plane?"

"In Khartoum."

"What will it come here for?"

"To bring my wife and two children."

"Are you going to let your wife and babies go up in that thing?"

"It will bring my wife and babies just as soon as you make a place for it to sit down."

The Mabaans were "talking it up" now. They had seen mysterious commercial aircraft flying overhead. They had never understood how the planes got up so high and stayed there. They had heard that men and women were in the planes. How small were these men and women? The planes that contained them were only specks in the sky.

The head chief spoke. "We'll clear the place," he said.

Mabaan from different villages came at different times to work on the airstrip. Before it was ready, well over a thousand people had toiled on it, a thousand trees had been cleared and eight weeks had elapsed. Tree-root holes were filled in and the strip was finally smoothed by dragging a heavy beam over it, towed by George's old Ford truck. The end result was an eight hundred-yard strip, clear and level, better than most of the mission strips in the south.

In Khartoum a telegram arrived for us. It read: MY TRUCK CAN GO FORTY MPH ON AIRSTRIP AFTER FIRST DRAGGING. GEORGE Nine days later came another telegram, STRIP READY. FIFTY MPH OVER STRIP. CAR WON'T GO FASTER.

A week later I passed my WT operator's Morse test,

rather to my surprise and greatly to my relief. The
licence approved, we were free to start operations.
Exactly another week later we set off in the Rapide
to fly first to Malakal and then to Doro.

The early morning flight from Khartoum to Malakal
was smooth. This was nice for our passengers: Mal
Forsberg, Herb's wife, Mary Ethel, their two small
children, and another lady missionary.

As we flew I had to use not only Morse code but
also the international Q Code, which enables messages to be passed in shorter form and with less chance
of misunderstanding than ordinary words put into
Morse. All our departure and arrival times, altitude,
position and other information were transmitted in
the Q Code.

This flight began a special era for me. For the next
seven years the radio operator's compartment became
my home in the plane. From it I was always in touch
with the pilot just in front of me. During many difficult landings or take-offs, I'd find I was either praying
us safely down or praying us safely up. Our airstrips
were short, their surface and condition frequently
unknown, often soft and dangerous. Our plane had
its limitations for take-off, sometimes finding it difficult to climb steeply out of a small airstrip slotted in
amidst trees. It also had its limitations for landing –
only two small airbrakes to help slow it down on the
approach. They gave no extra lift like the flaps of
modern aircraft. Also our wheel brakes were the old-
style cable ones.

From my radio operator's seat I kept an eye on the
passengers and learned a lot about their reactions to
travelling in small MAF planes. I used to provide
them with tea from a Thermos. I enjoyed giving a

good cabin service. Anyway, I liked having a cup of tea myself.

On this inaugural trip as radio operator I was quite anxious. But the air radio operator at Malakal knew I had only just acquired my licence, so he sent his messages slowly, repeating them whenever necessary.

I later learned to like the radio work, coming to love the singsong of the Morse notes as they came through and enjoyed tapping back messages and responses in similar musical rhythm. I appreciated the coded talking back and forth with the Sudanese radio operators throughout the Sudan; they included me in their camaraderie. At the end of a hard day's flying it was nice to get the final Morse message from the operator on the ground: "GN OM" – "Goodnight old man."

Both the transmitter and the receiver were enormous. The transmitter had two eight-inch tall, old-fashioned thermionic valves, the kind that slowly warmed up to emit a bright orange glow. They were a total contrast to later miniaturized transistors. The set could operate at nearly full power even with one of these valves out of action. They threw out quite a bit of heat. I always said that you could have made toast between them.

When we landed at Malakal we found the officials as excited as we were about this first flight into Doro. They knew, as we did, that finding the mission in the featureless expanse of grassland was not going to be easy.

The district commissioner for the Mabaan area asked whether we'd be able to take government officials soon. We replied we'd be more than happy,

but the Khartoum authorities would have to authorize it first.

I went to see the air radio operator in his little hut
on the airfield and thanked him for his help. We
discussed procedures for this exploratory flight into
Doro and arranged to make contact every fifteen
minutes.

Only Steve and I as crew and Mal Forsberg as a
"guide" who knew the area were allowed by the Civil
Aviation authorities to make the first proving flight
to Doro. The strip must be tried out before we took
any other passengers. The women and children waved
us off, then waited in Malakal.

As we flew on our compass course to Doro, we
soon saw why, several years before, the RAF had
experienced problems in locating any of the mission
stations. There were no identifiable landmarks at all;
just an endless expanse of vague, flat, barren grassland
with occasional ill-defined trails, seasonal streams,
small groups of trees or patches of bush. We flew high
enough to get a good overview of the countryside. I
peered constantly through our drift-sight checking to
what extent any winds might be blowing us off track.
Steve adjusted our heading accordingly.

After an hour and a quarter, we should have arrived
over Doro, but could see nothing of it. Neither could
Mal. Steve was tense: was this going to be a repeat
of the RAF episode?

The eager air radio operator in Malakal came
through my headphones in Morse: "Can you see
Doro?"

"No," I tapped back. "Looking. Will call on sight
Doro."

Off to the right we picked out the winding thread

of what we thought must be the little Yabus river. Doro should be near it.

"I'm starting a square search procedure," called Steve. I passed the word back to Mal, still scanning the unrevealing countryside below.

Suddenly Steve called, "There's the strip!"

Only then did we spot the much less obvious roofs of the mission buildings nearby. The strip looked splendid, clearly defined with white markers along the sides. Herb and George had obviously seen us coming. They had a smoke fire burning to show us the direction of the wind.

Steve circled a few times, sizing up the strip and its surroundings, and then came in to land.

"QGV DORO QAL," I Morsed in Q code to Malakal. "Seen Doro – landing." We tightened our belts.

We could see Herb and George on one side and the many upturned faces of Mabaan tribespeople all along the edge amidst the debris of cleared brush and undergrowth.

As Steve brought the plane down, three goats, frightened by the motors, dashed right across the strip in front of us. George and two Mabaans leapt forward like the lightning ballboys at Wimbledon and scurried them off just in time. Steve put the plane down smoothly on the excellent strip.

Herb was first at the cabin door as I swung it open. Behind him were crowds of Mabaans, clutching their spears and wide-eyed with interest. Herb was a big man and he had a big smile as he greeted us.

"I have never been so excited in all my life!" he said. We could see that was true. We were excited too. So were the Mabaans. They were seeing a plane

on the ground for the first time at last. They looked
closely at us foolhardy people who travelled in such
a strange and dangerous vehicle.

We spent the rest of the day looking at the airstrip
and working on the plane. Early the following morning we flew back to Malakal. The Governor, John
Winder, wanted to discuss plans with us. He was
helpful and supportive but had three main questions:

"How has the flight to Doro worked out?" He was
satisfied with our report on that.

"Why don't you come and base in Malakal? That
would be the best centre of communications." We
understood his reasoning but were not yet sure.

"Should I be contacting the Civil Aviation authorities in Khartoum to get permission for my district
commissioners to be carried by your plane?"

We replied that the Civil Air secretary would be
the one to authorize that.

The same afternoon we flew back to Doro with
Mary Ethel and the children. It gave us great satisfac-
tion to see the Major family reunited. God was good.
Our regular operations had made a very positive start.

We had now to get to the Akobo area to meet the
needs of Don McClure and his fellow workers there.
Further flight requests were coming in. We needed to
develop the service as quickly as possible. We must
get ourselves a base in south Sudan. Then Steve could
bring his family from South Africa.

We didn't take the governor's advice to base at
Malakal. To put it bluntly, we couldn't afford to.
Mildmay's financial position had continued to
worsen and we had very little money of our own. We
decided instead to start at Akobo where we'd been

offered some spare temporary accommodation rent free. There was a telegraph office at the nearby government post. We wouldn't be too cut off.

A new alignment had been approved for the Akobo airstrip. It should be a bit more weatherproof because the soil was a little better. The district commissioner had men working on it from both the Anuak and the Nuer tribes in the area. As an incentive he organized a competition to see who could clear the most in the shortest time. The prize was a bull. The Nuers won.

When we landed there the new strip was smooth and even. For me, coming back to Akobo was like coming home. I always loved the picturesque, low, thatched houses at the mission and found the quiet river flowing lazily past tremendously peaceful. I liked to sit by it in the cool of the dawn, to have my time with God before the work of the day began.

So it was that Akobo, with the American Presbyterian Mission and the Anuak people, was our first MAF base in south Sudan.

Everyone there, including us, worked very hard during the week. When we weren't away flying, Steve and I would be working on the plane or trying to improve the airstrip. Saturday evenings were different. As the sun's heat waned we'd all relax and play volleyball until darkness stopped us.

On Sundays we'd go to the Anuak church services and on Sunday evenings have fellowship and prayer together, sharing one another's burdens, sometimes in English, sometimes in Anuak. One prayer by an Anuak leader was translated for us by Don McClure: "Lord God, bless the men with the aeroplane and

keep them safe. I don't know, Lord, how you keep up
with them, they fly so fast." We were grateful that
God could more than keep up with us: He was always
ahead.

It was at the end of November in the dry season
of 1950 that we came to Akobo. Steve and I spent
Christmas there. On Christmas Eve, a Sunday, we all
joined with the Anuak at the Akobo Mission church.
A lame Anuak woman arrived there on her hands and
knees, having crawled all the way from her village.
The missionaries took her back home in the Jeep.
They'd have fetched her too if they'd known in time.
I was impressed by the love and care they showed
in their dealings with their African brothers and
sisters.

The morning service was followed by baptisms in
the river. Men and women declared their new life in
Jesus Christ. Charms and gourds used in spirit
worship floated downstream as the Anuak cast them
off to signify their new allegiance. Africans and
missionaries then clambered into canoes and the
missionaries' three small boats with outboard
motors. We went six miles upriver to another Anuak
village where more baptisms and a Communion
service were held.

After an early morning service on Christmas Day
a big feast was prepared. A bull had been killed for
the communal dinner and large basins of *dura* (the
local millet) were set alongside the meat. Anuak and
missionary joined in the meal, dipping hands together
into the bowls. To our Western nostrils the smell of
the food was exceptionally strong so we ate with less
enthusiasm than the Anuak. But the fellowship was
tremendous. By mid-afternoon Steve and I were back

at the aeroplane, getting it ready for an early flight the next day. The demands of the work were ceaseless, but we had no complaints. It was good to be where God wanted us.

Now that we had a base, Steve could get his family. We took the Rapide on a long trip south to Nairobi carrying a full load of missionaries who needed a break from the Sudan heat. I stayed in Nairobi while essential maintenance was carried out on our plane.

Steve travelled on down to Johannesburg, returning with the whole family in a plane he had been employed to ferry to Nairobi. Finally we all flew to Akobo in the Rapide. There, one of the American mission families kindly made room for me in their house. The Stevens and their three girls (Merle, Pam and Coleen) moved in with another American family. The very first night they were attacked and bitten by invading army ants. Kay spent the next couple of days beginning to get acclimatized to housekeeping in south Sudan.

Then came the fire. Three nights after our arrival the house where Steve and Kay were living burst into flames. An oil lamp started it, igniting a long dry stalk which fell from the roof and sent a flame upwards into the thatch. In no time the roof was ablaze from end to end.

In the other house we heard the commotion and rushed out, horrified. It was a relief to find that everyone had escaped unhurt. But almost everything in the house was lost, including all the Stevens's possessions, even their passports. The fire blazed late into the night, a devastating experience for the newly arrived family. Steve and Kay moved to a little used (and not very well-repaired) government rest house a

mile away which the sympathetic district commissioner said MAF could occupy for the time being.

A flight to Nasir later that week carried news of
the catastrophe. There was an immediate response
from the generous missionaries. We returned to
Akobo with a plane full of clothes, kitchen utensils
and even a paraffin stove. We looked like a winged
removal van full of household equipment.

After a few weeks, Kay and Steve invited me to
move in with them at the rest house so that we
could be together. Kay had to work with very limited
supplies and hardly any equipment and now she had
me to cater for as well.

I appreciated all she did in that strange, difficult
and primitive environment. The roof of the government rest house leaked freely when it rained. Wide
gaps between walls and roof provided easy access for
various creatures. Mosquitoes and bats flew in at
night and you never knew when you might find a
scorpion or even a snake. I took photos of Merle
holding a large spitting cobra by the tail and of
little Pam dangling its severed head from a
string.

In the months that followed, airstrip after airstrip
was sited, cleared and brought into use. My flying
logbook and diaries tell of hundreds of exciting and
rewarding flights. A fresh sense of relief and mobility
came to the missionaries. Aerial surveys were carried
out to locate people who were still unreached. There
was new ability to help the Sudanese, either by bringing in doctors or by getting seriously ill patients to
medical care at some bigger centre. We saw the whole
area opening up. Later, with the agreement of the

Civil Aviation Department, our planes were used by the Provincial Government too.

Our Rapide became a welcome sight to many. We put a name on its nose in Arabic: *Asfur Allah, God's Bird.*

11

Hard Rain, Soft Airstrips

One Sunday, early in May 1951, storm clouds began to gather in the skies all around Akobo. It was oppressively hot and humid. When night came the bright new moon was soon blotted out by approaching storms. Spasmodic lightning illuminated the wide horizon. Answering thunder echoed close by. Later in the night a strong wind blew up.

Steve, Kay, the children and I tumbled out of our beds on the veranda of the decrepit little rest house just as the storm hit. Rain beat furiously on the corrugated iron roof above our heads, making such a din that we could scarcely hear ourselves speak. It was even hard to think.

Crude canvas blinds had been rolled down over the wire-screened window openings and veranda to keep rain out. Now we rushed round rolling them up lest they should be torn off in the fierce wind. The beds got wet. Rain poured through gaps in the roof. The floors swam with water. We moved the most vulnerable articles on to chairs and tables. For two hours we listened to the heavy, tropical downpour.

"I wonder how our wooden plane is doing out there in all of this," I groaned.

Steven wondered too and added his own question. "What'll all this water be doing to the airstrip?"

Dawn came. Fifty millimetres of rain had fallen

and we found the strip was quite soft. We were due to take off to pick up a missionary in Malakal.

"We'll let the sun work on the strip for a couple of hours," said Steve. "Then we can see if it'll be safe for take-off."

We spent the time refuelling and cleaning the plane. About 10 a.m. we decided to go. But the plane taxied only a few yards before one wheel sank deep into a muddy crack in the cotton soil. I jumped out and, with help from some Anuaks who'd been watching, we pushed and pulled while Steve revved the engines. We managed to get clear of the hole and on to a better spot. I resumed my seat in the radio compartment.

"We can't taxi too slowly or the same will happen again," Steve called to me over his shoulder as he opened up the throttles for another attempt. This time we kept moving fast enough to prevent the wheels sinking into the mud and managed to get airborne before the end of the strip.

During the next three weeks another three big storms (as well as some lesser ones) struck Akobo. Nearly 200 millimetres of rain fell in that time.

We'd moved to Akobo in the dry season and had worked hard on the airstrip. But the rains were already threatening to make it unusable. Perhaps we could add sand from the river to improve the cotton soil and make the surface less vulnerable to the rains?

It was a mammoth task. Anuak and Nuer men dug the sand out of the riverbed whilst women carried it up the bank in four-gallon tins. (All the car and aviation fuel came in these.) The sand was emptied into the mission's pick-up truck and driven the half mile to the airstrip. Steve had grown up on a farm and was used to dealing with the soil. He supervised the laying of a narrow sandy carpet along the centre of the strip, just wide enough for the wheels of the plane. A wooden beam towed behind the mission Jeep scraped it all level.

It certainly made a difference, but not enough to cope with the rains as they became more regular. It would take several years of such treatment to render the airstrip reasonably usable throughout the wet season. Even with the sand, taking off from Akobo became like taking off with our brakes partly on. It was nerve-racking. The soft clinging soil didn't want to let go of the wheels.

The longer the rains continued the deeper became the softness of the ground and the greater the problem. We were in danger of being marooned. The new service we'd started could be brought to a total halt, just at the time missions were most cut off and most in need of us.

We didn't really want to move. We'd just begun to feel settled at Akobo, but we had to find a base with a better airstrip.

We chose Doro, 150 miles to the north, and we all flew across in the Rapide with our few worldly possessions. The Morrows had left Doro and SIM gladly lent their old house to the Stevens. I had an African-style *tukl* nearby, fourteen feet in diameter, grass-thatched, mud-walled. I shared it with the occasional scorpion and rat and with the rain that came through the roof during storms.

The soil on the Doro airstrip was considerably better than at Akobo and we worked hard on it. But one day we came out after a storm to be met by an amazing sight. The Rapide sat reflected in a half-

mile-long lake, its wheels awash. Better drainage was
vital, so Steve's farming experience was again put to
use. We found the lowest points in the surrounding
area and dug ditches to drain the rain waters down
to them, allowing the strip to dry out more quickly.

The work in those days was very experimental:
there was still much to learn about the different types
of soil. Conditions and problems varied greatly as
we passed through the wet and dry seasons. At the
beginning of the rains, for instance, the surface soil
would become slippery, whilst the undersoil was still
firm. The plane might tend to skid, but the wheels
would not sink in.

Later on in the season, when the rain had penetrated deeper, a day or two of sun could bake the
surface into a hard crust, apparently firm but leaving
the undersoil still very soft. The wheels of the plane
were then liable to break through the crust into the
mud below. That could flip the plane on its back
when taxi-ing, taking off or landing.

Those on the ground needed to know when a strip
was safe because they were responsible for signalling
to us whether or not we could land. How soft could
it be before they warned us off? We tried to develop
tests for them. There was a "heel test": if you dug
your heel in and it went more than two inches deep,
it meant the strip was not safe.

One of the best tests was to drive a loaded vehicle
along the strip at about fifty miles an hour, as George
Morrow had done when they first made the Doro
landing ground. This showed up dangerous undu-
lations and also, if the vehicle left deep tracks, demon-
strated that the subsoil was wet and unsafe.

We'd already discovered that if we taxied too

slowly on a soft strip the wheels would sink into muddy spots and stop the plane altogether. Steve continued to use the technique of taxi-ing fast enough to prevent this and usually gained sufficient speed for take-off. Taxi-ing a little faster gave some lift to the wings, helping to reduce the weight on the wheels and lessen the likelihood of bogging down.

Stan McMillan, who had gone to the rescue of the Guths as they struggled to reach Melut, was now in charge of a SIM station at Abaiyat, which was in the middle of the Dinka plains. With him, as well as his wife and young daughter, were two single lady missionaries. The senior, Marie Anderson, came from Canada and had been there for some five years working among the people in the surrounding villages. The younger, Phyllis Bapple, had for three years worked as Mal Forsberg's secretary in Khartoum. Feeling God was calling her to work among the Dinkas, she had been posted to Abaiyat.

The Dinkas often gave their villages nasty names with the idea of frightening away evil spirits. Abaiyat means the Yath or village of the Devil. The local witch doctors there strongly opposed the Christian message. A number of years before, when the first missionary couple came, a curse was put on a leg of goat which was then given to them. They cooked and ate it gladly. The village people expected to hear the death wail during the night, but nothing happened. The next morning, when they saw all the family walking about, they were mystified and then chagrined. Finally they admitted that the power of the new God must be stronger than theirs. One witch doctor

became a Christian and burned her witchcraft para-
phernalia.

The work at Abaiyat, however, was always a
struggle. Sickness was prevalent. There were times
when a plane would have made the difference
between life and death. Two small children have been
buried there – Eileen and Bobby. Bobby's grave was
marked only by a bush, but I have stood by Eileen's
lonely gravestone more than once and thought of the
parents' grief.

An airstrip had now been cleared in the grass just
in front of the two mission houses; it immediately
relieved some of the stress of isolation. Before the
rains had started Steve and I had been asked to fly in.
Stan McMillan had become quite ill. We flew him
and his wife to Khartoum for treatment. The new
strip had been easy to use: there was nothing to get
in the way as you made your landing approach – just
the open grasslands.

Phyllis Bapple used to write home regularly to her
parents in America, giving them the latest news and,
incidentally, a vivid insight into the conditions at
places like Abaiyat:

> June 11, 1951. With the McMillans gone, Marie
> and I are now alone on the station. On Thursday
> evening we had quite a hard rain, just before
> dark. We had to hustle to get the windmill and
> its water pump turned off so that it wouldn't
> get broken in the strong winds. Then there were
> shutters to be put up in the house and big holes
> to be filled in where rain was pouring under the
> foundations.
> At about 9.30 this morning it started really pour-

ing and kept it up all day. Our rain gauge showed
70 millimeters had fallen. It was interesting to
see the dry season cracks in the soil fill up. We
were expecting some of our people to come from
Melut and Paloich today. They were to be here
ready to go out on Monday when the MAF plane
comes. Now we are wondering if they will make
it. We are wondering too if the plane is going to
be able to land. If the ground is too soft we are
supposed to make a large "X" on the field with
sheets! We can't help but feel the responsibility
of it and are praying that we will know what to
do – either it will be so wet that we will know
to put the cross out, or so dry that we will be
sure that it isn't necessary.

Later: The sun came out and the ground started
to dry but word has been sent to MAF not to
come. The airstrip will still be too soft. But we
don't know if this message will reach them (it
has to go via Sudanese telegraph from Melut and
may not reach them in time). If it doesn't, we
must be on the job tomorrow in case they come.
If it doesn't rain again they should be able to land
by Tuesday or Wednesday.

Monday morning arrived bright and we again
tested the airstrip. We decided the plane
shouldn't land, though we felt it might just be
possible. After all, we are just girls and wouldn't
know for sure!

About the middle of the morning we heard a
plane and ran out to see the MAF plane appearing
in the distance. You should have seen us tearing
around getting the cross of sheets spread out on
the ground – we were so excited. The plane flew

quite low and we waved. Then it came over again lower and we began to be afraid that it would land . . ."

12

No Accident

"I wonder how much rain they'll have had at Abaiyat and what state the strip will be in?" I called to Steve. We'd just taken off from Doro in the Rapide and were heading for Abaiyat to pick up three passengers needing to get to Khartoum.

"They should know the ground signals to tell us if it's safe," Steve called back. "If there's any question, I'll test the ground with the wheels first without actually landing."

It was a forty-five minute flight. The whole landscape, for the ninety miles between Doro and Abaiyat, stretched flat to the horizon. The rains had changed the colours and the waterways since we'd flown in six weeks before. It made Abaiyat difficult to find. But just before 9 o'clock we spotted the two houses. At the far end of the airstrip a long darker streak through the grassland marked out one of the seasonal streams – the Arabs called them *khors*.

No mission station in Sudan had the airstrip closer to the houses than Abaiyat. The ground occupied by the mission was enclosed by a low hedge with the airstrip just outside and parallel to it.

As we circled we saw the two ladies run out of one of the houses. They were looking up at us anxiously.

"There's Marie and Phyllis – but where are the

passengers we're supposed to take to Khartoum?"
asked Steve.

I couldn't see them either. I raised my voice above
the engine noise: "Maybe they're still coming."

The girls disappeared indoors. We studied the
ground. Obviously there had been some rain, but we
couldn't judge how much. Within moments the girls
were out again, hastily arranging white sheets in the
shape of a cross. The message was clear: UNSAFE TO
LAND.

"They think it's too soft, but I'm going to test it,"
Steve decided.

I nodded: "OK, I'll tell Malakal we're landing." I
tapped out the message, received the reply and closed
down the transmitter. Then I gave my full attention
to what was happening below.

We realized that the two girls on the ground knew
even less than we did about how soft an airstrip could
be before being actually dangerous. But we also
realized that there must have been enough rain to
have made them fear it was unsafe. All the same, we
weren't prepared to give up just yet. Having come
this far, and knowing the need the missionaries had
to get to Khartoum, we felt we should at least make
some further tests ourselves.

We came in low over the strip, looking at it carefully. We could see it had been damp, but it didn't
look too bad from the air. The wheels touched lightly.
It felt OK. Steve throttled back further and the plane
settled more towards the earth. Still it seemed all
right. Gradually Steve closed the throttles and the
plane rolled successfully to a halt, though a little
more quickly than usual because of some softness in
the strip.

The two girls came running up as we clambered out. "I was never so scared in my life," said Phyllis. "I was shaking like a leaf."

They were still hoping the passengers would be able to arrive but had heard they had been delayed by the rain. While we waited, Steve walked up and down every foot of the airstrip to check it out. It still seemed quite good.

Soon after, our passengers appeared, their vehicle covered in mud. They'd had great trouble in getting through the miles of swamped trail from their station.

We boarded the plane, said goodbye and taxied out to take off. We had to taxi downwind towards the far end of the airstrip. There was a clear patch just beyond it which seemed to offer some additional length.

"I'm going to use every foot I can get," Steve said to me. "We may need it with a soft strip like this." He kept the plane moving briskly to the end and into the patch beyond where he planned to swing quickly round into the wind, fully open the throttles and take off.

But as we rolled into the additional "bonus" area the wheels suddenly sank into soft ground. The plane lurched, the tail came up and the nose went down, striking the ground with a splintering crunch.

For a horrible moment I thought the plane was going right over on to its back. But it stopped just short of complete disaster. It hesitated and then settled on its nose with the tail sticking up at an angle of forty-five degrees.

The cabin door, halfway towards the tail, was now quite high in the air. I scrambled out and jumped to the ground. Steve squeezed through the front cockpit side window. We helped our three passengers jump down. Apart from being a bit shaken they were unhurt. By now Marie and Phyllis had run up from the other end of the strip, concerned and breathless.

We found that the area of the accident, though dry on the surface, was soft and damp a few inches down, fed by water from the seasonal *khor*. In seeking to get those extra few feet of runway, our wheels had broken through into the wetter soil below.

We surveyed the damage. The nose had been forced into the ground and the front of it crushed. Both of the wooden propellers had snapped off. The plane was obviously not going to fly anywhere for quite a while. Our passengers set out back to their stations. All our plans had been disrupted.

I decided that, given time, I could repair the nose and all the damaged controls it housed there at Abaiyat. The broken propellers were a different problem. In the afternoon Steve, with a Shilluk tribesman as guide, set out for the Nile in Stan McMillan's old truck. He hoped to catch the postboat to Malakal where he could telegraph to Khartoum for replacement propellers to be sent down. That, too, would take time.

I stayed and worked on the plane. Its wooden construction was a help. There were a few pieces of good timber in the missionaries' storeroom. I took the very best of them and started the slow process of rebuilding the shattered nose structure and the flying controls.

We were anxious about the rains as big storm clouds hovered around us. The Abaiyat airstrip was already soft. If more heavy rain came before the plane was repaired, it could be trapped there for all of six months, leaving many people isolated. Fortunately, however, little rain fell by day at that point and no deluges came even at night.

Whilst working on the plane I lived in the empty McMillan house and Marie and Phyllis kindly fed me from their own sparse supplies. Phyllis had just passed her first Arabic exam, so in the evenings after we'd eaten I enjoyed the chance of some Arabic lessons from her to improve the little I'd learnt in Khartoum. We related easily and my Arabic made good progress. After a week the McMillans returned. They'd come back by river and then, though the roads were already nearly closed by rains, had picked up Steve and their truck and managed to get through to Abaiyat. They brought the replacement propellers.

I showed Stan the work I was trying to do. Eager to be of assistance, he made a rather rash offer: "You can have anything you need from this station that will help you." I thanked him and said I'd look around and see what there was.

There were certain things that I needed. Besides the pieces of timber I'd already found, I located some good plywood from packing cases. I even took screws out of Stan's furniture to use in the repairs. Mind you, I always tried to ensure that enough screws were left to prevent the furniture from falling apart completely, especially those big old wooden chairs we had to sit on.

Steve and I worked on the aircraft for another week. One afternoon a storm came moving across the Dinka plain straight towards Abaiyat. We watched it anxiously, and prayerfully too. To our amazement we saw it divide and pass on either side of the station, leaving the airstrip dry. The next day a disgruntled group of Dinkas appeared, complaining that the presence of the plane was keeping the rains away. They needed them for their millet.

Two days later we had the plane ready for air test. It flew well and we prepared to leave.

But before that I had a few other matters to clear up. First I needed to return to Phyllis some American newspaper cuttings she'd lent me.

"Here are your papers back."

"Oh, thanks. Did you find them interesting?"

"I enjoyed them, especially the cartoons . . . You'll find an extra note among them, by the way."

The note read, "I've fallen in love with you."

I had always wanted to be quite sure that I had found the right marriage partner: the one person God had for me. I'd been happy to wait until that became clear. It had now. Our delay at Abaiyat had been no accident.

The note left Phyllis dazed. She'd always thought I already had a girlfriend in England. It all seemed confusing. Her temperature went up to 102 degrees.

Marie became suspicious: "Is it that man?" she enquired. Phyllis admitted it was.

It wasn't easy to know what to do. Although she, Marie and I had talked freely during our evenings together, Phyllis felt she still scarcely knew me. And now the plane was due to leave the next day.

SIM mission rules were strict – especially as regards courtship! Mission leaders had a fatherly concern for all their members. They wanted to be sure their single missionaries didn't form unwise attachments. There wasn't much chance for Phyllis to see

me alone; it wouldn't have been considered appropri-
ate. She wrote me a note and sent it to me via their
house-helper:

"We need to talk privately, but I don't know
where."

I scribbled a quick reply. "I've left some of our
aircraft toolkit in the storeroom. I'll have to collect
them. Can you get the key? We can talk when I
come."

We did talk. But we didn't have much time. We
agreed to write to each other . . .

As Steve and I flew out of Abaiyat rain started
falling again. When we arrived back at Doro we found
that a message Steve had attempted to send to Kay
had never arrived. She knew only too well some of
the dangers of those early years. In the two and a half
weeks before Steve got back Kay had concluded that
there had been a serious accident and he must have
been killed. She was numb with disbelief when she
saw him alive and well.

Back in Abaiyat, Phyllis was still struggling with her
feelings.

"As soon as you were gone," she told me later, "I
knew I loved you!" But she still found it much more
difficult to be sure of the will of God than I had.

It was hard to believe that after being so certain
she was called to work among the Dinkas she should
now go in quite another direction. Was her love for
me tempting her to leave the work God had given
her? Her thoughts were in turmoil; for weeks she lost
her appetite.

After some weeks Marie said, "Perhaps it really is
God's will for you!'

Gradually, after that, Phyllis started knowing that it was. She had been asking for a sign and God then said, "My sign is peace." That peace had come. But not because we received letters from each other. Letters took ages to get through in south Sudan. The ones we wrote arrived months later.

Phyllis told Stan, as station head, about my proposal. He wrote to the field leader in Khartoum, asking in mock seriousness whether MAF was now in the business of robbing missions rather than helping them. When I next met Stan, I reminded him that it was he who had told me I could "take anything I needed to help me". I needed Phyllis!

Mal Forsberg had gone on furlough and a British-born Australian, Norman Nunn, had taken his place as field superintendent. When I told him of my intentions he warned me that Phyllis would have to get permission to become engaged from the General Director of the Mission, a Mr Playfair who lived two thousand miles away in Nigeria. Fortunately he was due to visit the Sudan shortly and Norman promised to put in a good word for us.

Mr Playfair was a powerful character: big in build, strong on theology, clear on principles and impressive in his firm leadership. He had been known to take a hard line in cases like ours.

Norman arranged for him to visit as many of the stations as possible, though this was difficult because it was late in the rainy season. Steve and I flew him into Abaiyat; I think he was satisfied with our flight safety standards. He also realized the plane was the only way he could have visited the station at that time of year.

He spent some time discussing general business

with Norman and Stan. While he did this I went to
see Phyllis. She'd lost thirty pounds but looked very
happy. She told me she loved me and confirmed God
had given her peace about it all. That was all I wanted
to hear, but there was just one more hurdle.

"What will Mr Playfair say?" we asked each
other.

We didn't have long to wait: he'd finished his discussions and came towards us. We stood together
while we told him how we felt. He looked at us for
a moment and then said:

"We think of MAF as being very much part of
our work. I'm more than happy to give you two my
blessing."

Relief! Norman had obviously put in his "good
word" for us. There and then we became engaged.

That day things moved with breathless speed for
Phyllis. Norman was in urgent need of a secretary
and she was given the opportunity of returning to
Khartoum. Otherwise it would have been months
before we saw each other again. The decision wasn't
difficult. The plane had to be back at Khartoum in
time to land before dusk so we had to leave quickly
and Phyllis had only three quarters of an hour to pack
and join us in the plane.

On arrival at the SIM headquarters in the capital,
Norman phoned the mission doctor:

"We've had to fly Phyllis out of Abaiyat, Dr
Balzer," he said in a grave voice.

"What's wrong?" asked the doctor.

"Heart trouble," replied Norman, still speaking sol-
emnly.

The doctor grabbed his bag and came swiftly, to

find Phyllis slimmer, but quite healthy – and very happy.

Twenty-five years later I was flying in a MAF plane on a medical flight over Dinka territory. We were helping to combat the dread disease of kala-azar which was decimating the people. The American Government had sent some military doctors to work on the project. One of them was in the plane with me. As we flew at five thousand feet I pointed out the lonely village of Abaiyat. There were no missionaries living there by then. Only the small Dinka settlement remained.

"My wife came from there, you know," I said.

He looked at me strangely but he didn't ask for any explanation. So I didn't offer one.

13

A One-eyed Pilot, a Defective Plane, a Strange Auction

It was close to Christmas 1951, two months after Phyllis and I had become engaged. Steve, Kay and I were still at Doro. There was a lull in flying as missionaries and their families prepared for another hot, sunny, Christmas in the bush: simple in the extreme, far from the pressures of the Western world.

Steve seized the brief respite to check the Doro airstrip where trees, scrub and anthills were always springing up. He took an axe, just in case he could make some minor improvement.

There was a small palm tree at the end of the strip. "I'll cut it down", thought Steve. "It will give just that much more clearance for the plane on approach." He swung the axe, severed its slender stem and bent down to throw it into the surrounding bush.

As he straightened up he knew something was wrong. He glanced down the airstrip to where the faithful Rapide was sitting in the sun. It looked somehow unclear. He put his hand over his right eye and stared down the strip again. The Rapide was there and clear enough. When he covered his left eye it became obvious that the vision in his right one was blurred. He tried his hands back and forth several times: the result was always the same. Walking down the strip, he turned off through the bush to the house.

"I'm feeling a bit dizzy," he called to Kay. "I'm going to lie down for a while."

After an hour's rest his eye was still blurred and he came to tell me. Together we checked his vision for general clarity and distance judgement. It seemed relatively unimpaired. We went up in the plane together and did several circuits; his landings were as impeccable as ever.

Shortly after Christmas we had a flight to Uganda and Steve took the opportunity to consult a British eye specialist in Kampala. Retrobulbar neuritis, inflammation of the optic nerve behind the eye, was the verdict. Some drops and tablets would relieve the condition. We were glad it seemed so easily curable.

Two weeks later, Steve, still concerned, visited an Egyptian eye specialist in Khartoum. His diagnosis was drastically different.

"You've got a detached retina, Mr Stevens."

That meant Steve was grounded and his licence could not be renewed. We were again without a pilot.

Steve wrote immediately to a Christian friend in the South African Air Force, Lieutenant Gordon Marshall. Like Steve, Gordon had won the DFC, in his case during the more recent Korean war. On his return to South Africa he and Steve had been staff instructors together at the Central Flying School just before Steve had left to join MAF.

Steve foresaw that Gordon, as a young single pilot, was likely to be posted to Korea again and might well not survive. What a waste of a life that could be used in Christian service, he reflected.

His letter arrived at a critical time for Gordon who'd been feeling a revulsion against the endless death and destruction of war. He replied at once: "I'll come," and resigned from the Air Force.

As soon as Steve stopped flying, the number of people waiting for air transport began to mount alarmingly. Many were now dependent on the plane. Once we knew Gordon was coming we accepted bookings again. By an amazing series of events, Gordon arrived in Khartoum only ten days after Steve was grounded. We again realized God had been preparing the way ahead.

When Gordon stepped out into the blazing afternoon heat at Khartoum following a long flight from South Africa, Steve, Phyllis and I were there to greet him. We hoped he could be ready to fly south in the Rapide early the next morning. Steve didn't see any problem about this. It was simply a matter of ensuring that Gordon was familiarized with the plane without delay.

For an hour and a half the two of them flew and practised landings together as Steve passed on all he could of his accumulated experience. Gordon enthusiastically mastered the idiosyncrasies of the ancient Rapide. Even after dark there was no respite. He and Steve spent hours poring over maps, working out distances and courses for the next day's flying.

We were airborne early next morning with six passengers as well as ourselves.

Gordon described this abrupt initiation in a letter home:

There was hardly a landmark for 400 miles all the way to Doro. But Steve knew the way like the proverbial back of his hand. He pointed out uncharted landmarks, enabling me to find the landing strips as we flew around the south. For five days I flew with Steve and Stuart all over the area. I had found myself suddenly transported from my homeland to the centre of this young mission field. God's servants welcomed us with open hearts.

We flew back to Khartoum carrying the last group of passengers we were to fly for some while. By now the faithful Rapide was due for its major annual overhaul.

In February 1952, Phyllis and I were married in Khartoum. It was strange and a little sad that both our families were so far away. But we had no lack of wedding guests: Sudanese, Nigerian, Armenian, Greek, Syrian, American, a New Zealander, Australian, Canadian, South African and British. Our marriage certificate was headed, in English and Arabic: "The Non-Mohammedan Marriage Ordinance."

After a brief honeymoon at an oasis twenty-five miles to the south, we moved into a room at the SIM headquarters. The plan was to overhaul the Rapide at Khartoum airport and our room had to double as MAF office during this time. Phyllis had both Bible and business college training. She soon took over accounts, paying invoices as well as typing innumerable letters to the MAF office in London, to the Sudan Government and to missions. She also ordered spares for the plane. Some of these had to be stored in our room; we kept a propeller under the bed.

Although the overhaul proved to be very demanding and time-consuming, we both enjoyed being in
Khartoum again, especially being involved with the
church and young people. We always found the
mainly Muslim Sudanese Arabs in the city very
friendly and helpful. We had many good friends
among them, in the hangar and elsewhere.

Steve had returned to Doro with his family to start
building us a house. Mildmay had no funds to provide
a house for us at this stage so I committed most of
what remained of my wartime savings to this project.
We were grateful for Steve's willingness to undertake
the onerous task of construction. We knew that soon
we'd need to build a hangar as well to protect our
plane from the severe effects of the weather.

Gordon and I began the Rapide's overhaul in the
Sudan Airways' hangar. We'd start at 6 a.m. each day.
A little later Phyllis brought us our breakfast and
stayed on to do what she could. Young people who
attended the SIM chapel in Khartoum gave us a hand
from time to time. The plane had to be stripped down,
the fabric removed, the timber airframe examined
and revarnished. The electrical wiring had to be
renewed, control wires checked or replaced and the
whole plane re-covered with new fabric. We estimated it would take three or four months.

The work was slow. We had to push ourselves to
keep going in hangar temperatures of well over forty
degrees Celsius. The more work we did the more
problems we found. Knowing how many were waiting for our services, the strain mounted. I was ill for
several weeks and finally went into hospital for a
week with a suspected ulcer. After treatment the
doctor suggested I should leave the country, but

instead we kept on with the overhaul. I don't know whether I had an ulcer. I've certainly never had one since.

The fuselage of our Rapide stood on jacks in one corner of the hangar. All the fabric was off, the wings and tail removed.

"Is that a plane or a boat?" asked a British engineer from Sudan Airways. He wasn't joking. What was left now looked more like a boat than an aircraft, the varnished plywood underbody more like a hull than a fuselage. We toiled on unremittingly as the three or four months stretched out to six. Paint and thinners ordered for proofing and repainting the fabric arrived from Britain with most of the tins leaking and empty. We were seriously delayed.

The Rapide had suffered from two years of exposure, standing in the open through extremes of climate. Pouring rain and high humidity, then searing heat and drying sun had affected all its timbers. No wonder we found splits in the outer and inner wing spars. We tried to get replacement wings. We couldn't. That was the final blow. All our labours had been in vain. We would not have a flyable plane in the near future. Once again the missions would be without an air service.

Mr Watts, the chief engineer of Sudan Airways, was one of the next people to come by.

"Do you think you will ever get flying again?" he asked. The deputy chief was with him. Although an avowed Jehovah's Witness, he had been coming to the SIM chapel with us on Sundays and we had often sat and talked with him about the things of God. He turned to his boss:

"These chaps expect God to work miracles. He probably will."

The miracle, when it came, wasn't what we expected.

Mr Watts returned a little later:

"Is this of any interest to you?" he enquired. He passed me a notice of an aircraft auction from the Iraq Petroleum Company giving details of a Rapide for sale in Lebanon. The notice called for offers. Sudan Airways weren't interested since they were operating much more modern Dove aircraft. But Mr Watts had remembered us.

Gordon and I looked at the information. We knew that, in the long run, a Rapide wouldn't meet our needs. We would eventually require aircraft constructed of metal rather than wood and we'd have to seek permission from the Sudan Government to be allowed to operate smaller, single-engined models. At that time, however, we had neither the funds nor the permission for such a change. What we did have were all our spares for a Rapide and government consent to fly one. So at this juncture another Rapide would be ideal.

But how to pay for it? The plane on offer was worth £5000 – far beyond our means. There was no hope of money from Mildmay. I myself had only £200 left out of my savings. Though Gordon said he'd match this, and Steve and Kay offered the same, that still made only £600. We were all poor as church mice and this would make us poorer. Moreover, we'd have to offer it for a plane we'd never seen and which was a long way off.

We talked it over: "Six hundred pounds! We can

hardly make an offer as low as that, it's just ridiculous."

"There's nothing lost, apart from sounding pretty foolish."

"Let's at least put a bid in even though we don't think it will be accepted."

We decided we'd make the bid. I ended my letter to the Iraq Petroleum Company: "We realize that this offer is extremely low, but it is all that we have available."

We heard nothing for a month. Then we learned Pakistan Airways had bought the plane with a far higher bid than ours. We weren't surprised. Another option gone.

A month later the Iraq Petroleum Company cabled: WILL ACCEPT YOUR £600 TENDER IF YOU CAN PAY IN LONDON. Now we were really surprised. We were being offered the plane at our own price.

We still had to decide if this was really right. Everything was at stake. The £600 meant we would be paying out the last money we had. If the plane turned out to be a dud, all would have been lost and we'd have nothing with which to carry on. Ought we to return to the UK and stir up interest in a new plane rather than risk all in another old Rapide?

Steve and Kay were down at Doro and out of touch with us. Gordon, Phyllis and I prayed together, seeking God's guidance. Gordon showed his usual sympathetic concern, pointing out that three years of hectic work had left me extremely tired and run down, whilst Phyllis had been living in a hot and difficult country even longer. (British Government officials in the Sudan went home for a month every year because of the conditions.) He wondered whether the programme should close for a while so that we could get away on leave, rather than finding another plane and continuing immediate service.

My own anxiety was whether, having used the dregs of our resources to buy our tickets to Lebanon, we might find that the plane was in a shabby, scarcely serviceable state. Each of us felt the tension from a different angle. We just had to know what was right.

By early afternoon, Phyllis and I had separately come to the conclusion that it was right to buy the plane. Gordon remained far from certain. We wanted unanimity. So we prayed on through the hot afternoon, literally sweating it out. In the end God showed us all that we were to go and get it. We had real peace.

Three days later, in late March 1953, Gordon and I flew to Beirut. There we learned why Pakistan Airways hadn't acquired the Rapide in the end: their country would not allow them the necessary foreign exchange.

The Iraq Petroleum Company had an efficient air transport section. They'd used Rapides to monitor their oil lines across the desert. From our first glance we saw the Rapide was immaculate; the best we had ever seen. The rich oil company had spared nothing to keep it in perfect order. Instead of repairing unserviceable parts they'd replaced them with new ones. It had recently had two new wings and a complete re-cover. Its next overhaul would be relatively trouble free.

Gordon and I flew it back to the Sudan rejoicing.

PART III

DEVELOPMENT
(1953–1965)

14

An Emperor and
a Chartered Accountant

Although we were still feeling the strain of the past months, it was with a renewed sense of God's goodness and guidance that we returned to Khartoum. The burden of our inability to meet the needs of the missions in the Sudan was lifted.

Everyone was excited at the arrival of the new Rapide and marvelling that the plane was in such excellent condition. Sixteen requests for flight bookings already awaited us.

On the first flight south we carried four MKs returning home from a mission boarding school in Egypt for their school holidays. MKs? That's the mission term for that unique breed, "Missionaries' Kids". These particular MKs had to be away from their parents in the Sudan for nine months every year. The three months they had at home were too precious to be wasted in slow road or river journeys. We could dramatically reduce their travel time by airlifting them direct to their remote stations.

Among them was Denny Hoekstra whose father, Harvey, was the translator at Akobo. Denny often hung around our plane. We were destined to see considerably more of him in later years.

The flying over the next months was varied. We

saw the opening up of new stations, the carriage (now approved) of government officials and our first entry into Ethiopia across the borders of the Sudan. That was again due to Don McClure who wanted to begin new work among the Anuak in Ethiopia.

To get permission he started, characteristically, right at the top, securing an audience with Emperor Haile Selassie. When the day came for him to go to the palace in Addis Ababa, however, even the courageous Don admitted tremors.

> I almost wished I was back in the wilds of the Sudan, facing a jungle lion instead of the Lion of Judah [one of the emperor's titles]. I laid out before him our hopes and plans for the Anuak people, carefully working up to the crux of the whole matter – his permission to work unhampered among the Anuaks in Ethiopia. After I had spoken for fifteen minutes, he said, "Thank you for coming and thank your mission for undertaking this work among the Anuak. I am deeply interested in these people of the lowlands and want to learn more about them. I will grant you immediate permission to open this work . . . When can you start?*

Harvey Hoekstra and his family followed the McClures to Ethiopia soon afterwards. They wanted our help, but we had no permission to fly there.

"I'll get you permission," said Harvey, and he did.

That first flight into Ethiopia took only fifteen minutes across the mountains, but it saved the family

* W. Don McClure *Red-headed, Rash and Religious* pp. 112–113, A. G. Halldin Publishing Company, Pennsylvania USA 1954.

two days of rugged travel by Land Rover.

In contrast to the exciting progress in Sudan and Ethiopia, we now began to face some divergence of policy with Mildmay, our parent organization in the UK.

The Mildmay Movement was not a mission society as such, but a home-based organization without the framework or the policies needed to support the mission we had now become. Its financial situation had continued to worsen and it would not easily understand or respond to the cost of flying planes in faraway Africa.

The Movement had initially taken on MAF to nurture it and literally see it "get off the ground". That had been achieved, and we were always to be grateful. But it was now time for the child to leave the parent and develop its own independent life. It was with real regret, and only after much correspondence, that this was ultimately recognized.

"Does it have to be?" wrote Dr Cochrane.

"We see no alternative," was our reply. Murray Kendon, still in New Zealand, agreed.

This change brought an increase in our own work and responsibilities. We now had to articulate MAF's principles and policies in a new way. We needed to set up a home base that could support the work overseas with prayer and finance: no small task. On a human level we were on our own. But we believed that God had guided and that He was with us.

At this point Bill Knights, who'd been administering the work in the UK, wrote to tell us he'd become engaged and would be leaving MAF. We already knew that Murray Kendon would not be returning to London and Jack Hemmings had left. There was a vacuum at home. What should we do? One of us at least needed to go to England to sort things out, establish a sound support base and encourage our existing prayer partners.

The annual airworthiness overhaul for the Rapide from Lebanon would be due soon. After our previous experiences I considered that it would be as cheap to fly to the UK and have the overhaul done commercially as try to do it ourselves or get it done by someone else in Africa. My parents lived in Cardiff where a good aircraft maintenance firm offered a very reasonable quote.

There were other factors too. The Stevens were finding life tough. Our house was still unfinished; it had been difficult to get supplies for the building and the rains had closed the roads earlier than usual. Their youngest daughter, Coleen, had been seriously ill with dysentery. Kay was pregnant and also very ill; the mission doctor warned Steve it was imperative to get her out as he lacked facilities to handle any birth complications. Steve had bronchitis. On top of all these things, the SIM now needed the mission house where the Stevens were living.

As I thought about the situation I also knew that Steve's eye needed attention and that, since Kay should really be right out of the Sudan for the coming baby, England would be the best place for them too. The UK situation was urgent. Phyllis and I needed to make contacts with churches and Christian friends who'd be interested in supporting us. Though Phyllis had some little support from family and friends who'd helped during her four-year term with SIM, I had no regular income since my small salary from Mildmay had stopped.

Then there was furlough. Maybe it was now time Phyllis and I went to the UK and then on to the USA. Phyllis had already been away for more than the usual missionary term. If we could find an aircraft engineer-cum-radio operator to replace me, the flying in the Sudan could continue, with Gordon as pilot, once the plane's overhaul was complete.

We had an engineer in mind: Alastair Macdonald, an ex-Fleet Air Arm officer who had gone to Thailand to do a survey for MAF. He'd followed in my steps in marrying an American missionary out there. Perhaps he and his wife, Margaret, could come to Sudan to replace Phyllis and me during our furlough.

We concluded that it would be best if we all flew to the UK in the Rapide: Steve, Kay and family, Gordon, Phyllis and I. We couldn't operate in the Sudan until the plane came back anyway, so no one would lose by our absence. We felt this was God's will and planned accordingly.

It was 4th August 1953. I was piloting the Rapide on one of the stages of the flight to the UK. As we crossed the Sinai peninsula, I saw its dramatic mountain beneath us, reaching up 8000 feet out of the desert, and tried to imagine what it must have been like when the Israelites were camped there on the forty-year journey to the Promised Land. Thirty minutes later we were above the Gulf of Aqaba, heading north for Jordan.

I handed over the controls to Gordon for landing, resumed my seat as radio operator and tried to contact Aqaba airport. Getting no response, I glanced back at our plane's full cabin. Phyllis had been serving coffee and biscuits: nice to have someone else doing the stewarding for once.

I tried the radio again, still without success. I looked out of the cockpit window to the airport below. Aqaba town stands at the top of the Gulf, adjacent to the southern tip of Israel. An RAF transport plane was making its final approach over the waters to the airport. As it touched down we saw something was wrong. It skidded sideways and stopped in a cloud of dust. Fire engines and an ambulance dashed out. The undercarriage had apparently collapsed on landing. No one seemed hurt but the runway was now blocked.

At that moment six twin-engined Dove aircraft bearing the markings of the Jordanian Air Force arrived and started circling. Like us, they were waiting to land.

Gordon started the usual left-hand circuit over the airport to see what would happen. The scene was reminiscent of wasps buzzing furiously over a jam pot. The Doves kept flashing past us, but going the opposite way round. I again tried in vain to establish radio contact with the control tower. Finally, one after another, the Doves landed on a strip parallel to the main one.

When the last one was down, Gordon brought our Rapide in on the same strip. As soon as we disembarked, a very tall, fierce British brigadier, complete with handlebar moustache, pilot's wings and a row of campaign ribbons left a knot of other pilots near the Doves and descended upon us. He strode up to Gordon. He was obviously the commanding officer, but clearly no dove himself. He was extremely angry.

"Are you the captain of this aircraft?" he barked.

"Yes, sir," said Gordon, recognizing his rank.

"What do you mean by doing a left-hand circuit over Aqaba? Haven't you read in 'Notices to Airmen' that we do a right-hand circuit here?"

"I didn't know that, sir," said Gordon.

"You may have caused an international incident. If you fly a left-hand circuit here you fly over Israeli airspace."

"I am sorry, sir," said Gordon.

Still furious, the brigadier strode away.

We survived the welcome, refuelled and pressed on, flying high enough to get a good look at the Holy Land to our left. We flew parallel to the Jordan valley and as near as we dared to the Sea of Galilee. But we kept away from the Israeli border. We had no permission to enter their airspace. As we came to the northern tip of Israel, Gordon altered course slightly westward to fly over Mount Hermon towards Beirut.

Suddenly I felt the Rapide bank steeply to the right, away from Israel. I shot an enquiring glance at Gordon. He called to me:

"Did you see those two Israeli Spitfires coming up after us? We must have clipped the border!"

I looked back. The Spitfires were already turning away. We were no longer over their territory. If we'd stayed a moment longer they'd have forced us to land in Israel. That really would have produced an international incident.

At Beirut we learnt that two commercial airliners had crashed just recently in the Mediterranean. We flew on through Greece where there had been an earthquake. The environment seemed distinctly hostile! We refuelled at Nice and our track took us across the southwestern Alps. The 12000-foot Massif du Pelvoux was to our right and, in the far clear distance, the snow-capped peak of Mont Blanc. For the first time since our Gemini crash five years before, I felt afraid of the mountains. It wasn't as though we were high above them in some giant airliner. We were in our small biplane, clearing them by little more than a thousand feet.

Maybe we'd not been so wise in all flying to the UK together, though we'd really not had much option and certainly no money to send anyone by commercial airline. But nearly all our active MAF staff were assembled in this one frail wooden craft, kept aloft only by the faithful running of its two Gipsy Queen engines. If even one engine failed I knew all too well that, with our full load, we would drop quickly among the mountaintops.

I remembered what it was like to hit a mountain; these were much more jagged and cruel than the green slopes of Burundi. I wished Gordon had chosen a course around instead of over them. But he had faith in the plane and in the steady running of our carefully maintained engines and we flew safely on. Many friends in Sudan, Britain and America were praying for our journey.

In contrast it was both comforting and exciting crossing the English Channel, to see at last the welcoming White Cliffs of Dover in the bright summer sunshine. It reminded me of my first sight of them at my homecoming from Germany after the hard-fought war in Europe. We touched down at Lympne, just inland from the Kent coast. Then we cleared customs and flew on to South Wales and Cardiff.

This was home for me, and it was exciting that Phyllis could at last meet my parents and sister who came to the little airport to greet us. Phyllis's own home, however, was still 6000 miles away. I looked forward to going on soon to meet her family too.

When Bill Knights left to get married, Phyllis, Gordon and I moved into the small flat just outside London which he had vacated. There we worked through all the MAF home-end records, updating the addresses of our 3000 prayer partners, dealing with accounts, receipts and thank yous. But who was going to carry on when we went on furlough or returned to Africa? How could we maintain our work, let alone see it expand, without adequate coordination of supporters at home?

That was where Herbert Adams came into the picture. We should never have met but for the Brethren Assembly in Cardiff where I'd been a member since college days. They'd given us a warm and sympathetic welcome home and taken a deep interest in our work. If they ever forgot about MAF my gentle but determined mother soon reminded them.

One of the leading elders there, an eminent Cardiff businessman, suggested that a friend of his, a recently retired chartered accountant living in London, might be interested in helping us. "He's a very fine and godly gentleman," he told us.

As soon as we saw Mr Adams, we realized that, superficially, we were as different as chalk and cheese. We were young, tanned by the Sudan's sun and the work of MAF had become our life. He was in his sixties, white-haired, with a fresh ruddy complexion; he'd had a sedentary career in the Civil Service and knew little about MAF. But he had a heart for God and for His work. He agreed to come to the flat for several days and find out more. A month later he became our Honorary Home Secretary.

What encouragement his involvement brought us! What a gift he and his wife were to the work. For a while their home became MAF's postal address. They took over the acknowledgement of letters from the prayer partners, dealt carefully and sympathetically with the correspondence.

"Day after day we'd find our hall floor by the letter box covered with a mountain of letters," Mrs Adams told me later. "Our home life was drastically changed."

We came to the conclusion that Steve and Kay, whose baby had now arrived safely, should stay in England. We needed someone with overseas aviation and mission experience to help carry the burden of the work at home, to deal with any candidates for MAF service and to promote interest among supporters.

Our own hopes of furlough were dashed: we learned Alastair Macdonald wasn't yet free to leave Thailand. Phyllis wrote to her parents and her much loved but seriously ill sister to tell them of our decision.

"Stuart and I feel we must return to the Sudan for a time. This is the hardest thing to write to you, especially as Doris is so ill, but I believe you will understand."

She went on to explain: "Since our arrival here we have had constant letters from the Sudan telling of needs for the plane and the problems because MAF is not flying. As we were praying, God made it very clear we should return until someone can replace us.

The work on the plane here is finished and we are all ready to go."

It was winter when we left England and headed back to Africa. Much had been accomplished. A MAF UK home office had been established and a new phase was beginning.

The trip back was surprisingly uneventful.

15

Changes In the Wind

Sometimes Gordon and I scarcely had time to eat. Back in the Sudan we'd resumed our busy schedule. New airstrips had been opened up, the authorities in Addis Ababa had given us permission to fly regularly into Ethiopia and our flying hours had doubled. Phyllis was often left on her own, always with masses of office work and accounts. We'd now made our base at Malakal, living first at the American Mission and later at a government rest house at the airport.

Even before we'd left for England it had become obvious that Malakal, not Doro, should become our Sudan base, as Governor John Winder had always suggested. The SIM at Doro, still in need of accommodation, was glad to buy and finish our house there.

In God's providence, we'd learned much by basing initially at Akobo and then at Doro. We'd seen first-hand how different missions operated and shared in the trials, problems and needs as well as the successes of the missionaries themselves. We'd gained invaluable experience in building and maintaining mission station airstrips. I would not have missed those experiences for they provided a priceless foundation for the years to follow.

John Winder still encouraged us to find land and build our own houses at Malakal. While in England we'd contacted an aluminium company producing cheap prefabricated accommodation units. They were relatively crude: small, boxlike shells of corrugated aluminium, but we believed they could be made into effective houses. Gifts to the work of MAF having increased, we were able to purchase three units and have them shipped to the Sudan. This was timely, because our housing needs were increasing.

In March 1953, the plane developed a serious propeller-shaft oil leak at Nasir and was grounded for several days while I worked on it. We never minded being at Nasir, though. The missionaries there always made us feel very welcome. One of them, Jean Maxwell, had actually been born there – her parents had been missionaries themselves. After qualifying as a nurse she had returned to Nasir to work.

Gordon had met Jean a few times before. This time it was different – he fell in love with her. He determined to tell her before we left.

Sunday afternoon was hot. The Sobat river ran right by the mission, and Gordon thought: "I'll go for a swim." He was soon midstream and drifting with the slow current. Suddenly he noticed someone on the far side sitting on a sandbar surrounded by Nuer children. "Who's that?" he wondered. Then suddenly realized. "It's Jean! Here goes!"

He quickly swam across and sat beside her.

"Jean, I've fallen in love with you!" he said. She was speechless with surprise. ("It was a one-way conversation," Gordon told me afterwards.)

Before we left Nasir, however, Jean had agreed to write to Gordon – just as Phyllis had done with me. Later they, too, became engaged.

The similarities with our own engagement were so marked that, for a moment, I did wonder if missions might see us as robbers of some of their best staff rather than helpers in their work. Maybe Stan McMillan's letter to Norman Nunn wouldn't be seen as a joke after all!

I needn't have worried. The inter-mission marriages only brought us more closely into the mission family. Gordon and Jean had a colourful wedding at Nasir attended by missionaries, local Arab traders in their flowing robes and Nuers in assorted costume. Many of them had known Jean since she was tiny. Chuck Jordan, the agriculturist, presented the couple with a bull. No Nuer wedding would have been complete without it.

The next news was that Alastair and Margaret Macdonald were arriving from Thailand. The political situation there had deteriorated and opportunities for MAF were not opening up. It had become clear to them that the greater opportunity was in the Sudan. Alastair had bought a small single-engine plane, a Piper Pacer, from an American missionary. Like others of us, he'd used savings from his wartime salary. He flew the plane the 6000 miles from French Indo-China. We were glad to welcome him and Margaret to the Sudan team.

Everything was wonderful. Alastair learned Morse and I initiated him into its use in the air. With two planes we now had the ingredients for a continuous service. The government had gained such confidence in our operations that they were prepared to let us operate the single-engined Pacer as well as the Rapide.

Given this permission to fly single-engined aircraft, we could go ahead with the plan to replace our fabric-

and-wood Rapide with two small, all-metal American-made Cessnas. These would be more economical and more reliable in tropical conditions. With their large tyres, lighter weight and better take-off, they'd also perform much better on short, swampy airstrips.

It would take time to raise enough money to buy two of them, but that was our target. The Presbyterian and Reformed Churches in America, in response to requests from their Sudan missionaries, gave me permission to speak in their churches and seek funds for such a plane. American MAF didn't see this as poaching on their territory.

Phyllis and I could at last be released for furlough. Little had Phyllis known when she left home that it would be six years before she got back. She was excited and eager for me to meet her family. We were feeling very tired too, but it looked like a full schedule ahead. We knew we needed to spend some time with American MAF near Los Angeles and with mission leaders in New York. It was important to make contact with friends and churches who had been supporting us personally. And, of course, we were keen to take advantage of the opportunity to tell these churches about our need for a Cessna.

En route to the States we were back for a while with my parents in Cardiff. I spent six grinding weeks peering through a magnifying glass to edit three new MAF movie films from material I had taken during our time in the Sudan. But there were times of refreshment, too, as we enjoyed the first spring we'd seen for years. The beautiful woods were full of primroses and celandine; later there were buttercups, bluebells and daffodils. It was a sight for sore eyes after so many years in the desolate swamps and dry deserts of the Sudan. We felt we were in heaven.

Then came the telegram from Gordon and Alastair:
BOTH PLANES DAMAGED BEYOND REPAIR AT MALAKAL. It
seemed as if the bottom had dropped out of our world.

An abnormally vicious storm had struck the airfield with winds gusting up to 120 mph. The planes
were torn loose from their tie-downs, the Pacer
thrown over on its back and completely wrecked, the
Rapide carried a hundred yards before dropping to the
ground, breaking its wings. MAF was out of action
again at a single stroke. We'd had enough money to
buy the planes originally, but not enough this time to
insure them against damage. We had lost everything.

Now we needed a Cessna even more urgently. It
was with heavy hearts we left for the USA.

The warm and excited welcome from Phyllis's
family did something to lift our spirits. They took
me into their hearts and made sure there would be
no lack of well-made tea for their English son-in-law.

We were exhausted when we reached California,
far more so than we had recognized. Looking back, I
realize we'd been through a great deal, physically,
mentally and spiritually. I found it hard to meet large
groups of people in churches. For the first two months
I simply wanted to hide, or even to cry. Then, at last,
we gradually started feeling more ourselves. It was
just as well; there was so much to be done. Correspondence from MAF in London and the Sudan was constant and required carefully considered decisions and
answers. Phyllis and I ran a mini-office.

"Let's go over to MAF headquarters," I said to Phyllis. "We need to meet Grady Parrott."

MAF USA was only sixty miles from Phyllis's

home so we took advantage of the easy contact. It was especially good to meet Grady at last. He made us very welcome and we spent long hours discussing many aspects of MAF work. American MAF was very much larger than our group and now had operations in both South America and Indonesia, regions very different from our south Sudan swamps.

"What do you think now about merging our two MAF groups?" I asked Grady. It was an idea we'd aired in letters once before.

With his greater experience, he was cautious. We concluded there were more problems than advantages in setting up an overarching international organization with its inevitable complications and inherent communication difficulties. We agreed, therefore, to retain our autonomous national identities. We'd each continue to be responsible for our own areas of operation while still maintaining close fellowship with each other. We felt this was God's pattern for us and our main MAF groups have sought to follow it since. We had many helpful meetings with Grady over the ensuing years.

The planned contacts were made with mission leaders. At the many church meetings people responded with interest and contributed towards a new plane for the Sudan. Gradually funds accumulated, though nothing like the £6000 needed for a Cessna, an astronomical sum in our eyes at that time.

Meanwhile God had His own ways of keeping our Sudan operations going. We hadn't been in the USA long before the SIM offered to buy a replacement Rapide, to be owned by them but operated by us. They wanted our service resumed without further delay; otherwise some of their missionaries would be stranded and the government might demand their withdrawal from the more isolated areas.

Gordon and Alastair traced a Rapide in East Africa, which SIM bought, and MAF resumed intensive flying. Then they heard of an old wartime RAF "Blister" hangar standing idle in the desert at Wadi Halfa. After some hard bargaining, the government sold it cheaply. Alastair went north and supervised its dismantling, shipping and eventual re-erection at Malakal. Although open at both ends it gave considerable storm protection as well as shelter from the sun and rain. It proved invaluable, too, for routine maintenance which, until then, we'd had to do in the open.

The Macdonalds and Marshalls had been living in unsuitable and uncertain rented accommodation. During our absence they had to move seven times. MAF urgently needed a site to erect its own houses. News came of three adjacent building plots to be auctioned in Malakal – ideal for our proposed new base. Unfortunately there was a lot of local competition for them from well-to-do Arab traders and particularly from a wealthy Nuer politician. If they all turned up at the auction the price could soon soar beyond our slender means.

On the auction day there was a heavy tropical storm. Everything stops in Malakal when it rains like that. But, soaked to the skin, Gordon and Alastair arrived at the Provincial headquarters at 10 a.m., the appointed time. The Sudanese district commissioner, who was to conduct the auction, was there. The Nuer politician was not.

"I'll wait ten minutes because of the rain," said the

DC. But only one other person, a lone Arab trader, appeared.

The auction was brief: the three plots went to MAF at the reasonable price of £125. Just as the proceedings closed the politician arrived. Too late; in spite of a heated argument the DC held firm: "The three plots have been sold to MAF."

Gordon and Alastair hired local labour and, like other missionaries before them, started to learn new building skills.

Further good news arrived a little later. SIM's General Director, the helpful Mr Playfair, wrote saying they now wished to make the Rapide a gift to MAF. Shortly afterwards the American Mission home board offered a large donation towards the purchase of the first all-metal Cessna. We rejoiced again.

From the USA, Phyllis and I returned to England. There, to our delight, God gave us our first child, Rebecca Anne.

When we got back to Khartoum in August 1955, Norman and Mattie Nunn at the SIM headquarters gave us a warm welcome, with a room and a crib all ready for Becky. We felt we'd come home again. The loving fellowship of our Christian friends in the Sudan had not changed.

The political climate, however, had changed a great deal.

The old Anglo-Egyptian Sudan was moving rapidly towards independence. But all was not well. A garrison of southern soldiers mutinied against their northern Arab officers, whose dominance they'd begun to fear, killing over a hundred Arab soldiers and traders. Northern troops retaliated, the mutiny was suppressed and its leaders executed. The remainder of the garrison fled into the bush and formed a guerrilla force.

Some southerners wanted secession from the north and an autonomous, independent south. Others would have acceped a federation whereby the south could look after its own affairs whilst remaining part of the whole Sudan. The ruling northern government, however, wanted neither. They declared a state of emergency in the three southern provinces, including the Upper Nile Province where we were based.

Fervent Islamic elements took the opportunity to assail Christian work. The Arabic press blamed missions for causing the trouble, claiming that the teaching of Christianity had alienated the previously animistic southerners from the Muslim north.

When we got to Malakal we found that the Marshalls and Macdonalds had almost finished building the first of the prefabs and organized it for us to live in – our first home. The Macdonalds then went on furlough and I immediately joined Gordon in flying the Rapide. Whenever we weren't flying we were building our base. When we were flying, it was our wives who supervised the building crew of untrained Shilluks, Nuers and Dinkas. Quite a task, but they did well.

In November 1955, all British troops left the Sudan. Independence was imminent.

16

New Government, Pilots and Planes

15th January 1956. I stood in a crowd of Sudanese outside the *Muderia*, the provincial administrative offices at Malakal. The simple long, low buildings looked cool and quiet, well shaded from the sun by the big overhang of their screened verandahs. The offices faced a row of palm trees fringing the Nile where the shining water made a beautiful and peaceful picture.

The great glistening river of history flowed impassively towards the north. The Nile had witnessed the life of the Sudan for thousands of years. It had seen the suffering caused through the centuries by the brutal slave trade amongst the villages along its banks and deeper inland too. It had seen the lines of shackled captives forced to trudge wearily northwards to be sold.

The Nile had carried the paddlewheel steamboat of General Gordon who had done so much to suppress the cruel exploitation of the south. Further north, at Abba Island, the Nile had watched the rise of the Mahdi, the Muslim "Messiah". Only fifty-five years before it had seen the coming of Kitchener's boats and troops, the setting up of the colonial government in Khartoum, the start of joint rule by Britain and Egypt.

Now it was witnessing a new phase of history. In front of the Muderia the condominium flags were flying for the last time. The new Sudanese Provincial Governor, Sayed Osman, came out and stood before them. A bugle call and Egypt's green flag slowly fluttered down its pole, followed by the Union Jack. Another bugle call and the flag of the new Sudan slowly ascended. It bore three horizontal stripes: blue symbolized the Nile, yellow the northern deserts and green the southern swamps. Independence had come sooner than had been expected. The Sudan was the first of many African countries to gain independence over the next few years. It was a day of exhilaration, gladness and celebration – certainly a day of history and hope.

The river flowed on. What was it yet to see?

The previous day our own plane had been chartered by the government to fly the new flag to such outposts as Doro and Akobo. We were glad to cooperate in the legitimate administration of the Province in any way we could. The government was now relying quite heavily on our services, accounting for a third of all our flying.

They paid us for such services, which helped to keep our operation viable even though we did not charge them a profit-making fare. At one stage they had tried small planes operated by pilots from Sudan Airways. But the pilots, very naturally, hadn't liked the kind of country that we were used to – the isolation, the navigation difficulties, the dangers of storms or the soft airstrips which were normal hazards to us. After a while they'd withdrawn their services. The governor then discovered it had cost the Province administration more to use the national airline than to employ MAF. So he turned back to us.

This meant that we were very, very busy. Gordon and I continued our double life, alternately flying and house-building. In the rainy season we'd start flying soon after dawn, hoping to finish by early afternoon when towering tropical thunderstorms would fill the horizon and make it difficult and dangerous to continue. Back at Malakal we'd resume our building.

The prefabs weren't exactly "instant houses". The aluminium shells could go up in a day but that was only the beginning. The interiors and roofs had to be lined and insulated from the heat, otherwise the sun would make them like ovens. The houses had also to be made proof against flies, snakes, scorpions and mosquitoes – quite a challenge when corrugated roof met corrugated walls. All the inevitable gaps had to be suitably filled. Mosquito screening was essential for windows and doors. Verandas were added to give shade and extra space, so were septic tanks and simple plumbing.

When all was done we liked our houses.

The Marshalls were due for furlough and, with the increasing flying, we desperately needed extra staff. I wrote to Grady Parrott. He replied:

"Could you use a lady pilot?"

A lady pilot in the Sudan? Could she cope with the rough working conditions and heavy freight loading often involved in our operations? Above all would the male-orientated Muslim government even permit her to come? It was unprecedented and certainly not in line with their culture and background.

The lady concerned was Betty Greene, one of the founders of American MAF. We already knew quite a lot about her and had no doubts about her ability and experience. She'd been a wartime ferry pilot with the WASPs, Women's Auxiliary Service Pilots, and had already flown for MAF in South America and for SIM in Nigeria.

We applied for permission for Betty to come, but we weren't very hopeful. The new Sudanese director of Civil Aviation was noncommittal and referred our request to the top Council of Ministers: they were the men who ultimately controlled the affairs of the country. We prayed. I'd dearly like to know what questions were raised, what arguments advanced by those six ruling Muslims and whether, in the end, they were unanimous. All I do know is that the director of Civil Aviation met me smiling:

"Permission for the lady pilot is granted."

Betty and I took over the flying from Gordon. In the two and a half years she was with us we grew to appreciate her in many ways. She was an outstandingly skilful, professional and hard-working pilot. Tall and elegant, she was a real friend and her humour and encouragement meant much to us, as did the wealth of experience she brought with her.

By August 1956 our first Cessna 180 had been purchased in the USA and was dismantled, crated and shipped to London. It was now time to dispose of our last Rapide. So Betty, Phyllis, Becky and I flew in it to England. A buyer was found at Croydon.

While waiting for the Cessna to arrive at London docks, we stayed at the Foreign Missions Club in

London. One evening I had a phone call.

"Hi Stuart, this is Harvey Hoekstra, speaking from Michigan."

Surprise. Harvey was on furlough and I hadn't expected to hear his voice, still less what he had to say:

"I've got an aeroplane here for you, Stuart. It's a Cessna 180. Let me give you the details . . ."

The plane was four years old and seemed in good shape. Harvey had aroused the interest of a group of Michigan businessmen in the value and needs of MAF. They had put up the money and were ready to buy the plane.

"Can you use it?" Harvey asked.

"Yes, we can! And thank God for it!" I replied and went quickly from the phone through the club corridors to share the amazing news with Phyllis and Betty.

The next day I wrote to Grady Parrott: "Would it be possible for American MAF to pick up the plane and handle its shipment to us?"

Grady replied with action, going personally to Michigan to collect it.

Even that wasn't the end of the story. Charlie Mellis, the secretary/treasurer of MAF USA, went further:

"Stuart, I think we can do better for you. If you agree, we can sell this second-hand plane and, because we get such a good discount from the makers, we can then buy you a new one for the same price."

Miracle upon miracle. We could have danced for joy.

We now had the prospect of two brand-new planes to replace the older, larger Rapide. I've often thought

about those two Cessna 180s. The first took two years
of persistent prayer and work to obtain. The second
came in a flash. We could thank God for both of
them. I realized that if the first had come as easily
as the second, we might well have become spiritually
proud: "When we pray God answers us – we must be
good." We learnt that while very often we may have
to wait (and wait for quite a long time) God can,
when He wishes, provide all we need in a moment.
Both the provision and the timing are in His hands.

While we were in England selling the Rapide and
preparing to assemble the dismantled Cessna, there
was another joyful event for us. We welcomed a son
and named him John.

The crate containing the parts of the first Cessna
was eventually delivered to Heathrow airport. There,
in a British Airways hangar, I unpacked it. I'd seen
Cessnas briefly in the USA but had never before had
anything to do with them at close quarters. Here was
a crate, full of tightly packed components, large and
small, including very many little parts with no sign
of where they were supposed to fit. They weren't
labelled and I had no assembly manual, no parts book,
only a pilot's operating manual.

It wasn't like putting together some amusing but
inconsequential puzzle. This was a carefully designed
flying machine. It had to go together absolutely correctly, every component in its right place, every control wire running where it should and precisely ten-
sioned, every flying surface set in the right
aerodynamic position, every fuel line and electrical
cable properly connected, every nut, bolt, shim and
washer in the right place and properly torqued.

The British Airways Christian Union engineering

staff came to my assistance when they were off duty and helped me greatly with getting the wings and other parts into place. But they were no more familiar with Cessnas than I was, being accustomed to handling big airliners. The responsibility for getting it right was mine alone.

The Cessna 180 was much smaller, of course, than the Rapide. It had only four seats, including the pilot's. The 230 hp engine gave it plenty of power. It was all metal, a clean high-wing monoplane with a single wing strut on either side instead of the multiple struts and bracing wires of the Rapide. Its silver polished aluminium was enhanced by a red and black flash along the fuselage and red tips on wings, fin and tail. The undercarriage consisted of two simple, flat spring-metal legs; the wheels had large low-pressure tyres. Inside, the instrument panel was well equipped with small, compact, recessed instruments.

The original Gemini was neat and beautiful; the Rapide had an antique elegance, but the Cessna was much more effective and efficient than either of them. We were to find this type ideal for our work through many years to come.

When it had been assembled, Betty and I pushed the little aircraft out of the hangar to be fuelled. An airport official looked at it quizzically.

"An unusual plane for Heathrow. Didn't know they allowed these little kites in here." He handed me an invoice for a landing fee.

"But this hasn't landed here yet!" I objected.

"Whatd'ya mean? Did it come up through a hole in the ground?" said the official. He wasn't used to planes being put together out of a crate. He reluctantly withdrew his invoice.

The day for the air test came. Heathrow was already one of the world's busiest international airports. It was generally available only to big airlines and certainly not to little single-engined Cessnas.

"Could we have permission to fly Cessna 180 N3757A on air test, please?" I asked.

The all-important airport commandant himself had to be consulted. Fortunately he consented. Betty filed a flight plan at air traffic control, we again wheeled the shiny little plane out of the hangar, made a final preflight inspection and clambered in.

"Heathrow Tower, this is November 3757 Alpha. Taxi clearance please."

Runway directions were given and we moved nimbly to the take-off point. The controller had made a gap for us amid the stream of large commercial aircraft. We kept our distance. Their blast could blow us over. Betty made a final check of engine and controls, set the wing flaps to twenty degrees and radioed: "Permission to take off please."

"November 3757 Alpha, clear to take off."

Full throttle; we accelerated down the runway, sensitive rudder movements keeping us accurately aligned. The Cessna quickly gathered speed, eager to prove it could fly as well as its heavyweight brothers. Like an agile young bird it soared skywards, more than a mile of runway still left unused.

We gained height rapidly and Betty trimmed for straight and level flying. We tried it "hands off" the controls – it flew steadily on. Then some turns, this way and that. It handled beautifully. All seemed fine. Engine, cylinder-head temperature, oil temperatures, oil pressures were all OK. Thank you, Lord.

Windsor Castle was beneath us as we turned back

to Heathrow. The air traffic control again made room among the airliners for us to land.

After the flight Betty checked back in at the control tower, apologizing for having interrupted the busy commercial traffic. She'd obviously made a hit:

"Oh, we enjoyed it," the chief controller said. "Such a change from all the big airliners that come in here!"

The plane was ready. However we now faced some problems. There was war in the Suez area and our most direct and convenient way back to the Sudan through Egypt was blocked.

Betty and I discussed the situation with Phyllis: "I think we two will have to fly the Cessna across the Sahara," I said. "In that case you and the children will need to go by commercial airline."

It would be much too dangerous for Phyllis, Becky and John to fly the Sahara route in a small plane. Besides, we'd have to carry a heavy emergency water supply and other safety equipment for crossing the desert; there wouldn't be the spare weight available to take us all.

But money was still short and we couldn't find a cheap enough fare to get Phyllis and the children to Africa. We finally decided that we'd all go back together, taking another route. Even so, there would be Betty, Phyllis, myself, Becky and little John – all of us plus our supplies in a tiny, four-seat plane. The trip out to the Sudan, a long one at the best, was going to be twice as long this time. We'd have to go down the west coast of Africa to Congo, then fly across central Africa and approach the Sudan from

the south. Eight thousand miles and lots of refuelling
stops.

It was the only way and we prepared for it. We'd
be two weeks in the plane. Betty and I in the front;
Phyllis and Becky in the back, and, in the luggage
compartment (accessible behind the back seat) John
in a carrycot. There'd be very little room for all the
things babies need. Very little room for any weight
at all. We ended up literally weighing things on a
letter balance, calculating down to ounces, not just
pounds.

It proved an epic flight, though I've space to tell
only a little about it here. We stopped at many bizarre
and outlandish places along the West African coast,
spending nights in strange hotels or little rest houses.
We'd wash the children's nappies at night and Betty
and I would spread them on our knees during the
next day's flight, turning on the cabin warm air to
help speed the drying. Two things made life easier.
John at last started sleeping through the night and
Becky cooperated with the potty which cut down the
washing.

Huge jungle canopy trees spread out in every direction beneath us, between them seventy-foot saplings
waiting to grow into forest giants themselves. Tall,
lighter green palms filled any gaps. And below all
this, shadowed and dark, lurked an impenetrable
undergrowth. A small plane could drop down through
the treetops and disappear among the tangled creepers
and dead trunks. Even if passengers survived, they
might never find their way out.

With twelve days and 5000 miles of flying behind
us, we had settled into a good working routine. It had

taken Phyllis the first day or so to get the rear half of the cabin sorted out and less claustrophobic, and Becky had at last stopped being air-sick.

The plane had performed well. I'd been amazed how clean the engine was. The inverted cylinders in the Gipsy Queen engines of our old Rapide had spewed oil around on every flight. The Cessna, with its horizontally opposed six-cylinder engine, remained clean. I could have maintained it with white gloves on.

As we headed down towards Pointe-Noire, where we intended to turn eastwards to Kinshasa and up the Congo river to south Sudan, the engine was continuing to run sweetly. Then suddenly – brupp-brupp-brupp. It spluttered and stopped. Immediately we sank towards the thick jungle beneath. The tall massive trees seemed to reach up to clutch at us.

I looked back at Phyllis. She was white, her hand grasping Becky's arm. The sudden silence was unnerving. Unaware, our baby John slept on. Betty and I were too busy trying to assess what was wrong to speak.

With the instinctive reaction of an experienced pilot, Betty's hand went down to the fuel selector valve between the two front seats. It was in the OFF position. In a second she had it switched on again: to the BOTH TANKS position. We waited. Tense moments. Brupp-brupp again. The engine picked up with a roar. Betty put the plane into a steady climb to regain the height we'd lost. We continued on our way.

While Phyllis had been dozing, Becky's little hand, coming from the back, had turned the fuel cock off. She'd seen, with fascination, how Betty changed the tank selection from time to time and decided to have a go herself. Rather than turning it to a full tank, she had turned it completely off.

Two days later we flew into Juba in south Sudan and then, at last, on to Malakal. We were home.

What a welcome! The mission and MAF people rolled out a red carpet made of crepe paper.

"Praise God for a wonderful trip," Phyllis wrote home: "and for His enabling and undertaking." To which I said "Amen".

Our flying continued to increase. Out of our first twenty-six days back Betty flew twenty-three. A radio telephone (RT) network had at last replaced the old Morse wireless telegrapy (WT) system in Sudan for air traffic control. As in other countries, a pilot could handle the communications through voice conversation on the RT. A Morse operator was no longer needed. I missed flying as radio operator, but I was now free to concentrate on the administration of the programme and the development of MAF's operations generally.

A few weeks after we returned to Malakal, we were joined by another family from American MAF: Ernie and Dorene Krenzin with their two boys. Ernie was highly skilled, a "natural" both as pilot and as aircraft engineer. He had considerable experience with Cessnas and it was good to have him when our new plane arrived.

Soon after, American MAF's secretary and treasurer, Charlie Mellis, together with his family came and stayed with us for over two and a half months. They were on their way to New Guinea. I'd had much correspondence with Charlie over the years and he'd always been ready to share and advise, so it was good to meet him personally and further strengthen the links between our two groups. As well as talking a great deal, we travelled together across Central and West Africa, looking into needs and possibilities as we went. Finally, we picked up our second Cessna which had been shipped to Nigeria and assembled by SIM mechanics there and flew it back to Sudan.

With two planes, the effectiveness of our service grew still further. One mission leader was saved sixteen days' travel by boat and car when he needed to visit a succession of stations in Sudan and Ethiopia. A family had taken nine days by winding river to get out from their station; our Cessna took them back in an hour and a half. Our passenger miles went up by seventy per cent and the outreach of the missions was greatly enhanced. We were carrying more and more Africans, including Sudanese officials. Among them was Colonel Nimeri, who later became President of Sudan.

On one flight our Provincial Governor noticed a little book peeping out of the pocket on the back of the seat in front of him. He was soon leafing through a New Testament in Arabic which he read for an hour or so. When Betty landed the plane at Malakal he asked whether he could have a copy.

"Do take that one," she said.

We always prayed that literature carried in our planes would be of value to our passengers.

Another time the governor turned up at our hangar when I had one of the planes in pieces inspecting it. He was surprised at my thorough examination of every part.

"Do you do all that even when you don't know that anything is wrong?" he asked.

"This is preventive maintenance, sir. It's not like a car. If this stops in the air you can't get out and push."

He appreciated the point, though this wasn't the way most people looked after their vehicles in Sudan.

On another flight he was travelling with a prominent Muslim religious official from the north. It was our practice always to pray before take-off, but to avoid offence on this occasion we went out to the wing tip and quietly had our prayer there. Then Ernie, who was piloting, climbed in and prepared to start the engine.

"Aren't we going to pray?" demanded the governor. He was used to our normal pattern and felt something was missing. Somewhat abashed, I had to explain that we had prayed already outside.

Our planes flew many hours helping to eradicate the disease of kala-azar, which had swept through the Upper Nile Province decimating the population. Carried by sandflies, it attacks the spleen and is fatal if untreated. Gordon Marshall, now back from furlough, flew medical staff into the affected areas. The mission nurses became expert in recognizing and treating the disease. Our plane constantly carried supplies of Pentostam, the drug used to combat it.

Abaiyat became the centre of the epidemic. From the numbers of new graves in surrounding villages, you would have thought that the Dinkas had been attacked and overrun by a hostile tribe. At one place where Gordon landed, a Dinka from a small settlement nearby appeared with a bag of pebbles.

"These are the people who have died in my village

in the last few weeks," he said. "I put a pebble in the bag every time someone was buried."

Gordon counted 145 pebbles.

Government and people alike appreciated the help the plane was able to give. Again, we were glad to serve them.

17

Wider Horizons

Some things still hampered our work. With two planes we could reduce waiting times for flights, but no amount of planes could reduce the rains.

A mission family at Akobo with a seriously sick child urgently needed to get to Khartoum. But their airstrip had been swamped by continuous downpours. Because the plane couldn't land they had to come out by boat. It took them three days, sometimes crouching in torrential rain as they moved along the winding rivers. Only when they reached Malakal could MAF fly them swiftly to the capital.

"Why don't we fit floats to one of our planes?" suggested Ernie Krenzin. "Then we could land on the rivers at Akobo, Nasir and many of the other places."

We applied to the Sudan Civil Aviation for permission. There was much necessary discussion. Were the rivers safe for this? What about floating debris? Would we endanger canoes? Eventually the department agreed and we ordered a pair of floats from America.

When they came, Ernie removed the undercarriage from one of our Cessnas and fitted them in its place. The floats were large and long, really enhancing the plane's appearance as it stood high and proud upon them. Its launch on the Nile caused great excitement.

The doctor at Nasir wrote of its first arrival there:

We told the Nuers that we were going to have a plane land on the river right in front of our mission. Many of them just didn't believe it, but they crowded the riverbank the day it came. The plane is always beautiful to us, in its black, silver and red, but today, with the silver floats on, it was magnificent. The floats skimmed into the water and the spray flew up as it gradually came to a graceful stop on the river. It taxied to the shore and was tied up. To see Ernie and Betty get out in their bright orange life jackets added flavour to it all.

Wherever the float plane landed it caused a sensation. In Malakal both southerners and northerners thronged to the riverbank to see it operate. "The plane with slippers on," the Arabs called it, thinking of their own pointed foot wear.

"It's like having an airstrip all the way beneath me," said Ernie when he returned from his first trip following the rivers to Nasir and Akobo.

In a wheel plane during the wet season we always wondered what would happen if we were obliged to make an emergency landing in the swamps. With the float plane we could land on any river or even put down safely on wet grass. It also gave new access to places with no airstrips at all, especially along the Nile and its tributaries.

There were, of course, particular dangers. We had to watch for currents, winds, canoes, floating grass islands, submerged logs, and, not least, crocodiles. Once Gordon felt a bump as he landed at Malakal and saw a hippopotamus moving away. It had come up at the sound of the plane, just to see what was

happening, and the float had struck its head. It probably went away with a headache; it certainly left
Gordon with one. The float was holed and quickly
started shipping water. He taxied to the bank just in
time. Alastair Macdonald, also back from furlough,
hauled the plane out of the water and up to the hangar
for repair.

Phyllis and I had lived in remote, isolated places and
were well aware that MAF could be a lifeline,
especially in emergencies, for Africans and missionaries alike. Now a day came when this was brought
home to us even more strongly by personal experience. I lay in bed in the heat at Malakal with mumps
– no joke at my age, as I soon discovered. I developed
serious complications. My temperature rose to 103,
stayed there for several days, then soared to nearly
105. I was constantly vomiting, dehydrated and felt
desperately ill.

"Dr Balzer is at Doro now," Betty said to Phyllis.
"I think I ought to get him."

I was never so glad in my life to see a doctor as
when I saw Reuben Balzer bending over me. Soon a
drip was in place and I was in his care.

"If I hadn't come, Stuart might have been under
the ground before long," he told Phyllis.

He stayed until I had turned the corner and started
a long, slow recovery. I had learned for myself what
it was really like to have MAF fly in help.

By the end of 1956 our base at Malakal was nearly
complete. Three houses were almost finished. A
smaller guesthouse, an office and a store were well
on the way. After eight years without any radio contact with the mission stations, the government

finally granted us a licence for both ground-to-ground and ground-to-air transmissions. That further relieved isolation and opened up a new era for us.

Now we could check the state of the airstrips before we arrived, our base could easily be called when needs or emergencies arose, flying schedules could be discussed and adjusted. Contact could even be made with the plane while it was airborne. Stations that previously had to send a runner miles on foot to the nearest telegraph station could now contact us quickly and directly. The whole mission family, separated by hundreds of miles of unfriendly country, could be united day by day over the radio.

Our horizons were widening in other ways too.

When Charlie Mellis had visited Malakal, in addition to contacts we'd made for future MAF work in West Africa, we'd later flown south to East Africa. The Africa Inland Mission was enquiring about MAF help for outreach in the Northern Frontier district of Kenya.

"As a mission we need air service," said Dr Davis, the AIM Director from the US. "But we don't want the technical problems involved. Will you start a service for us here in East Africa?"

I remembered the area well from our original Gemini survey. I knew we now had the resources to help them – having heard from Steve that interest and giving were increasing in the UK. So I agreed. We ordered a third Cessna 180, destined for Kenya.

Then Steve came out from England to join me in an intensive survey of the southwest and south of Ethiopia. The needs there still concerned us, but they required much more investigation than those of

Kenya. We felt this was the moment to explore them.
Betty flew us from Malakal to Dembi Dollo just
inside the Ethiopian border. From there, Steve and I
travelled by land for eleven days with workers from
several different missions.

Most of the terrain we covered was at least 6000
feet high, with mountains up to 10000 feet – not
unusual in Ethiopia – but very different from the
Sudan. Gone was the flatness, gone were most of the
swamps. Rugged trails were strewn with jagged rocks
and two-foot diameter boulders. We often had to hang
on for dear life in the Jeeps. The lens on my old Leica
camera jolted apart. Our Thermos broke. Sometimes
the vehicle was poised so steeply on a road that we
thought it would topple over backwards or sideways.
All this was commonplace in this region.

The people in these wild highlands were also
different from the Sudanese. They wore many more
clothes in the cool high altitude, were more
reserved, more suspicious. Sometimes we would
hear hostile cries of *"Ferangi! Ferangi!"* "Foreigner,
Foreigner".

In a single two-day expedition we crossed thirty
deep ravines on unbelievably high and flimsy bridges
made out of tree trunks precariously tied together
with rope. Each one had to be checked in advance for
gaps or structural weakness. Narrow as they were,
they had no parapets to prevent us plummeting into
the rushing torrents below.

Very different was the river Dabus. It was in a broad
valley and was too wide to be bridged. It could be
forded by a Jeep only during six weeks of the dry
season. When we arrived it was still chest deep and
a quarter of a mile wide.

ETHIOPIA, MAF's EARLY DAYS
Showing a few of the airstrips used and mentioned in the text

N
W — E
S

KHARTOUM

Red Sea

Asmara

Danakil
Desert

DJIBOUTI

SUDAN

White Nile

Blue Nile

Chali
Asosa
Doro

Dabus River

Malakal

Aira

ADDIS ABABA

Nasir

Dembi Dollo
Gambela

ETHIOPIA

Akobo

Gila River
JIMMA

Jemu

Surma

UGANDA

KENYA

Scale
km 0   100   200
miles 0   50   100   150

"What happens now?" we enquired. The missionary showed us.

We covered the Jeeps' engine distributors with
waterproof plastic bags, put heavy grease over the
sparking plugs and ignition fittings and attached long
upright extension pipes to the exhausts, bringing
them well above the tops of the Jeeps.

"That should prevent the water from stopping the
engines," we were assured.

Someone had to go ahead to find a shallow enough
path. I volunteered to walk in front, probing the river
bed with a long stick.

"There may be crocodiles," I was warned. The Jeeps
followed me closely and one of the missionaries kept
a powerful rifle ready. We all made it safely
across.

Some hours later we at last reached a mission
station where the Swedish missionaries had not seen
another white person for eight months. We quickly
realized how isolated these stations were and how
difficult of access. The need for an air service was
obvious. But could we hope to find airstrips among
these precipitous mountains? We eventually discovered we could – in every one of the places we
visited. But they were to be very different from our
flat strips in Sudan.

Back in Malakal I drew up the order for our fourth
Cessna.

Eight months after that, in October 1958, Betty
Greene returned to America. The governor at Malakal
held a special farewell tea party for her. She had won
her way into the hearts of all those she flew. They'd
appreciated her dedication, her flying skill, her

gracious manner and her care for her passengers. We were all sorry to see her go.

Changes also quickly followed for Phyllis and me. We weren't too sure about them at first.

We were now facing the need to administer three operational fields instead of one. We all felt that a central headquarters was required to coordinate our work, not only between the fields, but also between Africa and the UK. Most of the coordination, administration and planning had already fallen to me and it was agreed that I should be the one to continue this at the new headquarters.

It was decided we should be located in the UK because of the need to have a strong link with the home end. So Phyllis and I prepared to move to London.

In November we wrote to those who supported us:

> We feel our work is nearly finished here in the Sudan. It is strange to think of leaving our Nile-side MAF base. We have grown to love the people, the vast open country, the winding rivers and all those, including the missionaries we have had the privilege of helping. But we go to serve a wider sphere – one that will include not only the Sudan, but Ethiopia and East Africa as well.

Ten days before we left Malakal there was a military coup. The Commander in Chief of the army seized power. After less than three years the first independent government of the Sudan had fallen. Martial law was imposed; we found soldiers with machine guns posted at the Malakal airfield and around our hangar. The coup didn't prevent our leaving.

Very shortly after we'd gone, Gordon was called into the Provincial Governor's office together with some of the other missionaries. The commanding officer of the local army units, the chief of police and the Malakal district commissioner were there. The governor outlined the official position:

"Because of deterioration and chaos in the country, the government has been overthrown and replaced by the military. The motives are the welfare and the progress of the Sudanese people."

He continued: "The new government will work for the unification of the country. All political parties have been dissolved. Party politics are a thing of the past and are not allowed. Any discussion of the south becoming a federation is outlawed." Turning to Gordon, he gave a final instruction: "From now on, MAF must present two copies of its weekly flying programme to the army chief and the governor in advance."

Gordon was disturbed to learn that, under martial law, the MAF planes could be commandeered at any time for use by the army. In the event, there was no marked increase in demands for flights from either the government or the army. But the political climate continued to change. In MAF we knew we were guests in the country; it was our duty to be as helpful and cooperative as possible.

At the farewell service held in Khartoum for Phyllis and me, Mal Forsberg recalled:

"Eleven years ago you came to the South Sudan. You told us about your plans to help with an aircraft. We needed that help, but at the time the proposals all seemed so visionary. Now we have seen the vision

become a reality. We thank God for all that has meant
to us."

We also received a note from the American Mission
addressed to all of us in MAF. They had passed a
minute at their annual meeting:

"We express our thanks to God for the blessing
which has been ours through MAF and for the good
relationship with government officials which exists
as a result of your service. We appreciate what you
are and what you have done for us."

What greater encouragement could we have had as
we left the Sudan?

The MAF headquarters were now located in the
Stevens's large house at South Woodford on the edge
of London. They lived upstairs. The ground floor
served as the office. Phyllis and I eventually found
accommodation nearby.

The work in the UK had many different aspects.
There was constant correspondence with our overseas fields. Policies and standards of every sort had to
be decided and developed. Aviation, legal, personnel,
financial and many other matters had to be dealt
with. Problems needed solving, financial and personal
resources for the work had to be found, publicity
developed, films and filmstrips produced. In addition,
there were speaking engagements all over the UK
and, for me especially, there was travel to Africa as
well.

Dealing with applicants for MAF services required
many hours of careful interviewing, advising and
selecting by both Steve and myself. Not all were
trained pilots. One was a schoolboy of fourteen who
felt, even then, that God was calling him to fly for

MAF one day. Others were already qualified and experienced. Early on we had an application from a Navy pilot. Both he and the schoolboy eventually came into long-term service with MAF.

To our own films about Sudan Steve added some from American MAF, one of which had a particular impact. *Mid-Century Martyrs* was the story of pilot Nate Saint, who, with four missionary colleagues, had sought to contact an isolated and hostile tribe in Ecuador – the Auca Indians. After months of prayer and careful preparation they flew in Nate's Piper Pacer to a river sandbar in Auca territory. At first good contact was made. Then, without warning, all five were speared to death. This story made an indelible impression on thousands of Christians around the world. Hundreds dedicated themselves to God's service as a result. The schoolboy who came to see us was among them.

Steve arranged for Marj Saint, Nate's widow, to come to England for a month to tell the story first-hand. At Westminster Chapel, the huge hall, with its three tiers of balconies, was packed out. Marj spoke for three-quarters of an hour. You could have heard a pin drop during the whole time. When she finished there was a great sigh from the audience. God used her all over the country and on radio and TV.

These opportunities for greater publicity built up support for MAF. But we had learned financial prudence over long years of penury. We were constantly aware that, whatever our resources, we needed to use them wisely.

"Before you buy anything with MAF money," Steve used to say, "ask yourself – 'If it was my own personal money, would I spend it on that?' "

It was a good test. It's all too easy to waste money, even in a Christian charity.

We knew, too, how self-sacrificially some of the money was given. As we opened gifts from supporters we were often humbled. There were pensioners who did without a holiday to send us something, a man who gave a large part of his life's savings, a school-child who sent in her pocket money, a businessman stirred to contribute substantially. We were grateful for God's supply through His people.

After we'd been back in England for a while, we welcomed our third child, Priscilla. Now we felt our family was complete and thanked God for the way He had given us each one of our precious children.

With the coming of Priscilla, it was necessary for Phyllis to begin to hand over some of her accounting duties to new staff. MAF was not just a mission. It was an aviation organization as well. Expenses as an air operator can be frighteningly high, financial liabilities unexpectedly large. Effective control was essential. Mr Adams looked after the home accounts whilst Phyllis's job had been to consolidate the over-all accounts and monitor and coordinate the expenses of operations in Africa. I'd relied on her to keep me aware of what each programme was costing and of our financial situation as a whole.

New pilots joined the work in Sudan, amongst them Tony Holloway, the Navy pilot we had interviewed. Ernie and Dorene Krenzin and family moved southwards to start the new work in Kenya. The Cessna 180 we'd ordered arrived and Ernie was able to rent a hangar at Wilson airport, the small-plane airfield in Nairobi. The new Nairobi-based pro-

gramme was soon in full swing, reaching up to the
desolate Northern Frontier area of Kenya, southwards
into Tanzania and westwards as far as the Congo.

Calls continued to come from Ethiopia. The American Mission working there appealed: "There are
countless untouched tribes and areas within our
reach. We feel a real responsibility and need to locate
them. Will MAF be able to help us in reaching them
soon?"

18

Highlands and Lowlands

Ethiopia always fascinated me. It has a wonderful profusion of almost every form of African tree, flower and vegetation. In complete contrast to the flat, flat Sudan, its mountains rise up from a great moat of desert and swamplands like a mighty, inaccessible fortress.

The vast highlands are a huge volcanic plateau with striking conical mountain tops and enormous isolated blocks of rock. They are cut through by deep river valleys and ravines, with chasms dropping thousands of feet. The whole country could have been designed to hinder travel and access. It seems to cry out: "You shall not pass!"

In many parts surface travel is possible only by foot, packhorse, donkey, mule or, in certain regions, camel. This has made it very difficult to reach many of the inhabitants. Even if they are reached, it can still be difficult to continue to live safely amongst them given their virtual isolation from the outside world.

The people of Ethiopia differ widely. The Sudanese Arabs used to call the country *Balad el Habish*, land of the mixed peoples. In the 1950s many tribes were still so inaccessible that neither central nor provincial governors could administer them. In some cases, particularly in the south and southwest, even their locations were scarcely known.

If Ethiopia as a whole was one giant fortress, each of these tribal locations was a mini-fortress, hidden in the mountains, lost in the forests, inaccessible in the swamps or unsought in the fiercely hot lowland deserts.

The Mesengo, to take a single example, had never been accurately located and their language was unknown. They generally kept to their own area; none had ever visited Addis Ababa. Subject to many tropical diseases, they lived in fear and superstition in the darkness of the deep rain forests and, even more, in the darkness of domination by evil spirits. Century after century they had remained in gloom.

"We've got a pilot for Ethiopia," I told Phyllis one January day in 1960 when I came home from the Woodford office. "I've had a letter from Grady Parrott about an American couple, Bob and Betty Hutchins who've been serving with Australian MAF in New Guinea for seven years. He told them about our need in Ethiopia – didn't expect them to be very enthusiastic – but they were. They're ideally qualified for Ethiopia. Bob's flying experience is just what we need. He's had about seven thousand hours in New Guinea. What could be better?"

MAF supporters responded to the challenge and funds for a plane built up within seven months. Compared with most people, the Hutchins received visas to enter Ethiopia miraculously fast. By November they were there.

"Have you just arrived in Ethiopia?" an old-time missionary asked Bob and Betty at the SIM guest-house in Addis Ababa. "Do we really need a plane

here? We've got along all these years without one."
Then he added, jokingly: "If you fly me I won't have
any good stories of long mule-back journeys through
the mountains. What will I tell my supporters?"

Bob and Betty found some of their other initial
contacts and experiences equally discouraging. Difficult Amharic language study had to be rushed
because of their need to get the new programme
started. Then there were the repeated visits to government departments to get permissions, involving tedious waits to meet the right officials. There seemed
so many restrictions.

It was a relief, after some months, to move down
to Jimma, 150 miles southwest of Addis Ababa,
where the SIM allowed them to use one of their
houses. We felt this would be the best base as it was
central to the American and European missions who
had requested our help. Bob was soon in action,
though not yet providing flights. As in the Sudan,
finding airstrip sites was the first requirement and
he travelled out on mule-back week after week to
locate suitable places. When they were cleared he
returned the same way to inspect them. Only after
that would he be ready to fly in and make trial landings.

As soon as the Cessna 180 for Ethiopia arrived and
was assembled in Nairobi Bob flew it back to Jimma.
Flying started at once alongside the search for more
airstrips. Enthusiasm for MAF was mounting.

"Even those who'd first questioned the value of a
plane were now very happy to have it!" Bob told me
later.

Right from the beginning medical work and emergencies featured strongly in the flying. Sometimes, in

the absence of airstrips, Bob dropped medical supplies from the air. At other times, where there were places to land, he carried missionaries to outlying areas to hold clinics amongst the tribespeople. Previously the long distances and shortages of medical staff had severely restricted such help. Now it could be provided on a regular basis because so much travel time was saved.

On a visit to one of the newly cleared airstrips a big crowd gathered. The missionary used the opportunity to preach on the words of Jesus: "I am the way and the truth and the life." When he had finished, one of the leaders of the people, an old man, stood up and said:

"We are happy that you can come here. We have brought our children. Teach them and heal them. It is true what you have said. Our old people are all gone: we do not know where they have gone. They are lost. Now you have told us of God and of His place, heaven. It is good. Teach our children. Come back."

Jemu was a mountain out-station. The missionary who visited there came from a well-established mission station, fifteen minutes' flying time away. He wanted an airstrip at Jemu itself so Bob trekked in and selected a site. Since the missionary concerned was an experienced ex-military pilot it was left to him to clear it.

On the first flight in Bob carried only cargo. It was a "one-way strip": you could land only in one direction – up the steep slope. But worse, if the plane's climb was reduced because of a full load and you misjudged your final touchdown, the surrounding hills left you scant chance of going round again: you were committed.

Bob landed successfully, but didn't like the strip. There were still several rolling humps in it. He unloaded his cargo and then flew over to the main mission station and found the missionary.

"I'm sorry, the strip isn't ready for regular use," Bob told him. "We've got to get rid of those humps."

"Let's fly back right now," suggested the missionary. "Then you'll be able to show me exactly what needs doing." They headed back.

Just as Bob came in to land a dog, chased by a number of Ethiopians, dashed across the strip. In spite of the difficulties, Bob managed a very tight go-around. On his second approach he touched down further along the strip, beyond where the people and dog were still standing. Suddenly the aircraft's wheels hit one of the humps. The plane bounced. Before they knew what had happened it was on its back.

They both scrambled out safely. But the new plane was extensively damaged, beyond any possibility of repair on the spot. It would have to be taken apart and carried for weeks over rough mountain trails. Even then, where could it be repaired and rebuilt and who could do it?

It was a very low point for Bob and Betty. Bob blamed himself for what had happened. The plane was out of action just as missions were beginning to rely on it. It was a disastrous beginning. When I heard about it I could really understand how Bob felt. Memories of the Gemini crash and of how we felt then came flooding back.

This time a solution came quickly. Missionary activity was being restricted in Sudan; our two planes

there could no longer be fully used. One of them was
loaned to Bob and the Ethiopian service continued.

As the work expanded, however, the pressure on
Bob and Betty intensified.

Visits to Africa had now become a regular part of my
work. In November 1962, I arrived in Khartoum at
the start of a six-week tour through the three fields:
Sudan, Ethiopia and Kenya. On my flight to Addis
Ababa the Ethiopian Airlines' plane had a large group
of Russian passengers.

As we got off the plane I stood by for a moment to
watch them disembark. I couldn't help being aware
of the struggle for the soul of Ethiopia. In very general
terms, well over a third of the Ethiopians were
Amharas and Tigrinya: a people of Semitic origin and
mostly members of the ancient Ethiopian Orthodox
Church. Approximately another third, mainly in the
north and east were Muslims. The remaining people,
chiefly in the south and west, were nearly all either
animists following their own tribal religions or Evangelical Christians.

Now hundreds of Russians were pouring into the
country to give technical and medical assistance and
at the same time importing a powerful message of
Communism. Christianity was already there. So was
Islam. To which faith would Ethiopia give her
allegiance?

As I checked my luggage through customs I was
met by two missionary friends from Sudan days,
Chuck and Mary Alice Jordan, now serving in Ethiopia. On the way into town, they described the remote
Ethiopian station where they had been able to continue their work among the Nuer just this side of the

border with the Sudan. They told me how much they
depended on MAF to get in and out of their distant
centre.

After a day in Addis Ababa, I went down to see the
Hutchins at Jimma. For ten days I accompanied Bob
on his flights. In the evenings, back at base, we discussed plans for the future or worked through the
programme accounts.

As we flew out, day after day, over the rolling tree-
clad mountains, the grandeur and drama of the
country was always breathtaking. Although there
was sometimes smoke haze from dry season grass
fires, flying was comparatively easy. But it took little
effort to imagine what it was like when clouds and
rain shrouded these lofty mountains and deep valleys.
Sometimes we'd be flying barely a thousand feet
above high mountain tops or plateaux. Then suddenly
the ground would fall away thousands of feet into the
deep rift valleys. It felt like being catapulted off the
edge of a precipice and suddenly suspended high
above the distant forests below.

The airstrips were as dramatic as the rest of the
country. I was thankful that we had Bob, with all his
experience of the New Guinea mountains, to start
the programme here. He was used to this kind of
flying and this kind of airstrip. It was often impossible to find any flat, straight areas long enough for
even our small planes to land; steeply sloping airstrips were quite normal.

Landing at one of those ascending strips, I watched
with appreciation the way Bob handled the plane. We
made our final approach over a ring of green hills,
touching down accurately at the bottom end of the
strip. As soon as the plane was on the ground Bob

gave the engine almost full power to carry it up the
steep incline. At the top he closed the throttle sharply
and we stopped on a small levelled area. Good judgment and precise timing were essential for safe landings in such conditions.

The country and the airstrips were not the only
unusual features. The people who lived in these
remote regions were very strange to us too. At one
airstrip in wooded mountains we landed among the
Surma people. When we first flew over, the men,
painted in white powdery ash, were fighting a dangerous mock battle with six-foot long staves all over the
landing area. They stopped and moved away to let us
land.

It was then that I noticed the women. They had
brown clay discs, between six and ten inches across
cut into and distending their lower lips. I was startled.
But I had to recognize that their normal traditions
were different from mine. After all I was as strange
to them as they were to me. They couldn't imagine
life without either the fierce stick fights of the men
or the large lip discs that made their women so distinctive.

We flew over another heavily wooded district.

"In one tribe down there," Bob said, "before a
young man can be accepted as an adult member in
the tribe he has to murder a man of another tribe and
bring part of the body as proof of the killing."

Again I thought about different traditions. Do more
"civilized" people do much better with their wars
and rivalries? But I couldn't suppress a shudder.

I remember sitting later in a mud-walled thatched
hut in one of these areas – a newly reached one –
talking to Solomon, a fine Ethiopian teacher-evangel-

ist who had come from another tribe to work among the Jemu people. He and his wife were as much foreign missionaries as anyone from abroad, for the culture and background of the Jemu were strikingly different from their own. Solomon's example was to be followed by many others in years to come. It was exciting to know that MAF was helping to get them into these previously isolated places.

At the Gila river station near the Sudan border, we rediscovered Don and Lyda McClure heading outreach in a new area of the Anuak. The swampy lowlands were so like the Sudan that I felt I was back there. It was good to see the McClures again and catch up on their tireless activities. As we sat talking, Don looked around their mission house and remarked:

"Do you realize, Stuart, that apart from a few items, everything in this house has been flown in by the MAF plane?"

Over the years that followed I made many journeys to our different centres in Africa. It was inspiring, on every visit to Ethiopia, to see marked progress not only in MAF but, still more, in the work of the missions and the indigenous churches we were there to serve.

While the doors in Ethiopia were opening still wider, others were closing. Disaster was striking in the Sudan. The kala-azar epidemic had caused many deaths and now yellow fever threatened. The mission nurse at one of the newer stations near Doro was the first to suspect it. It was confirmed by the doctor in the American Mission area to whom she relayed the symptoms over the mission radio network.

The province government was immediately
informed, the danger of an epidemic was recognized
and messages were quickly sent to Khartoum. MAF
was asked to take a pathologist into the area and then
to fly in doctors, medical staff and mission nurses.
Thousands of inoculations were given, but at first the
area of epidemic widened. More serum was flown in
to inoculate those still uninfected until eventually
the progress of the plague was halted.

Then another disaster loomed, different but poten-
tially still more serious. Bitter fighting escalated
between northerners and those southerners who
wanted autonomy. The northern Arabic newspapers
again suggested that missions were stirring up
trouble. Islamic fundamentalists naturally wanted
missions out of the way.

"Only one Dinka station will be left open. All the
others, including Melut and Abaiyat, are closing,"
one missionary reported when she visited us in
London. "The northern government is taking over
dispensary work throughout the south; they no
longer want the missionary nurses there. Work permits are not being renewed and some are being asked
to leave."

Gradually the government further limited the work
of missions. Direct Christian work was curbed, medical and educational projects taken over. Eventually
the Missionary Societies Act ruled that all religious
workers must get a licence from the government. It
put severe restrictions on the national church as well
as foreign missionaries.

The Sudanese church had been firmly planted in
the Malakal area among the Shilluk, at Akobo and
beyond, among the Anuak, at Nasir and in the sur-

rounding region among the Nuer. At Doro the Mabaan had appointed church elders, at Chali-el-fil the Uduk church was strong and thriving with a godly pastor. At Melut two pastors to the Dinka had been ordained and, in the Nuba mountains to the west a strong church existed, with good leaders. Further south, among the peoples of Equatoria and Bahr-el-Gezel, the church was well and widely established.

MAF had played a part in much of this.

Suddenly the Minister of the Interior announced, "All missions are to be expelled." In most cases the missionaries were given only a few days to leave. Doro now had a crowded and well-equipped hospital, a leprosy settlement and educational work with literacy classrooms. All were closed.

At Chali-el-fil we'd been flying in copies of the newly translated Uduk new Testament. Uduk Christians took them and distributed them throughout the tribe. The last words the missionaries heard as they drove off amidst the dust of the dry season road were those of the Uduk Christians singing a hymn:

> I have decided to follow Jesus,
> No turning back, no turning back.
> The Cross before me, the world behind me,
> No turning back, no turning back.

What the words were to mean for the Uduk was yet to be seen.

So it was that all across the south Sudan, with similar scenes of drama and sadness, stations were emptied one by one. Some missionaries had thirty-six hours to pack and leave, others only half an hour. Some friendly government officials regretted the evacuation order. They were impressed by the good spirit of the missionaries. One missionary wrote:

"After all, we were guests of the Sudan. These happenings show the wisdom of always having a minimum of possessions!"

The MAF programme there had already been slimmed down. Gordon and Jean Marshall had transferred to Kenya. One plane and just two families were left: John Ducker from the UK was pilot and Hugh Beck from Canada was engineer. The intense work and the political and climatic pressures over the months had been very wearing. Needing a holiday, the two families flew down to Nairobi. They had scarcely arrived when they heard of the Sudan expulsion order. MAF was included, with only seven days to clear up and close down the entire operation. This involved our base at Malakal, our hangar, workshop, spares and equipment at the airfield and our fuel stocks spread throughout the country.

It wouldn't have been wise to take the MAF plane back to Malakal. It might have been impounded. John and Hugh returned there by commercial airline together with Gordon. They held a large auction at the hangar, selling off most of the movable property and personal effects.

The Provincial Government were sorry to see MAF go and the governor expressed his appreciation of our service. The chief of police gave a dinner for the three men before they left. As Gordon, John and Hugh finally drove away, our faithful Sudanese helpers, some of whom had been with us for over eight years, stood around weeping.

"They looked like lost sheep," reported Gordon.

"We were weeping too," he admitted. "It was a hard parting." It was March 1964.

John joined Gordon in Kenya. Hugh went to Jimma to work as engineer in the Ethiopian programme.

In the Sudan, as the political deterioration accelerated, many southerners fled into Ethiopia, Uganda or Congo. Others made raids on government posts manned by northerners. This in turn provoked a campaign to subdue them. Many, including Christians, were imprisoned. Army units throughout the south became increasingly active and anyone resisting was jailed. At Akobo, the Anuak village elders were accused of hiding rebels; all the men in another Anuak village were similarly accused and shot. Southerners who were literate, wore clothes, had held a government job or worked with any commercial firm were particularly suspect and liable to be killed. Thousands died.

Nuer, Anuak, Shilluk, Dinka and others escaped by fleeing across the Sudan's borders. At Juba a whole church congregation was machine-gunned. Near Malakal, the American mission station at Doleib Hill was burned down. At Melut a Sudanese pastor called Gideon, working among the Dinka, was charged with assisting the rebels. The army found the list of church members.

"These are rebels you are helping," they asserted. He and his four church elders were shot and their bodies flung into the Nile. The great river silently witnessed another sad episode in the Sudan's long and tragic history.

19

Where Cloud
and Mountain Meet

It was summertime in England. Twenty-four-year-old Tom Frank was working as the attendant at a small filling station just outside Great Yarmouth.

A middle-aged couple, who had stopped for petrol, spotted two Auster aeroplanes and a small office marked Anglian Air Charters in the adjacent field.

"Are there any pleasure flights for today?" they asked Tom.

"Yes," he replied.

When they went to book tickets, it was Tom who sold them, and when they went over to the planes it was Tom who escorted them and helped them get strapped in. Then it was he who climbed into the pilot's seat.

"What! You again?" the husband enquired, rather taken aback.

"Yes, the pilot is having a day off," said Tom, "so they're letting me have a go."

In spite of their qualms, they enjoyed their flight around Yarmouth. It was all in a day's work for Tom who'd done the trip nearly five thousand times.

After a spell at Manchester University, Tom had trained as an RAF jet pilot during his two years' National Service. He had also become a Christian.

He was expected to go into the family business on leaving the Air Force, but instead chose to study at London Bible College and aim for MAF. We required a minimum of five hundred flying hours in light aircraft, so for four years he flew every summer at Yarmouth to build up his experience. As the owner of the charter company also owned the petrol station, Tom cheerfully took on the attendant's job as well. He said it helped to break the monotony.

Meanwhile, at Jimma, Bob and Betty continued to manage the flying programme on their own. Betty's days were busy as she had to educate their son Bruce. Most of the time she also had the MAF radio on, monitoring Bob's flights and receiving his position reports and landing information. She would receive flight requests and, if necessary, relay emergency calls to him in the air. The programme accounts filled her "spare time". MAF wives all over the world play a vital part in the operations.

For Bob, too, the work was growing steadily as needs increased and the number of places served multiplied. New airstrip sites were requested but they couldn't be identified or cleared until he was free to trek in overland. An additional pilot was clearly required.

By 1963 Tom Frank had completed his preparation for MAF service. He and a second plane were on their way to Ethiopia. Bob and Betty were due to return to the US but waited to ensure Tom could become thoroughly familiar with the programme. Alastair Macdonald came with Margaret and took over as programme manager. A further British pilot family came too – Les and Elaine Brown, who'd gained MAF experience in Kenya. Hugh and Norma Beck had already arrived, following the closure of the Sudan.

In the Sudan, the British Embassy negotiated with the military government about our MAF houses and hangar. The governor at Malakal was willing to help and our prayer partners prayed. Suddenly the government agreed to buy our base properties for the army and made a fair payment. At first the money seemed of little use because it was in Sudanese pounds in a Khartoum bank. It seemed unlikely that the Sudan exchange control would allow us to take it out of the country. But permission was granted – a second miracle, just when we needed the money to build a new base of our own at Jimma. Our assets had not been lost; God had transferred them.

In our 1964 December newsletter, telling of the suffering and restrictions in the Sudan, I was also able to write: "This is the day of opportunity in Ethiopia. How long this door will remain open we do not know. It is open now and no cost or effort must be spared to bring the good news of God's love and to show His care to many people in this land."

The next thirteen years were to bear this out.

Tom Frank sat in a hut by the mountain airstrip at Aira. Rain poured off the corrugations on the tin roof. Beside him was an Ethiopian lying on a stretcher, his left leg heavily bandaged and supported by cushions, his eyes closed, his breathing deep and noisy. Tom had flown from Jimma that morning in response to an urgent radio request from the German missionary there. The injured man must be flown to hospital at once.

The weather hadn't been too bad when Tom had left Jimma. Now the missionary looked out at the rain, then at the patient, then at Tom, who knew only too well what he was thinking. The man on the stretcher, a leader of the church at Aira, had fallen while repairing a roof. He had lost a lot of blood, was weak and in great pain.

Heavy clouds shrouded the mountain tops all around, making flying impossible. Minutes went slowly by. Then Tom pointed to a distant ridge: "The cloud base is starting to lift over there, we should be able to make it now." He was still wary. He'd been in Ethiopia now for three years and learnt much in that time. Two years before, he'd had an accident here at Aira, so he checked the strip with extra care, finding one soft patch he must avoid. They carried the patient out and gently fastened the stretcher to the floor of the plane.*

A brief prayer by the missionary committed the flight to God. Rain spattered down on to the windscreen as Tom took off, but the slipstream soon drove the water away and cleared his view. A gentle pull on the control column and the plane was racing upwards towards the low ragged clouds just above. He headed it towards the gap he'd seen between clouds and ridge. To enter the cloud even for a few seconds in such a mountainous area could prove fatal.

Once through the gap, he turned the aircraft towards Jimma. Around him the rain had stopped, the cloud base was higher. He was able to gain more

*Tom described the events of the day to one of the MAF wives. I have included some of her graphic account of this incident. See Elisabeth Longley's *Over the Mountains of Ethiopia* pp. 31–38, Mission Aviation Fellowship, London 1966.

altitude. Over to the right it looked as though the
sun was trying to break through. But he didn't like
what he saw ahead – a vast mass of dense, black
storm clouds, with jagged streams of lightning.
Beyond this lay Jimma, itself probably in the throes
of a deluge which would make landing impossible. He
called the MAF base there. The storm made reception
difficult and there was a continual crackle of inter-
ference, but he could just hear Norma Beck's voice
answering him.

"Can you give me the Jimma weather, please,
Norma?" There was a pause. Norma's radio room
overlooked the airstrip.

"It's raining heavily here," came the reply. "The
cloud base is still very low."

"Roger, Norma. The weather ahead of me looks
bad. I'll try and skirt around it to the east and find a
break to get me through to Jimma. I have an urgent
medical evacuation case on board; please make sure
there's a vehicle ready at the airfield."

Tom looked out at the ground below, then at his
map; he made a pencil mark on it and turned the
plane towards some clearer weather just to the north
of the stormy area, noting the time in his flight log.
He set the line of his compass against the new direction. It was thirty degrees off track and would take
him over some particularly wild, mountainous
country. It wasn't one of his usual routes and he
didn't know the terrain below. He concentrated carefully on his map, trying to make sure he knew his
exact position.

Half an hour later he was still heading in the same
direction. Jimma was now well to the right, but still
the angry mass of black storm cloud hung low in that

Minnie and Murray Kendon, London

With Jack before take-off for Africa

Croydon Airport 13 January 1948 with "Gemini" ready to leave

Refuelling stop at Sudan border en route to Eritrea

At Bulape, Central Congo with local chiefs

Congo chief, Bulape

"Gemini" wrecked in Burundi mountains

England 1950, with Jack and Helen and "Rapide" before departing for Suda

The Stevens family in Sudan

With Steve and "Rapide" at Doro

Marie Anderson trekking near Abaiyat, in South Sudan swamps

Accident at Abaiyat

Repairing the damage

The Uduks and missionaries wave as the Cessna 180 arrives

Mabaans watch Gordon refuel at Doro

We cross the Dabus river during the Ethiopia survey

Doctor Balzer and pilot Hennie Steyn help a patient flown to Doro

Marshalls, Macdonalds and Kings together at Malakal

Sloping mountain airstrip in Ethiopia

Dropping supplies to Harvey
Hoekstra at Godare

Our family in 1964, just before
returning to Africa

Cessna 185 amphibian with medical launch on Lake Chad

Moissala Church, Chad, where all the men were shot

Joel and Hannatou with their eldest daughter at Tataverom

Baptisms in Chad

Tanzania: reaching remote people

Masai warrior and Pastor Lemashon

Steven King'ori servicing MAF aircraft

Marcos and Zufan Habtetsion and their children in Nairobi

Beech 99 makes its first landing with medical supplies in Zaire

Charles Wilson and a church leader

Max Gove at Headquarters

direction. He radioed his position to Norma and again asked for the latest Jimma weather.

"Still no change, I'm afraid, Tom. I'll let you know as soon as I see any improvement."

Another half-hour. He noticed a slight improvement in the direction of Jimma. The inky blackness of the clouds had given way to a sombre grey which seemed to fuse into the ground below as the rain reduced visibility to little more than a mile. The important thing was to know exactly what lay beyond. Again Tom sent his position report. Again the reply came back: "No change."

He made some quick calculations. His fuel was running low and unless he could head for Jimma in the next ten minutes he wouldn't have enough to reach his nearest alternative strip. Still no word from Norma. He picked up the microphone:

"Any change in the weather yet?" There was a pause again. Norma knew this was a critical stage.

"I'm afraid there is still no improvement, Tom."

His heart sank. The patient had been lying peacefully dozing on his stretcher, but now he had awakened and looked up pitifully at Tom, obviously in great pain. Tom glanced at the clock on the instrument panel. The decision point had come. The weather in the direction of Jimma had improved a little, but if the weather at the airport was still closed, it would be a risk. Such risks were never justified, even by the critical condition of his passenger. Tom turned the plane towards the clear weather, away from Jimma and towards his alternative airstrip, a wild desolate place among the mountains some twenty minutes' flying time away.

Just at that moment Norma's voice came through

his earphones. "The cloud is lifting clear of the hills in your direction, Tom!"

"Thanks, Norma, just what I needed to hear."

He banked the plane and quickly turned on to the heading for Jimma. Soon the rain was beating loudly on the windscreen and the swirling rain clouds scudded backwards only just above the cockpit. It grew quite dark inside the plane as it lurched and shuddered in the turbulent air left by the passing thunderstorm. Ahead, the outline of the mountains showed faintly through the murky greyness. Yes, it was safe to proceed. A few minutes later the plane touched down on the wet runway at Jimma.

Hugh Beck ran out and, sheltering under its wing, waited for Tom to join him. They quickly pushed the plane backwards into the hangar. Tom unfastened the harness holding down the sick man's stretcher, Hugh backed the MAF Land Rover as close as he could to the door of the plane and they drove the patient to the hospital. Some weeks later, well on the way to recovery, the man was flown back to Aira.

In one hectic week of flying, Tom carried out forty-five flights, often in similar rainy conditions. He summed up the experience in a letter to us:

> It's quite sobering to look back on the week and reflect how many missionaries have come to depend on us. Sitting on the ground waiting for rain to stop, I thought of what the delays would mean and the large number of people who'd be affected. One station could be without urgent groceries; another without essential building materials; two vital planning meetings could

have lacked key members and been unable to reach decisions; in two different places patients were waiting for flights to hospital. The ramifications were endless. It's wonderful to know that the same God who has given us this job is in control of all the circumstances affecting it. I am slowly learning to become "panic proof".

The whole matter of safety and margins is of vital importance for any aviation operation. Very often it's essential to decide whether it's safe to fly on or necessary to turn back. In Ethiopia, where cloud and mountain meet, we could not for ever be turning back. We had to learn when we could get through.

There were many types of airstrips. There were strips that had curves and bends; strips that sloped sideways as well as up and down; strips producing optical illusions; mountainside strips with dangerous wind turbulence; strips that precipitated you into the air over vast gorges where the ground dropped away with awesome abruptness. There were strips perched on high ridges which would frighten the ordinary pilot (and sometimes did when we carried visiting flyers); strips that were hard to recognize as airstrips at all. All these were our pilots' daily lot; landing after landing had to be carried out on them and judgment after judgment made about them.

In many areas, there could be up to fourteen landings during only a few hours of flying, with off-and-on loading of passengers or freight in between. But it was well worthwhile. Though the flights across high mountains and deep valleys were often very short, they saved many miles and hours, even days, of slow, difficult, dangerous and expensive land travel.

MAF pilots are not endowed with superhuman skills and endurance, they are ordinary people. They have simply felt the call of God to MAF and have worked hard, sometimes through long years of training, to gain their professional licences. Then they have painstakingly built up the skills necessary for bush and mountain flying. After joining MAF and arriving at their stations, they've been carefully taught to use each difficult landing strip, made familiar with each route. Both they and the planes they use are specifically prepared against accident. Our planes are equipped to enhance their safety: oversize wheels with modified tyre tread; an alternate fuel system for the engine in case of any failure in the standard one; full military seat harness, not only for the pilot but for every passenger; special navigational devices.

Each new area we had entered had taught us new things and challenged us in new ways. There were other countries now calling for our services. What new lessons and opportunities awaited us?

20

The Lake

One thousand three hundred miles westwards of the Sudan and halfway between Khartoum and Timbuktu, lay a lake over 10000 square miles in extent: as big as the whole of Wales. Studded with islands, floating islands and permanent islands, it was a lake of thousands of fishermen – the Buduma and Kanembou. It was Lake Chad, where four African countries meet.

The Republic of Chad is landlocked in north Central Africa. It lies west of Sudan and south of Libya, forms part of the Sahara and, like the Sudan, has northern deserts and southern swamps. The people of its north and central region are Muslim. But half the people live in the south and are either Christians or spirit-worshipping animists.

Few were more concerned to reach the people of Lake Chad than Dr David Carling, a surgeon with the Sudan United Mission and in charge of a large leprosarium at Maiduguri in Nigeria near the Chad border.

There were ten African missionaries with their families working around the lake: eight Nigerian, two Chadian. All had been trained as nurses, some had been cured of leprosy. They were people of high calibre, experienced as evangelists or pastors. One of

them, Joel Bealoum, for example, spoke six languages: French, Arabic and four tribal tongues. He
apologized that his wife, Hannatou, could manage
only four.

Like Solomon, the Ethiopian missionary, these
men had gone into areas very foreign to them, to
people of different religion, culture and background,
facing as much culture shock as any Western missionary taking his family to Bangladesh or Afghanistan.
They were all supported by their own African
churches and their call to be missionaries had been
confirmed by their fellow believers.

These families were scattered in lonely places
along 120 miles of Lake Chad shoreline. At their
dispensaries they helped and healed the people and
told them of the love of God. David Carling's concern
was to keep in touch with them, to encourage them
and to give medical backup for their more serious
cases.

In spite of his heavy responsibilities at the leprosarium, he travelled regularly to and around the lake.
This was time-consuming, sometimes dangerous. He
first had to cover more than one hundred miles of
shifting sand and swamp to reach the lake shore
where he kept a thirty-one-foot motor launch equipped for medical work, called the *Albishir*, Bearer of
Good News. Once on the lake he faced the risk of
great storms in which the boat could break down and
leave him stranded.

He wrote to me about his concern to reach the
thousands of fishermen on Lake Chad: "The opportunities are tremendous, they are opening up on every
hand. But the difficulties are also numerous. One of
the main problems that I face is the travelling

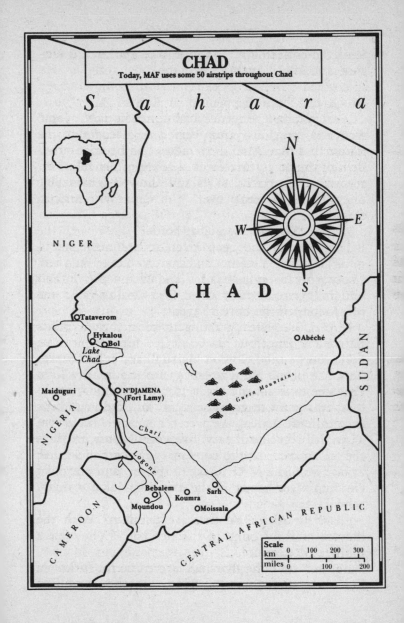

CHAD
Today, MAF uses some 50 airstrips throughout Chad

involved both in getting to the lake and then travelling around it. Can MAF help me?"

Much had been happening in Kenya. After years
of struggle, independence had come in 1963. Jomo
Kenyatta, previously imprisoned as a leader of the
nationalist Mau Mau movement, had become president of the newly decolonized country. He called for
reconciliation on all sides and showed remarkable
restraint as he took over. The country remained
stable.

Across Kenya's western border, however, the
Belgian Congo had been given its independence –
quite suddenly. Violence and anarchy had broken out.
Many Africans, missionaries (and even some of their
children) were brutally killed. The world's radio and
press reported the horrific events.

MAF USA were operating there and their pilots
flew many dangerous rescue sorties during that time.
For a short period Gordon Marshall and John Ducker
flew one of our Kenya planes into the nearby Kivu
Province to assist the evacuation of missionaries.

At this point there came a call for Phyllis and me
to return to Africa. We weren't keen to move yet
again. It hadn't been easy, five years before, to leave
the Sudan and come to London. Now we had settled,
at last we had a MAF house to live in, and our elder
children were happy in the excellent local primary
school.

"Back to Africa? With three children? With the
horrors of the Congo in the news?" Phyllis felt a
mother's concern.

But in Kenya the Marshalls were due for furlough.
We could administer the Kenya programme during

their absence. We could be in direct contact with the growing work in Africa whilst continuing our overall headquarters functions there. So it was decided that we'd go to Nairobi for the twelve months the Marshalls would be away.

In the New Year, 1965, we flew out by airline to Kenya with Becky, John and Priscilla, visiting Ethiopia en route. We felt happy in the assurance we were in God's will.

The work in Kenya was already well developed and had expanded into Tanzania (the former Tanganyika plus Zanzibar). Six MAF families were involved, including an aircraft engineer and a radio engineer from MAF USA. A good central maintenance, overhaul and repair base had been established in Nairobi, together with a radio repair shop able to deal with equipment for both aircraft and ground communications. All these facilities could handle major work for Ethiopia and other countries as well as for Kenya and Tanzania.

An Ethiopian Airlines DC3 freight plane had landed in Nairobi on Christmas Day 1964, a week before we arrived, its cargo destined for our MAF repair base. When its doors were opened and our engineers looked inside, they saw a big sign: "Happy Christmas!" It was draped across the fuselages and dismantled wings of two damaged Cessnas. The one wrecked three years before at Jemu had eventually been brought out. The other had been severely damaged in a take-off crash. We were thankful that we now had facilities to rebuild them.

We next started to introduce a different model of aircraft. Up to now we had relied on the faithful four-seat Cessna 180 together with the larger six-seat 185, both of them tail-wheel aircraft. Now we introduced a six-seat model with tricycle undercarriage – the Cessna 206. It had more cabin space and, with its large double loading doors at the back, was better suited to carry stretcher cases or freight. For the passengers it was altogether more comfortable.

At first we were not too certain about the performance of a tricycle undercarriage on some of our rough airstrips, feeling that the nose wheel leg might be damaged or broken. Nor were we too sure what would happen on really soft strips – would the smaller front wheel dig in and again cause trouble? But a lot of research had been done before we had ordered our first 206. When it arrived in Nairobi in June 1965 it soon proved to be an ideal aircraft. Its greater comfort and carrying capacity were a great boon, especially on long-distance flights over Kenya and Tanzania.

John Ducker had continued flying in our East Africa programme ever since he and his family had moved there from the Sudan.

"Would you like to fly with me up to Chad in the new 206?" I asked him. "From what Dr Carling is writing, there are real needs up there. We ought to investigate."

John was always ready for a new challenge. Our survey trip would cover over 4000 miles in two weeks.

We had never been to southern Chad before. From the air it looked just like south Sudan, with curling rivers and great green swamps. We knew at once that it could not be an easy country for land travel.

We were still 500 miles short of David Carling's leprosarium in northeast Nigeria when we stopped in

southern Chad to visit several missions. I'd written
to tell them we'd be coming through their area and
would like to see something of their work. They had
been interested.

One of the first places where we landed was
Koumra. There we were particularly struck by two
things. First the airstrip, instead of being black cotton
soil, wet and soft, as in the Sudan, was made of bright
brick-red "laterite" as the French call it, or "murram"
as it was known in East Africa. This provided an
excellent all-weather surface.

Second, in all our travels we'd never met anyone
quite like Dr David Seymour. A missionary from a
Baptist group working in the area, this doctor was as
extremely American as John Ducker was extremely
English. At six foot he was as tall as John, but very
much heavier and broader. He was also big-hearted
and big in his ideas. He'd grown up in Chad, where
his parents had been missionaries before him, and
gone to school with the Chadian who later became
President Tombalbaye.

He regaled us with information about the people
and the region in phrases unusual for a missionary.
The vivid incidents he described were punctuated
with exclamations like, "Holy cow!" or "Oh, my
aching heart!" his hand appropriately clapped to his
massive chest.

As we walked over his large and well-developed
hospital he explained his philosophy:

"My aim is not to do the medical work myself, but
to teach the Chadians, men who've been recom-
mended by our Chadian church and who've already
had a five-year pastoral course in our Bible school.
Then I train them here for a further three years. By

the time they're finished the government recognizes them almost as it would doctors."

"Then they continue to work in the hospital here?" we asked.

"No, I send them into the areas around so they can be available to the people way out in the bush. They go there as witnesses and to help and heal the people."

We peeped into the operating theatre. Four gowned Africans, their white surgical face masks contrasting with their black skins, were engrossed in surgery.

"These men can perform Caesareans and deal with strangulated hernias," David Seymour told us.

We walked on through the rest of the hospital. The wards were full. We saw the houses nearby where the patients' relatives stayed to look after them while they were recovering.

In the cool of his house we studied a map of the area with David.

"I need to be able to get out to the dispensaries where we have men working. It's important to visit them regularly; they need support and encouragement. At present I go by car. But in the wet season, holy cow! It's very difficult and I often can't get through. There are other areas I want to reach as well, but there isn't time to attempt to do that by car. You could help me with a plane."

We were impressed. This unusual doctor and his work presented another challenge.

We visited other parts of the south of Chad and found self-supporting indigenous churches throughout. At a church service at Moissala, in an area where work had been started by Brethren missionaries, Chadian elders led and preached to a large assembly, then invited John and me to tell of our work and reasons for visiting Chad.

We saw people give their offerings: sometimes eggs, sometimes a hen, sometimes ears of dry corn, sometimes money. We heard of one girl who had a treasured pair of shoes. When the time for the offering came, she gave these. They were all she had to offer and there was little chance that she would be able to replace them. We were moved by the dedication of these people.

That evening, as we were having supper with the missionary couple, there was a knock on the door. Two of the elders came in.

"They say they have a gift for the men with the aeroplane," the missionary translated. "They heard what you want to do in bringing an aeroplane to Chad. They want to be the first to give something towards buying the plane to work in their country. They believe it could help the people and spread the good news of God."

They gave us a money gift for MAF. We were staggered. Here was a church in one of the poorest countries in Africa, a church whose people lived at scarcely subsistence level. Yet out of their poverty they wanted to help to buy an aeroplane for God's work in their land. Though our survey had hardly started, God had already put this seal upon it. Once more we were humbled by the commitment of African Christians.

The next day we flew into Nigeria. David Carling met us, taller than Dr Seymour and less broad, but with an equally deep concern for isolated people.

It was bright the following morning as we climbed aboard the 206 with him to explore the travelling

difficulties of this area. Heading towards the southern
tip of Lake Chad, we observed the different stages of
his journeys to the lake, by Land Rover, papyrus reed
canoe, or camel train. Soon we were flying over the
swamped countryside under clouds of drizzle. We saw
long stretches where deep, shifting sand would tax
even the Land Rover. Then we spotted a camel train
moving slowly along the primitive trail, and a little
later some Buduma tribespeople in their canoes
making their way towards the lake through the
papyrus-lined water inlets.

It was clear and sunny again over the lake. The
rippled water shimmered a deep emerald green produced by vegetation and natural minerals. Just off-
shore we looked down at one of the floating islands,
an irregular fringed grassy mass 300 yards long and
200 yards wide. At one end of it was a yellowish
earthen clearing with a few reed-thatched huts
shaped like beehives.

"The Buduma live around the lake, on the floating
grass islands and on the more permanent islands
further north," Dr Carling explained. "The Kanembou, who are a slightly larger group, tend to settle
around the shore."

As we flew on across the miles of water we could
soon see why the ocean-going launch was necessary.
The thousands of people scattered around the shore
or on the many islands had to be reached by water.
The sheer size of the lake and the frequent storms
meant that no smaller vessel could safely cross it.

After an hour's flying we reached the further eastern shores of the lake. Here was a close patchwork
of permanent islands, like pieces of a jigsaw puzzle
spread slightly apart.

"It's easy to get lost among all those islands when you're travelling by boat. It's like trying to find your way through a maze," David's voice broke through our thoughts. "This flight is doing in minutes what takes me several hard days in the launch." He pointed northwards. "Can we fly over the northeast part of the lake to try and find out where the people are living? It's been difficult to do that from a boat. Just looking along the shoreline doesn't tell you where the people really are. We've planned a new dispensary at Tataverom. I want to make sure that's the right place."

We flew up the east side of the lake. Tataverom lay on an almost invisible trail, an ancient slave route across the Sahel. The dry pale gold of the yellow sands contrasted sharply with the dark, liquid green of the waters. Just inshore were clusters of round Buduma houses and compounds. David's choice of Tataverom as a centre was confirmed.

We headed back south towards Fort Lamy, another hour's flight. Following the Chari river we soon had our first glimpse of Chad's capital. "A city in the desert" was the phrase that sprang to my mind when I saw it. We landed and went into the town. The whole atmosphere of the place, the French flavour, the Arab-style clothing of many of the people, its position on the edge of the desert, reminded me of the book *Beau Geste* and other stories of the French Foreign Legion.

We visited government departments, seeking to find out if we would be allowed to operate in the country. The French and Chadian officials were quite open to the idea, though there would be quite a lot of red tape. I put in a letter formally requesting permission to set up a MAF service.

We took David Carling back to his leprosarium in Nigeria and finally flew the 2000 miles home to Nairobi.

We'd learned a lot about surveys since our first one in the Gemini. We'd seen work develop in the Sudan. We'd surveyed and entered Ethiopia and Kenya. It was not difficult now to assess the needs in Chad. We were convinced that in the deserts, on the lake and across the swamps and distances of the south, there was a clear challenge for us.

I reported back to Steve and our Board in London:

"There is no doubt that there is a wide open opportunity for MAF in Chad. A great deal has been done over the past thirty or forty years by missions and the growing national church. But there are certain areas which, due to lack of workers and travel difficulties, have had to be neglected. This survey of Chad has been one of the most challenging and encouraging I have ever taken part in. I feel God is leading us to Chad."

PART IV

PROGRESS AND PAIN
(1965–1980)

21

The Hidden People

Gordon Marshall brought the Cessna 185 low over the dense forest trees. We'd removed the right-hand door of the plane before taking off and the wind was blasting in with a steady roar, adding to the engine noise. The interior of the cabin, all its rear seats removed, was filled with sacks. Standing amongst them, I fixed a rope to one of the cargo tie-down rings and then secured it round my waist, knotting it well.

The trees, about a hundred feet below, were flashing quickly by. Gordon pushed the propellor control to maximum safe revs. The sound of the engine increased as it sped up. He lowered the flaps, easing the throttle open at the same time to give more power and to stop us losing too much speed. Now flying fairly slowly, we levelled out. Suddenly I saw we were over a clearing.

"Now!" shouted Gordon above the wind and engine roar.

I pushed a sack out and watched it tumble towards the ground. Gordon opened the throttle and started climbing, then banked as we circled and came round over the clearing again. I pushed another sack out, very thankful that I had the rope round my waist.

Below I had a fleeting glimpse of an old friend: Harvey Hoekstra. I could see his familiar khaki shorts, short-sleeved shirt and white pith helmet.

Some of the forest dwellers were standing with him, all looking up and waving.

It was May 1966. Gordon and I were over Godare in the dense rain forests of southwest Ethiopia. Harvey and Lavina Hoekstra were working there with a people who the Ethiopian Government called the Mesengo. But the people themselves called their tribe the Majang.

A year before, the Hoekstras had trekked for seven days through unknown forest to reach this place. They had brought with them their three-year-old son Paul.

Right from their arrival there they'd relied on MAF for supplies. In three months forty drops had been made with food, medical supplies, tools, building material and so on. For the MAF crew this was exciting and exacting flying; for the Hoekstras it was a lifeline.

Since then Harvey had paid a large number of tribesmen to clear an airstrip and allow the plane to land. This had now been in use for some months. Gordon and I had flown to Ethiopia in the Kenyan Cessna 185 to collect first-hand news of the progress there, and share it with MAF's supporters at home.

We had been re-enacting the earlier supply drops for the benefit of a missionary photographer from Addis Ababa who was taking pictures from the ground.

We landed on the slightly upsloping strip. Rain and mist were settling over the forest-clad hills. Storms were close, so we tied the plane down securely. I saw that many of the trees around us were well over 130 feet tall. Some were twelve feet in diameter. Hanging vines writhed round them and dense bush surrounded their bases. Chattering black and white colobus monkeys scrambled up and down in the branches.

Harvey joined us, a group of Majang with him. We studied them with interest. They were rather like the Anuak, only shorter, handsome, with friendly smiling faces. They wore loincloths, leaves or occasionally shorts, with coloured beads, white, red, yellow and blue in rings round their necks, arms and waists. Some carried spears, others had ancient rifles brought back from distant trading posts. (Everyone in Ethiopia seemed to have guns.) Some of them held little musical instruments: small wooden bases on which they'd mounted thin metal reeds of different lengths. When plucked, these produced a curiously plaintive musical tune.

They greeted us: "Diggoi". We replied likewise: "Diggoi". Harvey seemed to be conversing easily with them.

The deep forest felt comparatively cool as we walked through it to the Majang-built house where the Hoekstras were living. It was very basic, the walls made of upright bark-covered poles tightly laced together with vine rope, the roof loosely thatched with grass, the unglazed windows just large openings in the walls.

Lavina laid a tablecloth ready for a meal. She could make a place seem like home even in the remotest bush. I was surprised to see her put some red roses on the table.

"Roses? Here in the jungle?" I asked.

"We brought a rosebush in with us."

"You mean Harvey allowed you to haul that in, all the way through the forest?"

"Yes, he did. We also brought rabbits."

"Rabbits! You didn't bring pets in as well?"

"No, they were for breeding for food. We brought chickens too and Harvey has developed a vegetable garden."

The story went back some years. The American mission had focused its concern on seven remote tribes in southwestern Ethiopia. Some were "lost" tribes, inaccessible to the government, traders and even other tribes. The mission had decided to send one missionary family to each of them, including some of the families who'd been forced to leave the Sudan. MAF had carried out aerial surveys to chart a few of the tribal locations. One of these belonged to the Majang.

A ground party of four missionaries, including Harvey, travelled 150 miles on foot through thick forest to reach the Majang territory. They struggled through heavy undergrowth and clinging vines, across rivers and streams, over slippery moss-covered rocks and often through squelching mud and driving rain. Much of the journey was so deep in the forest that little daylight was visible. Towards the end of their journey one of them contracted a dangerous blood infection. The team came out with Majangs carrying him on a stretcher. Though wearied by the trip the missionaries were sure God had shown them where to start work among these people. The site was on the Godare river, close to the home of Balte, the paramount chief of the tribe.

It had been one thing for a party of men to find their way through the forest to the Majang. It was a more formidable proposition for Harvey to go in with Lavina and Paul. But they did it, carrying supplies, a tent and bedrolls, a little MAF radio transmitter and a car battery to run it. Harvey told me the story of their journey.

"We started out from Teppi, the nearest government airfield. It took us several hours to get carriers organized and six mules loaded. Within a minute, hoofs went flying in the air and three mules kicked their loads off, scattering our things in every direction. Mercifully they were in a gentler frame of mind when we arrived at our first stop, ten miles ahead. We set up our tent with the light of a candle.

"A cloudburst struck at 3.30 a.m. We got cold and wet. Our rabbits and chickens drew hordes of army ants during the night. The ants weren't satisfied with just eating chicken and rabbit, either!

"Even at best the trail was barely passable. Vines, thorns and brush, fallen trees, and ten or eleven river crossings all slowed us down. Once I turned my head just in time to see Paul pulled backwards off his horse with a vine wrapped tightly around his neck. He had a bandage around his neck the rest of the journey. Lavina got thrown off her horse at one of the river crossings.

"On our second morning our carriers put down their loads and refused to go further. Things looked pretty bleak. Fortunately, they had a change of heart and returned to take our things on to the next village.

"Once in Majang country we found it different; local chiefs were helpful and rounded up whole families, with men, women and even children each carrying something. They'd take us on to a nearby settlement where they helped us to find new carriers.

"The last morning, we set up our transmitter and called MAF to come with supplies for us. The MAF crew couldn't see exactly where we were, down amidst the dense forest trees. But we were able to guide them to us by giving directions on the radio.

"They made two drops of blankets, food and grain. As they sped away the huge back clouds rolled in and heavy rain fell. When darkness came, we were exhausted, drenched and hungry. We slept that night in wet bedrolls with a single mosquito net stretched crossways over our three heads. We were glad when daylight broke.

"That morning Balte, the local chief, turned up with about thirty men and they built two glorified Majang shacks for us. Those first days brought scores of Majang out of the forest to see these strange white people. They moved right in with us; they came through the door and through the window openings, too. They stayed and watched everything we did."

When the airstrip was ready Tom Frank and Hugh Beck had made a further trek through the forest to check it. Then Bob Hutchins flew in and, after further careful inspection from the air, landed. As he taxied slowly up to the higher end, the Majang workers, cheering and clapping, broke into a run behind him. Soon everyone was around the plane talking excitedly in various languages.

In the months that followed, the plane regularly brought in food and supplies, and sometimes visitors or helpers. In particular it brought building supplies, including prefabricated sections from the mission's workshop, sixty miles away. These were carefully designed to fit into the small MAF Cessna. Bricks were made locally from mud and sand from the local river. Building at Godare progressed rapidly. A better house for Harvey and Lavina, a clinic, a church and a schoolroom soon sprang up underneath the giant forest trees.

Thing were still not easy. Once Harvey nearly lost his life. Returning from a preaching trip to another village, he found that all the Majang men at Godare, including the chief, were completely drunk. One of them tried to hit Harvey, another threatened him with a loaded gun. A third, called Ochor, nearly speared him, as the Aucas had speared Nate Saint in the Ecuadorian jungle ten years before. In God's providence, several brave Majang women knocked down the man with the gun before he could fire and Harvey was able to escape from Ochor's spear.

The next day the chief and the others were sober: minds were clear again. They came and clasped hands with Harvey, Majang fashion, to say how sorry they were. The man with the gun said he thanked God that he had not been allowed to do what he had wanted. Ochor clasped Harvey's hand in both of his to show his sorrow. They went out of their way to help the Hoekstras understand they must not fear them. Paradoxically, the aftermath of that terrifying episode showed how much the Majang had really come to care for Harvey and Lavina.

A year later there were over a hundred of them meeting regularly to worship God. Amongst those Harvey had baptized was Ochor who in turn helped many others to know Christ. A group of Majang chose five strategic places where they hoped to establish new congregations of believers and sent two of their number to each. What God has been leading the missions to do He was now leading the Majang to do as well.

Almost daily, Majang evangelists were taking out

sturdy little hand-turned cassette players with taped
messages prepared by Harvey. A new group of
believers was baptized. Others had to wait until they
made a break with their spirit worship and the shri-
nes in their villages.

Harvey wrote:

Instead of superstition and fear, men are beginning to live a new life of freedom in the love of
Christ. Where once they trusted in the sprinkled
blood of a chicken or walked under its carcass
to protect them from deadly smallpox, the
Majang are now coming to the clinic for
inoculations . . . Difficult medical cases, instead
of being left without hope, can now be flown
to one of our mission hospitals for surgery and
treatment. Where Jesus Christ is unknown there
is darkness, superstition and despair, but here in
the forest, where His name enters, light shines
and men are set free . . .

Through the early months we could not have
stayed here, apart from MAF's air drops. But we
came to this forest because a whole tribe lives
here who had never heard the message of Jesus
Christ. In one village, where I was out with the
tape player, the Majang turned to each other and
said, "Why have we never heard this word
before?"

22

"Magnifique!"

We were still awaiting authorization from the Chadian Government to start an air service. Even so, we decided that we should proceed with plans. We believed consent would come; both national church leaders and missions had encouraged us; God had already provided sufficient funds to purchase a plane; never before had we actually had the money so far in advance.

John Ducker, having completed his term in East Africa, had planned to return to England to resume teaching. However, when I had asked him to join me in the Chad survey it was partly because I knew we might soon need someone to start a regular service there and I believed that someone might be John. Now, to my delight, he and Mary agreed to take a short furlough, then go straight on to Chad.

Finding a suitable aircraft was more difficult, even though we could pay for it. The work on the lake and some of the southern rivers called for a float plane. But a normal wheel plane was necessary for the northern deserts and the relatively good sand and laterite strips in the south. With only one pilot, two planes made no sense. The answer was an amphibian, capable of operating either from water or from land. We researched data on many available models, coming back in the end to a Cessna. We fitted a 185 with amphibious floats equipped with hydraulically retractable wheels.

I was happy to see John taking over in Chad as both our pilot and programme manager. He had the experience: good disciplined training as a pilot in the Army Air Corps, a period in Norway for float plane training, then operations in the Sudan, a country similar to Chad.

The Duckers and their children were joined by Tim and Elisabeth Longley. Tim had served an apprenticeship at de Havilland Aircraft and was a very versatile engineer. Phyllis taught Elisabeth how to keep the programme accounts.

John and Tim flew the float plane from Nairobi, full of spares and equipment. A dedication service was planned at a quiet spot on the banks of the Chari near a major bridge just south of Fort Lamy. A number of Chadian pastors, elders, local Christians and expatriate missionaries were expected to gather for the service.

Somehow word about the dedication got around. At least seven thousand people turned out for the occasion. The bridge was packed, the river banks crowded.

At Fort Lamy airport, unaware of the crowd, John climbed into the amphibian, obtained clearance from the control tower and took off. He selected "wheels up" as he climbed away. Within minutes, to his amazement, he saw the tremendous throng of people. He circled above the river, then came down low, close to the bridge.

The excited crowd watched as he landed on the water, the floats cutting long twin darts of white foam. Throttling back, he taxied the plane slowly towards the shore, lowering the wheels underwater. As he came to the bank, to the utter astonishment of the Chadians, the plane taxied up to dry land. The excitement broke loose. They had never seen even a boat do this, let alone an aircraft. Where had the wheels come from? They hadn't been visible when the plane was overhead. The air was full of cries, *"Bravo!, Bravo!" "Magnifique!"* – and, with French accent and intonation, *"Formid-a-a-a-ble!"*

Radio Chad recorded the proceedings. Some of the church pastors spoke on the radio, some went on a short flight. The event was broadcast the following Sunday morning. Pastors voiced their enthusiasm for this new opportunity for outreach by the church in Chad. As we had hoped, the plane had become a symbol of advance.

Work started very quickly. Within a short time a complete network of routes was established reaching out from our Fort Lamy base all over Chad and into the Central African Republic to the south. To the west, frequent flights to Nigeria collected David Carling. Soon the plane became a familiar sight over the lake, landing around the shores, or making rendez-vous with the *Albishir* on the water. It considerably increased the scope of David Carling's work in the north and significantly helped David Seymour in the south.

The plane was a lifeline back and forth to isolated areas. The national Chadian missionaries as well as the expatriate staff could be flown out when they were sick, due for change or for furlough. It brought relief and encouragement. Missionaries, black or

white, were no longer inevitably cut off for long periods of time.

John Ducker had flown David Carling and two other
senior English missionaries to the western side of the
lake where the *Albishir* was moored. He'd left them
at the launch and, after arranging to collect them
again the next day, returned to Fort Lamy.

By morning the lake around the *Albishir* was rough
with strong winds. The three missionaries went
ashore in a little motorized dinghy to collect Joel and
another Nigerian missionary. When the five of them
set off back to the launch, the water was even storm-
ier. Soon waves were breaking over both prow and
stern. Suddenly a larger one turned the small boat
right over. Neither of the Africans could swim. Joel
clung in panic to one of the Englishmen and they
both sank, touching the shallow lake bottom. They
rose and went down twice more. Dr Carling, trained
in life-saving techniques, disentangled Joel then dragged him on to the upturned boat.

The pilot of the *Albishir* hurried alongside in the
launch. Leaving the controls he managed to haul Joel
– and the exhausted Englishman he'd been clinging
to – up the high side of the vessel to safety. But he
was unable to reach the others.

At that moment, quite unexpectedly, the plane
arrived overhead. John had arrived back at the launch
much earlier than arranged because of a strong tailwind. He quickly sensed the urgency of the situation.
Though the water looked dangerous, he landed at
once. The plane shook frighteningly as it hit the high,
drenching waves. It came to a stop right next to the
upturned dinghy. Gasping and amazed, the men in

the water suddenly saw the floats at their heads and tried to scramble on to them. John pulled them up one by one exhausted and shocked and got them into the plane. Without it, almost certainly, lives would have been lost.

In 1968 we brought in a second plane. Other pilots came and a second base was set up at Koumra, to help David Seymour further in his work.

Two Chadian missionaries were assigned, with their families, to the lonely desert area round Tataverom. One was Joel, the other was Paul, previously a Chadian army sergeant, now very much a soldier of God. The visits of the launch and the amphibian brought both medical supplies and encouragement. They meant a great deal to them.

It took courage to live in such an isolated place, facing loneliness, danger and sometimes hostility from an alien people. It was no small test of their faith and commitment, but they didn't waver. I was with David Carling on one visit, when he asked them:

"Don't you feel it's time you had a change from this difficult and lonely area?"

"No, we believe God has called us here. We want to stay," they replied.

We taxied away from the shoreline in the amphibian, took off from the lake, then circled back over them. As we looked down we saw them standing below with their families, waving up at us, lonely figures in the surrounding desert sands. We were humbled again by the measure of their dedication, glad that we had the privilege of serving such as these.

The work of the medical evangelists and the

national church progressed. Both in the north and the south people came out of real darkness into a totally new lifestyle as they accepted God's love and forgiveness. A sultan in the Guera Mountains was dramatically changed. A witch doctor near Koumra, bitterly opposed to the missionaries and African pastors for many years, publicly announced his conversion, openly burned his fetishes and medicines and did his best to reimburse those he'd cheated of money or goods. At Tataverom the first-ever baptismal service was held. Seven were baptized and a small church started: a significant event on this one-time slave route across Africa.

But the atmosphere in Chad was to become more and more hostile — the need of contact and encouragement even more imperative.

23

Not Without Cost

The palm trees below us were bending before a violent storm. A herd of elephants was stampeding. Other terrified animals were running wildly through the tangled forests vainly trying to escape the tempest. As we tried to locate the airstrip at Obo, the name of the region, "the lost corner" came ominously to mind: a heavy grey curtain of rain all around us blotted out almost everything.

We sighed with relief as the tiny town appeared. The headwind was so strong as we came in to land that it took full power to get the aircraft on to the strip. There was no trouble stopping: as soon as the throttle was closed the plane rolled no further.

Cecil Davis and I were returning to Nairobi after a visit to Nigeria and Chad. Cecil (an ex-US Air Force major) was with us for three years from American MAF. He'd helped us significantly in Ethiopia and was now assisting me in the overall administration of our African programmes. An experienced pilot, he was flying the Cessna 206 on this journey.

Storms still buffeted us throughout our return flight to Nairobi, getting even worse as we approached it. This was dangerous marginal weather, somewhere between instrument flight and visual flight conditions. The tower operator had just cleared us for landing when another aircraft suddenly broke through the cloud ahead, coming straight towards us. Cecil abruptly broke off his approach, called the tower and headed for the tallest building he could see in the murk over the city. He started circling it: at least we could see where we were until the weather lifted enough for us to get back to the airport.

Our flight from Obo had taken four hours.

"The fuel gauge is telling me I should get this ship on the ground pretty soon," Cecil called across to me. He radioed the tower again. The controller cleared us for an approach from the northwest. As we returned to the airfield Cecil took one glance at the weather and called to me again:

"Can't make it from that approach, the weather's too thick there. I'll have to go in from the opposite direction. We'll land downwind." The tower operator didn't like it, argued, but finally agreed.

By now we were on final approach, our flaps fully down. I felt we were being whisked along by the tailwind at an alarming speed. Then another danger loomed. There were inches of rain water on the runway. Cecil stalled the plane on to it "with a big plop", as he put it later. We started aquaplaning. He cautiously kept tapping the brakes until eventually we stopped.

"I'm glad to be at home at last!" he remarked turning to me with a big smile of relief. So was I. Our wives, watching from the hangar, were equally relieved.

The long journey we'd just completed was just one of my regular administrative flights, maintaining contact with our different areas of operation during our time in Kenya. This period, from the mid '60s to the early '70s, saw some exciting events and tremendous advances in the work. But not without strain and not without cost.

Phyllis and I never felt as much at home in Kenya as in the Sudan. Strange, for Kenya was no hardship post. The mountains, the highlands, the mostly blue skies, the vast variety of trees, flowers, animals and scenery made it a beautiful country. Its climate was temperate. Nairobi, where we lived, offered many civilized benefits we'd lacked in the Sudan.

It had developed enormously since Jack and I had first landed there in 1948. It was still one of the main crossroads of Africa with good commercial communications in almost every direction. It was also the hub of much mission and Christian work and an important centre for the whole of our MAF activities in Africa. With the constant flow of people in transit through Nairobi there were many important contacts. But, instead of being at the front line of missions, we were now much further back. We missed living in constant and direct touch with the pioneer element which had challenged us in the Sudan.

My work continued to embrace the general concerns of MAF: keeping contact with the UK, with our people and programmes in Africa, as well as a steady correspondence with MAF in the USA on technical and personnel matters.

Rapid developments in our widespread areas of operation often kept me away from home. Phyllis continued to coordinate the field accounts and to train pilots' wives and others looking after the various programme accounts, sometimes travelling to the different MAF bases for the purpose.

In our local church she had a large Sunday school class of Kenyans, Asians and Europeans. It was not hard to hold their attention: in Africa there was a hunger to learn God's word often lacking in our homelands. I found the same with a class of teenagers. We jointly led a weekly Bible study in our home for adult Africans, most of them with very little Christian background. One was a charcoal seller, another a Kikuyu who worked in our MAF hangar, others were Sudanese refugees. We sought to show them how to understand the Bible and God's love and practical help for them day by day.

"I didn't know anyone could read and know God's word before," said one of them. "Now I'm beginning to understand it."

Others of our MAF people took similar opportunities for service.

Yet, amidst all this activity, we went through a spate of staff problems.

"It must be lovely to be working amongst fellow Christians and missionaries," wrote a friend from the UK " . . . like being in one big happy family."

It was and is wonderful to be working shoulder to shoulder with fellow Christians but, as in ordinary families, difficulties arise. People have said to me many times: "MAF does such a wonderful work." Knowing how often we all failed, I always have to reply: "It's what God in His grace has done – in spite of us."

Sometimes there were bigger problems, periods when we had to hang on in darkness seeking to know and trust God to lead us through. There were times when we prayed for hours, even for days, before we found an answer.

Christmas 1965 brought the first of several personal losses. My father died suddenly in Cardiff. My mother, aged eighty-six, and my sister, Joan, who was already suffering from rheumatoid arthritis, were faced with the urgent task of clearing out the family home which our parents had rented for thirty years. Even at that busy season, Steve Stevens spared several days to go and help them and my brother, Ralph, was able to drive them across to Joan's home in Cambridge, where mother settled happily for the next eight years.

We felt very far away: it was hard not to be there to help in this family crisis. Today we can get people home quickly when such situations arise. It wasn't so easy then and we didn't have funds for personal travel. Nor did my mother or Joan want us to take time from the work God had given us.

Six months after Dad died another MAF family paid a heavier and more direct price for their dedication. Squadron Leader Graham Macrae, who'd been commanding officer of the Queen's Flight, had resigned from a promising career in the RAF to help MAF with one of its greatest needs – that of encouraging, guiding and providing training for aspiring MAF pilots.

It was incredibly difficult and expensive for anyone in the UK to obtain a commercial pilot's licence and the five hundred hours of minimum flying time MAF required. As a result we had problems in finding pilots. Graham's concern was to help candidates to get good flying training without exorbitant costs.

Pilots from the Air Force or the airlines usually had the good disciplined training we required. Even these had to have had adequate light-plane flying as well.

Others had to go to a flying club, first to train as private pilots, then as instructors. Having gained further flying hours instructing, they then had to find jobs with commercial small-plane operators to get additional experience. But a good flying club was the essential starting point. Bad habits learned at this stage could spell disaster in emergencies later. Disciplined reactions in tight situations were essential.

Graham spent six months in East Africa gaining first-hand experience with MAF, then returned to England and joined the Bedfordshire Air Centre which we had identified as the most suitable place for our pilot training. It was run by an ex-RAF flying instructor who proved extremely sympathetic to our type of flying and training requirements. Graham worked hard there for five years, especially helping MAF trainees. To supplement his income, he became company pilot to a Christian construction firm whose director readily agreed that he could devote all his spare time to what he considered his prime task: serving God and training MAF pilots.

In mid-June 1966, I received a stark telegram from Steve in London: GRAHAM MACRAE KILLED IN MID-AIR COLLISION OVER LINCOLNSHIRE.

We learned later that it had been a million to one chance. He had been making a flight for his firm when his plane had been struck by a larger RAF training aircraft.

When we first heard we could hardly take it in. Then the shock hit us as we thought of the loss to

MAF and, even more, the loss to Helen, his wife, and their three children. It was hard to understand. Graham had been fulfilling a vital role in MAF. We had come to count on his love for God and qualities of leadership. His loyalty and devotion had involved a high cost. It was not easy to say whether he himself or his wife and family paid the higher price. To this day we remember them with gratitude and respect.

In Kenya, despite problems and pressures, our work went on growing.

The Northern Frontier District was a large desolate area some 300 miles east to west by 250 miles north to south. It was peopled by tough, resilient, semi-nomadic tribes, such as the Turkana, whose entire world revolved around their goats, camels and cattle. When we started the MAF programme in Nairobi the work we expected in this area had not opened up. The Flying Doctor Service of East Africa had already been helping the Africa Inland Mission in their medical safaris there, free of charge. Unfortunately that service could not meet the AIM's desire to spend longer periods with the Turkana. The mission needed additional time on the ground to tell them more about the teaching of Jesus and to establish dispensaries, schools and churches.

I sat one day in Nairobi discussing this problem with Dr Dick Anderson who led the AIM work among the Turkana.

"Can't we help you in some way or other?" I asked. "After all, that's what we originally came to Kenya for."

"The problem is the cost of the flights," he replied.

"If we had the money I would much prefer to use MAF."

"Suppose we go ahead and book the six-weekly medical and evangelistic safaris you want, Dick?" I said. "Then we'll have them in our diary and be able to give you priority. At the same time let's look to God to supply the finance. If the money doesn't come in, we'll just have to cancel the flight."

Dick was quick to seize the idea. Some of the local Nairobi churches were interested. The money was given and the flights were carried out regularly. None was ever cancelled for financial reasons.

This AIM outreach began to tackle the recurring problems of famine in that area. Agriculture and fishing were encouraged. Lake Turkana was full of fish, but the ill-fed people had been living around its shores without using this tremendous source of protein. It became possible to change centuries of tribal habit: they started to eat fish and their whole level of living improved dramatically.

It was shortly after this that the first man landed on the moon. Some of the pictures taken of the moon's surface reminded me of parts of the Northern Frontier District. MAF worldwide was now flying a distance equivalent to more than fifty return trips to the moon every year. God was using the wings He had given in an amazing way to bring new hope to many people. But, just as in space exploration, there were still human costs.

Mike Melville had trained under Graham Macrae and, after the usual long period of building up experience, had been accepted by MAF. With his wife, Ruth, and their baby son, Andrew, he came to Kenya. He was carefully familiarized with the work.

It was almost exactly three years after Graham Macrae's death. The clouds hung low over the Nairobi area as Mike took off with four passengers to fly across the great Rift Valley to the edge of Lake Victoria.

He knew that he needed to keep clear of the nearby Ngong Hills, shrouded in cloud at the edge of the rift. Those hills had claimed a dozen aircraft over the years. Jack Hemmings and I had only just escaped them when we left Nairobi on our first survey trip across to Congo and the west coast of Africa. Unfamiliar with them then, we had entered cloud near their peaks. It was a mercy that we'd avoided their knuckle-like tops and passed through a saddle between them. But it had been a near thing.

Well aware of the hazards, Mike turned away from the Ngongs and headed northwards to see if he could get around them into the clear valley beyond. Failing in that, he flew back along the edge of the hills hoping that the southern end would be clearer.

The low wispy cloud and drizzle all merged with the grey mistiness of the hills themselves. Near the end he turned to fly into the rift valley, as was normal practice in such circumstances. Then something went wrong. Maybe the confusion of mist and mountain deceived him and he thought he was clear of the hills. Suddenly the plane, at full cruising speed and power, struck the southern mountainside.

Air Traffic Control alerted our airport office that they had lost contact with Mike. Two hours later our MAF staff located the wreckage. All five occupants had died.

I was in England on a visit to the London office at the time and didn't learn about the accident until the next day. I flew out to Nairobi immediately. The funeral was at the mission station overlooking the Rift Valley, where Becky and John were at boarding school. They hadn't heard I was coming, but Becky suddenly spotted me: with an excited shout, she ran to me, followed by John.

Together we called at the missionary's house where Ruth was staying and prepared to go with her to the little station cemetery. I was deeply concerned for Ruth in her great loss. Her concern was for others.

"It's muddy down at the cemetery. Becky and John are going to need their rubber boots on," she told me.

We watched as Mike's body was laid to rest in a site which looked out across the land he had come to serve.

A week later Ruth wrote:

The Lord gave and the Lord has taken away; blessed be the name of the Lord. God has been preparing me for Mike's death; Mike's place was ready for him, may we be ready to go when the Lord calls. At the moment I plan to stay on here in Nairobi. God led me into the work of MAF before I met Mike and therefore I feel at complete peace that this is where He would have me stay. Until He leads along another path, with His help and guidance I shall carry on the work He has given me to do.

For some time before this I'd had an excellent personal assistant and secretary in Nairobi. When she married and left, Ruth Melville stepped into the vacancy. Her willing and efficient work was a real support to me at a difficult time. Some years later she remarried and, at the time I write, is still serving God in Kenya.

24

Fly While You Can

Dr Lionel Gurney was a man of prayer, with a deep love for people, especially Muslims. It was more than twenty years since I had roomed with him while learning Morse in Khartoum. Since then his vision, like MAF's, had become a reality. The caring Christian medical work of his Red Sea Mission Team had spread to several countries, including the Danakil desert and the Red Sea coast in the northeast of Ethiopia. We had the privilege of serving them there with our planes. Some of their lonely stations were staffed by women, some were in bandit country, some of the places they visited were in scorching areas below sea level. We admired their dedication.

In another desert area, this time in the far south, Bob and Morrie Swart, previously in Sudan, were working at Omo among the Geleb people. I always remember their airstrip, distinctively marked out in the sands with lines of bleached cattle skulls and bones: a reminder that life in that region was hard. For several years they lived in tents in the hot, windy desert while they built a clinic and a school. Only then did they start a house for themselves. Even building supplies had to be flown in by air when new work was being developed.

Chebera was 140 miles north of Omo and in Ethiopia's western mountains. In a single day Tom Frank

and Les Brown made thirty landings there with bags
of cement to enable the mission building to be
started. Like Omo in the desert and many other pioneer locations, Chebera, in the high mountains, relied
entirely on air support for its communications.

In another mountain area airstrips were opened in
the plateaux north of Addis Ababa. The Southern
Baptist Mission started an agricultural and medical
care programme among the Amhara. Places that had
previously taken days to reach by Land Rover were
now reached in minutes. One mission had the official
policy: "Travel by MAF. It's too dangerous by road."

When we started work in Ethiopia in early 1960,
three-quarters of our missionary passengers were
foreign, only one in four Ethiopian. By 1970 that ratio
was reversed. For every foreign missionary, we now
carried four Ethiopians going to show and tell the
love of God to tribes other than their own.

This certainly represented the pattern for the
future. Churches were becoming established in more
and more areas, amongst more and more tribes and
they were constantly reaching out.

For example, a long way to the west lived the Shankilla, a downtrodden people whose name means
"slave". Part of the huge Oromo tribe (who represent
nearly forty per cent of the people in Ethiopia) had
pushed up from the south, forcing the Shankilla
towards Ethiopia's relatively inaccessible western
border. As the Christian Church grew among the
Oromo, however, its leaders became concerned to
reach the previously despised Shankilla with the
gospel. MAF planes flew them in.

The town of Bonga was perched in high, heavily for-

ETHIOPIA
Showing a few of the 200 airstrips eventually used

ested mountains in the southwest. It was a very logical base from which to reach half a dozen different tribes; there were some quarter of a million people within a fifty-mile radius. Yet the SIM missionary there had to struggle to contact even two or three of these tribes a month. He could get only a few miles along the mountain trails in his four-wheel drive Toyota. He could then go a little further by mule. After that he had to scramble long distances on foot through high trees and thick bush. Bonga did have an airstrip and we used it to link the station to other main centres. But we could not fly to the close-by villages as there was nowhere to land.

One day a salt trader from an outlying village called Cheta came to Bonga and heard the gospel. It made such an impression on him that he begged for someone to be sent to his own valley. The church at Bonga dispatched an Ethiopian missionary who trekked across the mountains and found the people responsive. Trekking back he demanded, "Can't we have an airstrip at Cheta? Then we could get in, and stay amongst the people and do better work."

One of our pilots found a suitable site there, villagers helped clear it and we started flights from Bonga. The Ethiopian Christian who had first been sent there was flown in with his family. The church at Bonga also sent in a teacher. Soon Cheta had a school with a hundred pupils and its own church.

Much the same happened at surrounding villages. Across the mountainous ridges around Bonga, ten satellite airstrips were established. Each village had its own church; some had their own satellite churches as well. It was dramatic to see the positive change in the people. Only air travel had made it

possible to maintain regular contact with the
churches and evangelists.

There were similar developments elsewhere. After
ten years at Godare, Harvey and Lavina Hoekstra
moved out to Teppi, some fifty-five miles away. This
became a centre for reaching new areas among the
Majang and other tribes, with eight new airstrips
around it. Sometimes Harvey himself flew out to
them; more often the plane carried teams of Ethiopian evangelists and medical dressers who stayed in
these areas for several days. Whenever they went to
collect these men, our pilots heard their enthusiastic
reports of people who'd become Christians during
their visit, sometimes as many as thirty or forty.
Taking all the satellite outreaches together,
several hundred were becoming Christians every
week.

Harvey continued to provide a series of taped
cassette messages for the evangelists to use. This
was the beginning of a cassette-tape ministry later
employed in other parts of Ethiopia as well. Sub-
sequently he was to develop it further. It is now
employed in many parts of Africa, India and beyond,
with tapes in over thirty languages including Russian.
It all started at Godare and Teppi.

The church and missions had been increasingly planning their outreach around the availability of the
plane. The number of our aircraft in Ethiopia had
risen: first to three, then to four, later to five, six and,
for a while, seven. New people had joined the work,
too. Then, after five years, Alastair Macdonald left to
go to Chad and Tom Frank took over as programme
manager.

In 1970 Tom and his wife, Penny, moved to our UK office.

Other new pilots and their families were still arriving. One couple was Verne and Lorraine Sikkema. We'd first known them in the 1950s, when Verne was mission agriculturist at Akobo. Since then he'd acquired considerable flying experience and they joined our Ethiopian programme.

Another couple were Denny and Carol Hoekstra. Denny was the eldest son of Harvey and Lavina. He'd been one of our earliest MK (missionary kid) passengers in Sudan and Ethiopia. He and Carol had become members of American MAF and now they came to us to work in Ethiopia themselves.

Then there was Max Gove who arrived with his wife, Sue, and their first child. He was the schoolboy who'd originally visited Steve and me in the Woodford office when he was only fourteen. With hard work and determination he'd obtained the necessary licences and fulfilled the early call he'd had from God.

We already had an international team: British, American and Canadian. Now our first Scandinavian family came – the Kurkolas from Finland. Seppo Kurkola was an agriculturist, an accountant and a pilot, a very useful combination for MAF work in developing areas. By now we had eight families in Ethiopia. The work there was at its peak.

On the morning of 12th September 1974, Verne Sikkema was flying back from Omo to the MAF home base at Jimma. He radioed to give his expected arrival time. The reply he received was unexpected.

"Jimma airport has been officially closed, Verne."

"What am I supposed to do – stay up here all day?'
"Stand by, we'll call the airport and let you know."

Fifteen minutes later: "The airport will be open –
just for you. Then it'll be closed again."

When Verne landed he found the reason. Ethiopia
had seen a military coup, the culmination of more
than twenty years of growing ferment and discontent
in that great, but very mixed, nation. Emperor Haile
Selassie had been deposed. Everything began to
change.

The new military executive committee, the
Dergue, gradually took ruthless control. It soon
became obvious that it was a Marxist body. At first
it seemed that the relative freedom of missionaries
would not be affected. The work of the church, missions and MAF went on and was poised for further
advance. However, by August 1976, we were reporting to our prayer partners: "The Ethiopia flying programme continues, but in an atmosphere of considerable uncertainty." We reduced our programme fleet
to five planes by sending one aircraft to the UK to be
used in a special techniques course required for our
flying.

In Ethiopia, Stalinist-style terrors started to spread,
as they had in the USSR. Atrocities and bloodshed
abounded. Thousands died in Addis Ababa and
throughout the country. The church suffered greatly;
the Dergue was committed to its elimination.

In September, the government, suspicious of our
access to the troubled and divided country, grounded
all our aircraft. Missionaries in remote places faced a
difficult time. Several outposts had to be closed and
the staff withdrawn. In mid-December we were
allowed to start flying again. But local anti-mission

agitation, stirred up by the hostile government, continued to force many missionaries to leave the rural areas where much of our service was targeted. As a result, over the next four months, our flying dropped to less than ten per cent of its previous level.

The inactivity was costly: in aviation high overheads continue whether you fly or not. I visited Addis Ababa in January 1977 and talked with David Staveley who was now our programme manager there. Missionaries were facing increasing harassment and danger from the turmoil throughout the country. Rural outreach had stopped. Disturbances, executions and murders were increasing.

I had to go to look at conditions in the Sudan, where we were considering the possibility of restarting work. But in London I discussed the situation in Ethiopia with Tom Frank and asked him to visit there if necessary as his previous extensive experience would be valuable in deciding what to do.

Shortly afterwards, David Staveley requested that Tom should come. On arrival Tom found the consensus of the missions and of our own staff was that MAF should leave. It was a difficult decision. If we waited we might have all our aircraft confiscated by the Dergue. Staying could no longer effectively help missions or churches; the restrictions were too many.

David applied to the government for permission to fly our aircraft out of the country. Permissions were required for everything.

We were in constant touch with our aircraft insurers at Lloyd's in London. We had put additional cover on our planes for "war risks". The premiums had been reasonable and we'd felt it was a wise precaution, even at a time of financial difficulty. Once we warned our insurers, however, that our planes were in danger of confiscation, they were not prepared to renew the war risk cover after its expiry on 1st June 1977. If our planes were confiscated or destroyed before that they would have to pay. But not afterwards.

It was touch and go whether we would get the exit permissions in time. At the last moment, in answer to many prayers (including those of the underwriters, I imagine), permission was given. It seemed a miracle. The insurers were relieved. But the planes weren't out of the country yet.

Three aircraft from Jima flew up and joined two in Addis Ababa. It was the very last day of May when the planes gathered in front of the control tower to take off. Seppo Kurkola went to hand in the flight plans. The controller studied the stamped and signed permissions from the Civil Aviation Department.

"Ishi, ishi" (OK, OK), he said. "Everything seems to be in order." He paused and looked up. "But you want to take five aircraft out. You can't leave just like that! I must reconfirm these permissions before I let you go."

Suspense. He dialled on the old black telephone. He managed to get through to the Civil Aviation Department. A conversation in Amharic followed. He put the phone down and smiled. "You may go!"

The planes taxied out to the take-off point and stood in line, one behind the other. The first plane called for clearance from the tower. It didn't come – at first. Then at last it did. The second plane called for its clearance. But now the tower replied, "Just go, go, go." The controller seemed in a hurry. He didn't want to wait for any more formalities.

The five planes were soon flying in loose formation, southwestwards out of Addis Ababa, an unusual sight and sound in the early morning skies. Ethiopians below looked up and wondered what was happening.

As the capital was left behind our pilots listened on their radios, hoping there would be no call ordering them to return. Fortunately none came. Towards the southern border of Ethiopia, however, other calls did come. Most people who had seen the planes flying over would not have known what it meant, but Bob and Morrie Swart, the missionaries at isolated Omo, knew all too well. MAF had been their lifeline.

"Mike Alpha Fox, Mike Alpha Fox," came Morrie's voice. She was using the MAF call sign as she made radio contact with the planes on the mission frequency. "This is OMO river station. We are sad to see you all leaving, but we are grateful you're able to get your planes out safely. We're praying for you. Goodbye."

Other stations came on the air. They'd been listening out too. Their voices joined in the sad farewell.

Seppo told me a long time later: "I don't think I've ever been so moved as by those messages that day."

The next day one of Kenya's leading newspapers, the *East African Standard* had a front page banner headline: "Five Mystery Planes Arrive from Ethiopia." It was a while before the Nairobi authorities understood what had happened.

The aircraft were eventually dispersed to other programmes. The staff were dispersed too: some went on furlough, some came back to the UK to stay, others joined the operations in Kenya and Tanzania. It was the end of an era.

In seventeen years of work in Ethiopia a network of routes had been established into almost two hundred airstrips. Nearly four million miles had been flown. Many new areas had been penetrated and the church established in them. We'd assisted entry to more than thirty tribes. As one of our pilots said, "By the time we prepared to leave, nearly every unreached area had been touched with the gospel of Jesus Christ."

Even though the aircraft were now withdrawn, bridgeheads had been made. The church had been planted in previously difficult or hostile areas. Its work could go on.

At that time God impressed on me that our motto should be: "*We must do all we can, where we can, while we can.*" It proved true in Africa. It applies to all of us, wherever we are and whatever our stage of life.

Two months before our fleet flew out of Ethiopia, Don McClure, the man whom God had used to call us back to Africa and to the Sudan nearly thirty years before, was killed.

For some years he had been working among the Somalis. He had gone there originally following a request from the emperor who wanted a large centre established to help these troubled people in the extreme southeast near the border with Somalia itself. Now, well past retirement age, he and Lyda had launched out to meet this new need.

The end was abrupt. One night Don heard that plundering Somali guerrillas were close by. Always generous, he told a fellow missionary, "If they come here, I will give everything I own, rather than shoot one of them."

They shot him, the one who'd come to help them. On that dark night Don McClure completed almost fifty years of service in Africa. He had touched and affected many lives, including our own.

25

Yondo

Names were being changed in Chad. President Tombalbaye had decreed it. The nation must return to its traditional roots; all traces of the old French colonialism must go, even though a few French troops might stay to maintain stability.

The capital, Fort Lamy, became N'djamena, meaning roughly: "Leave us in peace". Many Chadians with foreign forenames, like Pierre or Alphonse, were ordered to replace them with authentic Chadian names. The "cultural revolution" seemed reasonably innocuous at first, similar to other African authenticity programmes in the newly independent countries around, where they were designed to foster national pride and identity.

Political unrest, however, spread throughout Chad. Tombalbaye was a southerner from the Koumra area. Northern Muslims, resentful of southern dominance, attempted a coup against him. This failed, but its defeat was followed by further tension and resistance. By 1973 Tombalbaye's policy was becoming more drastic as he sought to strengthen his hold on the country. Previous changes were superficial compared with *Yondo*.

Yondo was an ancient tribal custom involving initiation rites practised by Tombalbaye's southern Sara tribe. They included floggings, mock burials, drugging and other tests of stamina. Not everyone survived them. The rites were described officially as a way to God, a form of new birth.

Initiation camps were set up in the bush, the most notorious holding as many as one thousand four hundred people with over seven hundred initiators. Initiates spent up to six weeks in them, the first three without washing. Then they were taken to a river and bathed, the occasion of their "new birth". Ancestor and spirit worship were involved. All was highly secret. Oaths of allegiance had to be taken to the initiators, who had, in turn, to express their allegiance to Tombalbaye. This gave the president control over all who were initiated.

When people returned home from *Yondo* they were supposed to refuse to answer greetings from old friends. They were now "new people", totally divorced from their past. Some did not return. Some were held for further indoctrination. Some who tried to escape from the initiation camps were buried with their heads or limbs exposed: horrible warnings to those who considered resisting the president's decree.

Many Christians refused initiation. One evangelist was put into a metal oil drum in the burning hot sun. The lid was fixed on top and the drum beaten incessantly until, dehydrated and blistered, he died. Other Christians were found buried up to their necks in sand, their heads swarming with ants. Many pastors and evangelists in the area were imprisoned or killed.

Missions came under attack by the Tombalbaye-controlled national press. Radio Chad waged a vicious campaign against them. The Baptist missionaries were expelled from the Koumra area. Amazingly the

MAF plane was still able to go around from place to place, even to the distant outposts staffed by Christian Chadians, bringing encouragement at this desperate time.

The same year as *Yondo* was introduced the widespread sub-Saharan drought began to take effect. The rivers flowing into Lake Chad shrank. The lake level fell steadily, eventually dropping as if a plug had been pulled out. Within a year the vast lake was a third of its original size. Thousands who'd earned their livelihood by fishing had to move. Mission work adapted to the new situation. We made more landstrips around the lake area and the amphibian was changed back to a normal land plane. It could carry a bigger payload without the weight of the floats.

Soon after that there was a famine in the Guera mountains in central Chad. The area had become isolated because of bandits and impassable roads and MAF was the only way to get grain in. Ernie Addicott, who'd now been flying in Chad and Nigeria for the past five and a half years, added relief flights to his busy schedule.

At that time we were facing a pilot shortage and Ernie was on his own. An additional French-speaking pilot was urgently needed. Claude Jacot, from Switzerland, volunteered. He was a forty-six-year-old schoolteacher, but with more than 1600 hours' flying experience and professional pilot's licences. He'd flown a lot in the Alps and also in the Himalayas for the Red Cross. He and his wife, Annette, were deeply appreciated by all with whom they served.

Claude had initially come for six months, though he was prepared for further service. When Annette,

unable to cope with the heat in Chad, had to return
to Switzerland, she insisted that Claude remained to
finish his time.

In London, Tom Frank and I accompanied Ruby,
Ernie's wife, to the Foreign Office. There had been
trouble in Chad. Ernie and Claude had been arrested.
Ruby and her two daughters had caught the first plane
home. We wanted to find out what could be done.

A slim, grey-haired gentleman introduced himself
– the British Ambassador to Chad.

"We've had reports that your husband has been
flying illegally across international borders," he
began, addressing Ruby.

"He has been flying into some of the countries
around Chad," she replied evenly, "but always with
proper permissions." She went on to give a clear and
concise account of the true situation.

The problems had not arisen during an external
flight. Ernie and Claude had flown to the lakeside
town of Bol. On landing they'd been taken by the
gendarmerie, questioned, accused of antigovernment
activity and put under house arrest there. Several
missionaries were already imprisoned in N'djamena.

The ambassador promised the Foreign Office would
do all they could. "But we can't send the British Fleet,
you know!" was his final thrust.

Admittedly, that would have been difficult to a
country landlocked in the Sahel.

We put out a widespread call for prayer. After
several days, news came that Ernie and Claude had
been released. Back in N'djamena, Chadian officials
warned them strongly against any subversion. Then
our programme was allowed to resume fully. At such

a strategic time, when there was such fierce hostility against the church, this was astonishing.

By Christmas 1974, there were two weeks left before Claude was due to return to Switzerland and be reunited with Annette. He wrote to us from Chad.

"I believe I am in the right place. Our lives are dedicated to God. We are still candidates for future work with MAF if there is a place where the climate is more suitable for Annette's health."

It was at this point that he contracted hepatitis. With complications rapidly developing, he was admitted to the French military hospital in N'djamena. He went into a coma. Annette rushed back from Switzerland, but he never regained consciousness. Two weeks later I stood with Ernie Addicott by his grave in the Christian cemetery in N'djamena. He had died on 2nd February 1975.

"I have peace. I know Claude had done the Lord's will and that his death was within God's plan," said Annette. "Claude's six months of service with MAF were the happiest time of his life."

We kept in touch with Annette and often prayed for her.

The persecution of the church continued. Nine Swedish Pentecostal missionaries were seized in the south, brought to N'djamena and put under house arrest. The national newspaper and Radio Chad called them subversionists, spies, and mercenaries, but no formal charges were made against them. They were expelled from the country two weeks later.

Stories of Chadian Christians facing martyrdom

continued. In the south, Christians in village after village confronted the choice: to participate in initiation rites or pay with their lives.

One Sunday morning the church at Moissala was gathered for Communion. (It was from that church, ten years earlier, that the first gift had been made to us for a plane to come to Chad.) Suddenly soldiers burst in through the doors. All the men were ordered out on to the grass in front. There they were lined up and shot.

Seven other rural churches suffered the same fate.

I flew to N'djamena to discuss the situation with Ernie and Ruby. What should MAF do? Was the presence of missions adding to the dangers of the national church and stirring up the antipathy of the government even further? Would it be best for them if we pulled out?

I found Ernie fully involved in the flying programme. No second pilot had replaced Claude. Regular safaris, or *tournées*, as the French called them, occupied much of his flying. He'd spend a week at the lake helping David Carling; another week in the south with David Seymour and then with the mission hospital at Bebalem, visiting outlying churches and medical centres. A further three to four days each month were fully occupied in flying the greatly needed famine relief. Amid the prevailing persecution and distress, these *tournées* were still very important.

I flew south with Ernie. At one place I spoke to a Brethren missionary who, with his colleagues, had been under continual harassment. He catalogued their constant search for information:

"We've been listening to Radio Chad to find out the latest thing the government intends doing. We've been reading the local press and getting newspapers and *Time* magazine from abroad. We've been in a state of tension – thinking, discussing, listening, reading about it." Then some of the strain left his face. "But God has shown us that we are not to be worried about what the government, the radio, the newspapers or *Time* magazine are saying. We've come back to reading our Bibles instead: seeing what God says. That's what matters. This has given us so much more peace!"

Ernie and I met Pastor Moise (Moses), one of the African church leaders at Bebalem. At the risk of his life, he had refused initiation. I asked him if he thought it would be easier for the national church if the expatriates were gone. He looked at me, then spoke slowly and carefully:

"The Spirit of God must lead you. If He tells you to go because there is more important work to do elsewhere, then you must go. If the Spirit tells you to stay then you must not resist." He paused and quoted a saying: " 'If you keep the charcoal together the fire stays hot. *If the coals are separated the embers die out.*' "

I've never forgotten his words.

He told us later, "We need the missionaries to continue to encourage us. The translation work needs completing. There are medical needs in the hospitals. The evangelists in the bush need to be visited and encouraged."

Back in N'djamena we spoke to the church leaders.

"It's hard for our Christians to understand," said one pastor, "why some of the missionaries have left. We need their support at this time."

An elder added, "Few are trained, the church is

young and still needs help and advice. Missionaries, too, have told the outside world what is going on here in Chad. The international reaction has reduced some of the brutalities against us."

Local churches and missions all wanted MAF to stay. If we withdrew, said the missions, the lake work would largely collapse; much was still going on in that area in spite of the shrinking waters. Without the plane the southern *tournées* could not be continued, and the work in the Guera mountains would be adversely affected.

Ernie and I decided MAF should not only stay, but should increase its work. Since Claude's death and the many restrictions we had been using only one plane in Chad. We decided to move back to a two-plane, two-pilot programme.

Two months later there was a second coup in Chad – a major military one. It was successful. President Tombalbaye was killed. Another southerner, General Maloum, took over the government.

The senior members of the new military council had Christian sympathies. Previously expelled missionaries returned. Freedom came for Church and missions, such as had not been known for years. The demands for MAF service grew.

A second plane and another Swiss couple, Maurice and Josianne Houriet and their children, arrived. A further British couple, the Cliffords, followed. A year later I asked Ernie Addicott to join me at headquarters and delegated the overseeing of our operational programmes to him (as I had previously to Cecil Davis). Maurice Houriet became our Chad programme manager.

The church in Chad, however, faced severe problems. During the persecutions up to four hundred Christians had been martyred for their refusal to participate in initiation rites. But many thousands had yielded to the cruel methods of persuasion that were applied. Which of us would have stood up to seeing our wives and children killed before our eyes or to the threat of being buried alive ourselves? Now the church leaders faced a division between those who had refused initiation and those who had given in. These divisions were very slow to heal.

Difficulties continued for missionaries, too. One of the strong Muslim groups, the National Liberation Front (NLF), increased its rebel activities in the north and east. It abducted Dr Paul Horala, a French missionary working in the deserts of northeastern Chad. MAF at once flew 500 miles from N'djamena to evacuate his wife and four children, but Paul himself was held captive for five months before being released in North Africa. He had been tried for "activities under the Tombalbaye regime", accused of siding with the previous government. On his release he was given a certificate of innocence and the promise, "We will not trouble you any more." But the activities of the NLF continued to hamper church and mission work severely.

The Arabs in the north became increasingly divided by ethnic conflicts. In the south, too, tribal divisions asserted themselves. The country gradually became more and more chaotic. Soon there were eleven different armies at large.

The Chadian missionary, Joel, was at this time operating an effective dispensary among the Buduma at

Hykoulou, a large permanent island near the eastern shores of the remnant of Lake Chad. A hospital and housing had been built there by expatriate missionaries and when, because of rebel activities, the government had insisted these missionaries be withdrawn, Joel had been left in charge. He and his family still depended upon MAF for communications and supplies. One day his wife, Hannatou, was flown out to N'djamena for the birth of a child.

"You have a baby boy, Joel," John Clifford informed him next day on the MAF radio link.

But the day after that there was no response to the regular radio contact. Nor the next day, nor the next. Perhaps the battery they use to operate the radio is flat, thought our staff in N'djamena. Then their telephone rang. It was the Ministry of the Interior:

"Hykoulou has been attacked. A band of rebels stole the radio. Joel and the other Chadian nursing staff have been taken. They were told they would be killed."

Prayer went up; the rebels changed their minds, the staff were released after close questioning. Shaken by the attack, most of them left the dispensary and started a long trek to the safety of the nearest town. Joel and another worker, however, stayed to guard the station and await instructions from the church in N'djamena.

Before any instructions could be given, the rebels attacked again, with a much larger force. They ransacked the dispensary, burned down the main building and took Joel prisoner. Some months went by without news. Then there was a report that he'd been seen alive, that the rebels were using him to care for their wounded soldiers. A letter eventually came from him:

"I've been able to be a witness to Christ amongst my Muslim captors. I am in good spirits. Pray for my wife and children in this time of separation and uncertainty."

The rebel activity was more widespread than ever by now and was Libyan-backed. The work on the lake had to be closed and MAF's flying reduced, though the work in the south continued actively.

After seven months, there was further news of Joel. Weak and unwell, he had stumbled into a small town on the southern edge of Lake Chad, accompanied by an NLF officer and sergeant. His captors had come to respect him so much that they actually brought him back when they saw how ill he was. The Chadian Christians greeted him with joy and tears. To them it was like the story in Acts of Peter's release from prison.

In spite of his weakness, Joel was full of gratitude for God's help during his captivity. Several times the rebels had sought to force him to become a Muslim. Although he could have been killed for refusing, as others were, he would not comply. He wasn't killed and was soon regarded highly as a medical officer. The NLF made him a captain in their army. He had to travel with them wherever they were fighting, attending to the sick and the wounded and helping many.

Five weeks after Joel's release, unprecedented violence erupted on the streets of N'djamena. A third coup started. The Muslim prime minister of the ruling military council, Hissein Habré, a former guerrilla leader from the far north, seized power from the southern president, General Maloum.

A British ex-Navy pilot, Keith Jones, had just joined the Chad programme as the second pilot with Maurice. Keith and his wife, Lin, were living on the MAF compound in N'djamena with the Houriets.

Early on the morning of the coup, before fighting broke out in the capital, Maurice, unaware of trouble brewing, had flown off south for a medical *tournée*. Still before any violence had occurred, Keith had taken some missionary children across the town to a playschool. Before he could get back fighting had exploded. Habré's guerrillas were fiercely resisted by Maloum's army and terrible carnage ensued.

The MAF compound was right next to Habré's house which was being bombarded from the ground and from the air. Josianne, Lin and the Houriets' three little children were on their own. They huddled under a table for twenty-five hours. It was not until the next day that a Swiss doctor was able to take an ambulance across the town during a lull in the fighting and get them to a safer area. With unspeakable relief Keith joined them.

Still unaware of what had happened, Maurice flew into N'djamena a few days later. Fortunately he was able to land safely but fighting was still going on. An evacuation of some of the missionaries began. They drove across the town to the airport amidst the shooting. Keith made a series of evacuation flights to the south.

Maurice had to stay in N'djamena because he'd been carrying out a major inspection on the second aircraft just before the coup. It was in pieces in the hangar when the fighting began. While Keith flew the serviceable plane, Maurice worked on the other, frequently interrupted by bullets coming through the hangar. Eventually it was safely reassembled and flown south too.

At least five hundred people died in the fighting in N'djamena. One report claimed it was nearer two thousand. Fighting now spread all over the country. We could no longer operate: our MAF programme had to be closed. The planes were ferried out of Chad for service in other areas.

There, as in the Sudan and Ethiopia, we had done all we could while we could. The future was in the hands of God.

26

"Win them Now or Lose them Forever"

It was early in 1975. "We're going to start our own AIM air service," the Africa Inland Mission in Kenya informed us, " – in nine months' time."

We felt devastated. We'd always known there were some in the AIM who would have preferred to have their own air wing, exactly tailored to the needs of their large mission, rather than using MAF's inter-mission service. But we'd been informed they were not moving in that direction. So the news was a bolt from the blue. It was to serve AIM that we had initially come to East Africa and we had done so for fifteen years. Perhaps we had been conservative in our response to some of their requests for new sub-bases in the north. Now we were suddenly losing more than half our work in Kenya.

For the previous five years an AIM missionary, who was an excellent pilot, had been seconded to us. He was now well experienced in mission flying and AIM appointed him to set up their new service.

Whatever the reasons for our loss of AIM's custom, and whatever the lessons we needed to learn, we were to find that God would, as often before, use this apparent setback for His own purposes.

We soon felt very clearly that God was saying: "What about the other half of East Africa–Tanzania?" We seemed to have been released to respond more fully to the needs of the growing church further south. We'd already been flying into Tanzania from Nairobi for over fourteen years.

Billy Graham and his team had been amongst our passengers there in 1960; five thousand conversions had been recorded. Soon after that we'd had a temporary base at Dodoma for two years. We'd used existing airstrips in inaccessible places around the big country and opened up new ones. But up to this point we'd confined ourselves mainly to meeting specific needs in a few areas. We'd been too preoccupied elsewhere to probe and uncover the wider picture. Now we began to look at Tanzania in a fresh way. It was like opening a door to a new world of opportunity.

A few years before, Gordon and Jean Marshall had left Kenya and moved to South Africa. Gordon's father had died and his mother needed his help in planning her future; their children were at school there. They needed to be together as a family. There were possible needs for MAF work in South Africa too. We wanted Gordon to investigate them.

We started a flying programme in Transkei and I encouraged MAF South Africa to become autonomous and take it over.

This meant there were now three operational MAF groups in Africa. First, there was MAF USA led by its Africa vice president, Bob Gordon. Second, there was MAF South Africa. Third, there was MAF UK.

To avoid overlap and confusion we formed an Inter-MAF Africa Coordinating Committee to plan and survey new areas together, pool our experience and decide, prayerfully and objectively, which group could best take on any new programme. We re-evaluated old regions together too. The system worked well, though political restrictions prevented Gordon Marshall from joining us on surveys outside Southern Africa.

I asked Bob Gordon to join me on a survey of Tanzania.

A tall African, broad-shouldered and grey-haired, sat facing Bob and me, smiling a welcome. Underneath his dark jacket he wore a clergyman's collar and a purple shirt. He was Yohanna Madinda, Bishop of Central Tanganyika, the largest diocese in his country.

"I have a deep concern for the people in our Ujamaa villages," he said. "I want them to come to a personal knowledge of Christ as Saviour. Unless they are reached soon it may be too late. We may have ten years at the most."

What were these villages? Why the urgency to reach them?

In the past, the peasant farmers had lived in small clans tucked away in inaccessible places. Tanzania was a large country, four times the size of the UK and larger than France and Germany put together. It had a subsistence agricultural economy. President Julius Nyerere had promoted a new system called "African Socialism", which required the many scattered villages to combine as large collective ones.

Ujamaa meant "oneness and familyhood".

The tribespeople were to work together in these villages, providing their own food, water, health services and schools. The government would be able to reach them there more easily and teach them the Tanzanian socialist policy. Six thousand such villages were established, each with three or four thousand people. Two million had to leave their rural homes to go into these centres with their new mud-brick houses and corrugated-iron roofs.

When Jack Hemmings and I had first surveyed Tanganyika (as the country was then called) the Christian Church was quite small. Now, almost thirty years later, it had quadrupled. Especially in the towns the churches were full. Christians, with very few material possessions, expressed their trust in God with worship full of praise and thanksgiving. But many had remained unreached. Now the compulsory move to Ujamaa village had suddenly made them accessible to the Church as well as the government. The new villagers were displaced and disturbed: old systems of belief had become inadequate. They were more open than they'd ever been to hear of God's care for them. It was important to reach them while they were still receptive.

One of the Tanzanian pastors had said to us: "We win them now, or we lose them for ever."

Bishop Madinda felt that urgency very strongly: "We're in a five-year plan of evangelism. This year we have increased to a total of a hundred evangelists. The theme for our diocese is: 'Every Christian an Evangelist'. At present our church is growing by ten thousand a year."

"Where are these unreached villages?" I asked,

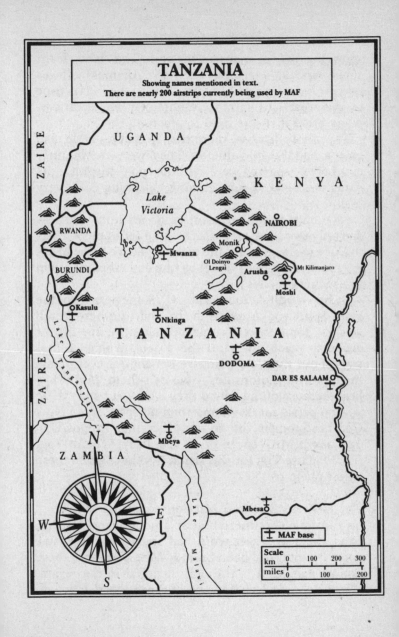

TANZANIA

Showing names mentioned in text.
There are nearly 200 airstrips currently being used by MAF

UGANDA

ZAIRE

KENYA

Lake
Victoria

NAIROBI

RWANDA

Monik

BURUNDI

Mwanza

Ol Doinyo
Lengai

Arusha

Mt Kilimanjaro

Kasulu

Moshi

Nkinga

Lake Tanganyika

ZAIRE

T A N Z A N I A

DODOMA

DAR ES SALAAM

Mbeya

N

ZAMBIA

Lake Malawi

W

E

Mbesa

S

✝ MAF base

Scale				
km	0	100	200	300
miles	0		100	200

spreading out our maps on his desk. The bishop leant across and showed us: sixty-five Ujamaa villages northwest of Dodoma; a large area of the Masai tribe to the west, still almost completely unresponsive; many other districts hard to reach.

The whole diocese, more than 500 miles wide, had only a handful of vehicles. They were exorbitantly expensive, spares were almost non-existent, the roads were bad, distances long, operating costs very high.

"We only have a few missionaries from overseas and only two have cars which could get from Dodoma to Dar es Salaam" said the bishop. "So we value MAF. It's much cheaper to travel by one of your planes than to use our vehicles."

Bishop Madinda looked at us: "Some years ago, the Holy Spirit spoke to my heart and to other church leaders. Sometimes I could not sleep for the urgent desire to reach out with the gospel. When we first started our five-year plan, we bought our evangelists little moped motorbikes – we call them 'piki pikis' here, because of the sound they make. But soon there was no petrol for them and then no spare parts. Now God has brought you to my office here in Dodoma. You ask if MAF could be of use. I say, 'Thank You, Lord! I praise You for the vision You have given these men to help us.'"

The German Brethren Mission covered a long tract on Tanzania's southern border, among a large Muslim tribe, the Yao. Their work had started in the 1950s, and a hospital had been built at Mbesa to serve these remote people. It is the only hospital in the region. When Bob and I visited the area we found it lower, hotter, wetter and more wooded than the typical dry Tanzanian plateau country around Dodoma.

When the mission first arrived, the local chief had vowed that none of his people would ever be Christians. For twelve years there had been little response. Then came two baptisms, the following year four. The number had increased through the ensuing years and shortly before our visit it had reached two hundred. From the beginning the church had been established on indigenous lines. Ninety per cent of the evangelism was already in the hands of Tanzanians and the church was now growing by fifty per cent annually.

Here again, the transplanting of people from the small tribal villages to the large Ujamaa ones had given new opportunities. Although it was a Muslim area, there was freedom to preach and churches had been started in many of the new villages. However, there was still much to be done.

"Have you considered developing village airstrips and using the plane for outreach?" I asked Herr Nusch, the senior missionary.

"My concern is with the problems faced by our staff in getting to and from Dar es Salaam and the coast," he replied. "They dread the travel, refusing to take vacations, even when they desperately need them for health reasons. The journey is so terrible that they feel worse after vacation than before they went. We need MAF for getting in and out of this isolated region." He continued: "I don't think local use for our evangelists is practicable. It would be too expensive in the light of the very low income of the national church."

We accepted his plea for an air link to the coast,

though I still felt that, one day, this large area could be greatly helped by local village airstrips. They had been too effective elsewhere to ignore.

We visited other churches and missions. Their responses confirmed the challenge we had received from the bishop. I reported to our board:

"There is an exceptional opportunity in Tanzania. MAF can significantly help to accelerate the development of the church. Surface transport has become less and less viable with deteriorating road conditions and economy. We should start a service in Tanzania immediately."

Who would go?

MAF pilot, Chris Emerson, then programme manager in Kenya, had had eight years' experience in Chad and East Africa. One day Nigel Reilly, a lean, bright-eyed young man, strolled into our Nairobi hangar.

"Do you need a pilot to help out in your work here?" he asked.

"Just what I've been praying for desperately", thought Chris.

The Marshalls had moved to South Africa. It was a year before any "spare" pilots became available from the closure of Ethiopia. We'd lost the AIM pilot who'd gone to start the AIM-AIR wing and we had loaned our other MAF pilot to the AIM Turkana work. Chris was on his own.

Pilots often came looking for work, but few of them with the Christian commitment or the flying background we needed for MAF. Chris wasn't certain about Nigel.

"What's your experience?" he asked cautiously.

"I'm a pilot with British Airways and I'm expecting a year's leave of absence," Nigel replied. "There's a slow-down in flying at present."

As they talked, Chris found that Nigel Reilly was a keen Christian. Although he flew the big jets with British Airways, he was also current in light-plane flying. He'd be getting half-pay during his leave, so his support would be largely provided.

Within three months Nigel had completed his preparation for MAF and was flying in East Africa. It's unusual for a pilot to come into MAF so quickly, even on a short-term basis. As it happened, he was to serve with us in several countries during his British Airways career and finally to leave the airline altogether and come into MAF long-term.

Six months after our Tanzania survey, Chris Emerson went for a few months to Dodoma where he was joined by Nigel. Others were soon to follow on a longer-term basis.

At first we thought of closing our Nairobi base entirely. Chris cautioned against this, realizing what a strategic position it held. It was too early to know whether the needs of all our previous clients could be met by the new AIM air wing. In addition we had housing there, major maintenance facilities and a Kenyan air operators' licence.

In the event, we never closed our Nairobi base: it was redeveloped along rather different lines. There were great needs for travel to and from surrounding countries: Zaire (Congo had changed its name now), the Sudan, Somalia and Tanzania itself. Much of the work from Nairobi later became long-range flying — a logistics programme, helping people get in and out of more distant countries. A good deal of local flying continued within Kenya itself for the non-AIM missions.

At times the new AIM-AIR operation and our own MAF services were able to assist each other when either of us was short of planes or pilots or facing unusually heavy demands. We had to watch we were not both flying the same routes at the same time or becoming wastefully competitive. This took working out as well as Christian grace and understanding. But through it all, mission, church and relief agency, flying in and beyond Kenya continued and developed.

27

"Why This Waste?"

It was only a few months after we had opened our new Tanzania programme. I was back at Abaiyat in the Sudan.

I was standing by the trees missionaries had planted there over a quarter of a century before, the only trees visible in the vast Dinka plain. But there were no mission houses. The place where I'd proposed to Phyllis had disappeared.

It was no dream. Thirteen years had passed since missions had been expelled. The station had been laid waste, the outline of the old airstrip was hardly discernible through the high grass. Surrounding Dinka or Arab tradesmen had taken all the bricks and building materials from the mission houses. There were only a few crumbling foundations and the remains of a small clinic. And little Eileen's grave.

A few Dinkas came by. "Are the missionaries coming back?" they asked. "There's no one to treat us when we are sick or hurt."

I had driven, with Bob Gordon and three missionaries, from Malakal to Abaiyat on another survey. We'd been allowed back into south Sudan to assess some of the great needs of the Upper Nile Province. The SIM had a new permission to set up a chain of primary health care clinics among the Dinka and Mabaan. An air service was again going to be vital to support the project. We were glad to be asked to help.

Wherever we went much had changed. Abaiyat's destruction was typical. The difficulties of travel hadn't changed, however. It was the dry season and we could go overland, but it was hard going. We had a Toyota and a four-wheel-drive Land Rover. Even flat out neither of them was able to do much more than twenty-five miles an hour because of the bone-shaking roughness of the cracked cotton soil trails.

There were few Dinka Christians in the Abaiyat area. The independent Dinka had largely ignored the teaching of missionaries. They had been decimated by fighting, by diseases such as cholera and especially by kala-azar. In one village, a few months before we arrived, three-quarters of the children and a third of the adults had died of it. Another had only one child left alive. Drought and famine added to the problems.

A hard drive from Abaiyat eastwards across the Dinka plain to Doro brought us to other scenes which, for me, evoked further nostalgic memories. I remembered the Christmas evening twenty-five years before when, with a few missionaries, I had walked back there from one of the outlying villages. The tropical moon had lit up the palm trees as we walked and sang "Oh little town of Bethlehem. How still we see thee lie." The stars were so bright that I felt I was walking into a Christmas-card picture of Bethlehem itself.

Doro was nothing like that now in the hot light of day. The little round African *tukl* where I'd lived as a bachelor and which had served as daytime quarters for Phyllis and me soon after our marriage was still there. The decrepit mission house, the veranda of which we'd shared with Steve and Kay Stevens, had survived as well, though more decrepit and lizard-haunted than ever. A giant baobab tree in the centre of the station had grown even bigger: it looked like a grotesque ogre, with a dozen branches sprouting from its squat trunk like angry arms raised in frustration at the hurt of the land and its people.

Doro proved more encouraging than Abaiyat, however. Though bush and trees had encroached on the airstrip, it could soon be operational again. And though the number of Mabaan Christians wasn't large, they were still meeting there, even after years of isolation. There was no church building. The church seats were rows of long treetrunks, lodged horizontally in the forks of short Y-shaped stumps, set in a clearing near the baobab tree. That Sunday we worshipped outdoors with the Mabaans, one of their elders leading the service.

We visited distant villages, going as far as we could in our Land Rover and then continuing on foot through the tall grasses. The villagers welcomed us and we conferred with their elders. They wanted medical help, they wanted teaching, they would clear an airstrip.

On the way back towards Doro we met a young Mabaan woman, bright-faced and smiling. She had not seen missionaries since she was a child.

"Let me sing to you," she said. She started a hymn in Mabaan that was familiar to us all. The light of God's love had not died away.

When I met one of our faithful Sudanese workers from Malakal, I asked what had happened to him since we'd left there. His story was only too like that of many others. He'd had to go into hiding. His wife

had become ill with malaria, she'd been admitted
to hospital in Malakal and died. His three children,
Rebecca, John and Priscilla – named after ours – had
died too. I thought of our own three children, alive
and well, now with children of their own.

The civil war had gripped south Sudan for many
years. Half a million southerners had hidden in the
bush. Over a quarter of a million had fled to surrounding countries. Thousands had been killed. The whole
administrative infrastructure set up by the British
colonial administrators had been lost. Hunger and
disease were rife.

Eventually Emperor Haile Selassie (before he was
deposed) and others had mediated in the Sudan dis-
pute. A "Peace Accord" had been signed in Addis
Ababa between the leaders of the north and south,
with a degree of federal autonomy conceded to the
southerners.

This Accord had now reopened the country to relief
work, though not to other traditional mission activities. In addition to the new health care that the SIM
was able to start in the Upper Nile Province, a totally
new relief organization was formed, with its operating base much further south, at Juba. It was called
ACROSS: Africa Committee for the Rehabilitation
of Southern Sudan. Initially MAF and three other
missions were involved, other agencies joining later.
ACROSS did outstanding work over the following
years. It set up dispensaries, reopened and staffed hospitals and ran urgently needed agricultural, relief,
rehabilitation and development programmes. Schools
were opened as well.

I often travelled with ACROSS staff, visiting the
southernmost provinces of Sudan to see the work.

Once when we stopped our Land Rover on a rough trail to greet local people, a large crowd of teenage Dinkas gathered round. Why were they gazing at us so intently? Suddenly I realized: this whole generation had grown up hidden in the bush. They'd heard of white people from their parents, but we were the first they'd ever seen. Again, it took me back to our earliest visits to some of Africa's remotest areas thirty years before. The clock had been turned back further than I'd realized.

"Drink of the Nile and you'll always come back to it again." The Arab proverb was certainly true of some in MAF. Needing experienced pioneers to reopen our Sudan programme, I asked Alastair Macdonald to be the project manager. He and Margaret came back to Malakal for two years to see the work started, renting an Arab merchant's house almost in the shadow of the mosque. Back too came other Sudan veterans: Verne and Lorraine Sikkema, followed by Hugh and Norma Beck.

We'd have liked to buy back our original base in Malakal but the army did not want to part with it. Instead the Provincial Government granted us a plot on the edge of the town, and we had to start again from scratch to build a new base. It took more than two years, with the desperately slow arrival of building materials, interruptions from the rains and the general difficulties of building on cotton soil. In contrast, we were able to reoccupy our old hangar very quickly. The governor, glad to see us back, soon had it cleared out.

As the programme built up, Keith and Lin Jones joined it, and later Nigel and Nicola Reilly. The Becks

and then the Sikkemas returned to East Africa. We
reopened a number of the old airstrips for SIM and
added new ones. The mission established six clinics,
staffed by nurses, stretching across the Upper Nile
Province from the Dinka area by the river, to Mabaan
country to the east. A doctor was stationed at Melut,
the main base of the primary health care project. At
Abaiyat, the nurses' house and health care centre
were built on the foundations of the earlier dwellings.

Further south, in the former American Mission
area, our planes flew once again to Nasir and Akobo,
helping the Sudanese church leaders. There were both
Nuer and Anuak Christians at Akobo. At Nasir the
Nuer church was strong, with some tireless evangelists reaching out to neighbouring areas. In all, we
served seven different church, mission and relief
agency groups, as well as flying for the Provincial
Government itself. With two planes and three pilots
we were as busy as we had ever been in the Sudan.

'We're grounded. The Northern government has suspended our operating permit," Keith Jones wrote to
us in August 1982.

Our base had been completed, with three good
houses and a much better hangar. We were ready to
serve the region more effectively than ever before.
Why were we being stopped again? I flew with one
of our MAF board members to see the Civil Aviation
authorities in Khartoum. An aviation lawyer of international reputation, well known to the Civil Aviation
Department, came too and did his utmost for us. All
in vain. We were allowed to continue to operate,
but only under crippling restrictions. Tension was
obviously rising.

The conflict in the Sudan escalated once more. The uneasy Peace Accord shattered and fighting broke out again. Our new MAF houses at Malakal were damaged by gunfire. General Nimeri's government collapsed, unable to stabilize the rapidly deteriorating economy or end the animosities between north and south. Strong Islamic elements in the north sought control and bitter civil war swept down on the south once more.

I made a final visit to the Sudan to talk with missions, churches and our MAF staff. We decided we had to close down our operation and once more withdraw. We'd been back in the Sudan only seven years. Had it all been fruitless?

"Why This Waste?" asked Roger Fothergill in the title of an article he sent us at this time. As our last pilot in the Sudan before it was closed he echoed the words of the questioning disciples, when Mary of Bethany poured her expensive perfume over Jesus's feet.

"We don't know why this waste," Roger wrote. "We have done all we can to serve Sudan, though sometimes we feel like Isaiah when he said: 'We have laboured to no purpose and have spent our strength in vain . . .' Amid the spiritual battle there will be wastage. It is part and parcel of the task. Much has been achieved. Christian work has been greatly encouraged. Our brothers in the national church have expressed their gratitude to us many times."

During those seven years the small Mabaan church at Doro had grown encouragingly. I well remember the happy face of one of the Doro pastors. Mabaan Christians had gone out from village to village and

more than a dozen other congregations had been established. Much more of the Bible was translated into
their language. In the Chali area, two hundred and
fifty Uduks had been baptized – an amazing number
for the tribe which, years ago, an anthropologist had
described as one of the most primitive in Africa.

Even among the resistant Dinkas an unusual spiritual hunger had appeared in some areas. The Gideon
Bible School had been established alongside the growing church at Melut. The faithful Pastor Gideon who
had been shot and thrown into the Nile had not been
forgotten, nor had his work been extinguished. The
School trained more than a dozen pastors and evangelists from among the Dinka, Mabaan, Uduk and other
tribes in the region. Roger Fothergill was right. Much
had been achieved.

Further south, in Equatoria Province, the work of
ACROSS carried on for another five years, even
amidst much fighting and guerrilla activity. Thousands were helped, including many Ugandan refugees
who had fled across the border into the Sudan from
their own war-torn country. As a member of the
ACROSS board I continued to visit south Sudan and
kept a close touch with what went on there.

The leader of ACROSS at this time was Charles
Wilson whom I came to know well during my fifteen
years' involvement with their work. His extensive
experience with ACROSS and with the many different nationalities involved was one day to prove
invaluable to MAF.

28

Flying Low and Long

The clouds above us had been very low, dark and solid. They forced us down to only 200 feet above the ground. It was another stormy flight made long ago – with Phyllis and Gordon in the old Rapide – one none of us will ever forget. Rain had struck our plane with a fierce drumming as we flew. A thousand needles of water seemed to be trying to pierce the taut fabric of the wings and fuselage. We could see almost nothing ahead. We could scarcely see the Nile below as we tried to follow every bend, fearful of losing sight of our only landmark. It had seemed an eternity before we reached Malakal.

To this day, when we fly in our small planes in conditions of continuous unbroken cloud, our MAF rules require us to remain below the cloud level, in sight of the ground, so that we can at least keep some idea of where we are.

From the mid '70s MAF came into a long period of operation under low heavy clouds. Occasionally there would be a slight lift in the cloud base. But there remained little room for manoeuvre and unrelenting demands for concentration. Sometimes, as the clouds pressed even lower, we were barely above the tree tops and possible disaster.

These clouds were not produced by the weather. They were clouds of financial difficulty, just as real and even more oppressively persistent. Flying a small plane, skimming just above the ground under a low cloudbase, can be very exciting at first. But after a while it becomes extremely tiring. Obstacles may suddenly appear, danger is very close, quick evasive action may be essential. The strain increases with time and, if the clouds never lift, you may be heading for disaster.

That's what our financial situation was like during those years. When, much later, many businesses and families began to undergo similar pressures in the long-drawn-out economic depression, I understood how they felt.

We had faced low finances often enough before – what was the difference now? True, we had often lived with little money, learning to trust God and finding He never failed us. But in those early years it was just the few of us together.

Now we had to learn the same lessons again, but for a much larger and more expensive organization and over a considerably longer period. We were now responsible for serving churches and missions in five different countries, an ever-changing kaleidoscope of dangers and opportunities. The challenges were enormous but financial support was needed to match them. I was used to challenge – but this was different.

Sometimes it was a nightmare: there were in fact many nights through the long months and years when I found it hard to sleep. The burden of the work would creep through my restless subconscious and wake me to concern and prayer.

What worried me was that the lack of money meant pressures on our staff and restrictions on what

we could do. I had a fear that we might fail in the
work to which God had called us. Everything involving finance had to be examined with a fine-tooth
comb. Where could we afford to go ahead? What could
be cut back? How would our people cope with the
restrictions? It was wearying and time-consuming
and sometimes I felt like opting out. Nevertheless,
as before, though the way was hard, God sustained
us. Even below dark clouds, hope had wings.

There had been considerable changes at our headquarters in the UK. In 1970 Steve and Kay Stevens,
having given twenty years of self-sacrificial service
to MAF, had moved on to become early members of
the National Festival of Light, forerunner of today's
CARE organization. It was in their blood to pioneer
in needy areas. Their vision and fellowship had been
of the utmost value in the early years of MAF. I don't
know what we'd have done without them.

I had asked Tom Frank to replace Steve as Home
Director. Then at the end of 1973 Phyllis and I also
moved back to England. Our planned twelve months'
return to Kenya had by then stretched to eight and a
half years! It was time to reinforce the UK base of
MAF again. Our overseas operations depended on supplies and support from home, just as any army overseas relies on its home country to provide for its
needs.

There were other reasons for our return. Our eldest
child, Becky, was already married and living in
Canada. But John needed to get into a job or further
study in England and it would be good for Priscilla,
who had just finished primary education in Kenya,
to complete her schooling at home. Every missionary

family has to face decisions about its children's education and location and find God's will.

Phyllis had acted as General Treasurer for MAF for nearly twenty years. For some time she'd felt that the growing size and complexity of the work called for a chartered accountant. Ken Taylor, who had been with us for a year in Nairobi, also returned to the UK and took responsibility for supervising and developing our financial systems. Phyllis continued for some years more as Accounts Administrator. Mr Adams, after twenty years of dedicated voluntary service to MAF, retired. We missed his godly presence.

The MAF offices were eventually moved out of London and our headquarters established at Folkestone in Kent where housing and offices were cheaper. From there, as General Director, I made constant visits to Africa to maintain my close links with the work.

"The work of missions is surely done now. Missionaries aren't needed any more, are they?"

"Aren't people like Bishop Yohanna Madinda from Tanzania and Bishop Festo Kivengere from Uganda coming to this country to challenge us? Aren't there the Luis Palaus from South America? What about people like Yonggi Cho from Korea?"

"Isn't the Church overseas growing more rapidly than it is at home? Isn't there a greater need here than out in Africa?"

"Who are we to send people to Africa anyway – look at the poor moral state of our nation and even our Church!"

Such sentiments were frequently voiced during the 1970s and early '80s. Interest in mission waned,

giving was drastically reduced, some of it moving
away from missions to other Christian relief agencies.

Giving to MAF declined just as our work and opportunities were increasing. There were other financial
strains. In five years the pound dropped to half its
previous value. Most of our aircraft, spares and other
aviation equipment came from the US. Fuel also was
priced in dollars. As a result our costs rose tremendously. Our services to churches and missions overseas had already been heavily subsidized: now we had
to provide bigger subsidies than ever to enable them
to use the planes.

Political turmoil, hostility and rapid change in
Africa increased our difficulties. Three out of the five
countries where we were flying saw serious coups,
disturbances, restrictions and costly evacuations.
Some underwent several changes of government. One
political event after another tumbled across our television screen, disrupting our work, bringing loss of
income and heavy additional expenses.

We'd had to leave the Sudan twice. The coup in
Ethiopia had severely restricted our flying. Planes sitting idle were expensive: heavy overhead costs continued while fare revenues dwindled to a trickle.
Restrictions and closure in Chad aggravated the situation, so did a severe fuel shortage in East Africa. The
new Tanzania programme brought additional
demands and expenses. Our bills were frightening.
For a period I had to ask that all orders for spares
from our programmes came through me so that I
could check them personally.

In the years that followed, the financial situation
fluctuated. For the most part we were forced to fly

very low and long and to cope with the resultant stresses. At one stage I had to ask that departmental budgets be cut by forty per cent. At another we went to "zero budgeting": departments had to justify minutely every item of expenditure. "Contingency Plans" and "Worse Case Scenarios" became realities. We came within a few weeks of being bankrupt. But we still believed God would work out His purposes.

Some changes were particularly painful. Peter Empson, one of our experienced pilots, had flown extensively in Ethiopia and had been a programme manager there. After Cecil Davis left he'd supervised all our operational programmes for me for three years. Then he'd come to England to start a training course, teaching pilots the specialized skills they would need for flying with MAF in Africa. Financial stringency obliged us to give up the course and Peter had to leave. It was sad to see him and his family go.

While all our managers had to live with the results and restrictions of this period, as chief executive I obviously took the brunt of the pressures. Leadership is lonely.

Hudson Taylor, pioneer of the China Inland Mission, and George Muller, the man of faith who founded the Muller Orphanges in Bristol, had never publicized their needs. They looked to God alone to move Christians to meet them. In MAF's early days we had been greatly inspired by their stories and reluctant to mention financial requirements to others. And God had supplied our need too.

But the situation had changed. People weren't giving. We spent much time agonizing and praying about what we should do. Should we only pray?

Should we tell our supporters more about our difficult situation? Or would that indicate lack of faith?

At this time a Christian organization I knew sent me information about their own serious financial position. I responded with a gift, then realized that I wouldn't have done so unless they had told me. Why shouldn't we do that in MAF? The way God had blessed us in the past might not be His way for the future. God was not limited to one way or another.

Over the years there had been other objections to making our needs known:

"We mustn't fish in other people's pools, we mustn't rob other missions."

"There is only one cake. We mustn't take more than our fair slice of it."

"MAF mustn't take advantage of the glamour of flying to attract giving away from traditional missions."

It was important that we should not compete, since our very purpose was to serve and help other missions. But our "low profile" approach was preventing us from doing just that. "MAF is the best kept Christian secret in the UK," someone claimed.

"We've got to go high-profile," said our board members. We realized that any publicity given to mission work helps all missions. We had always tried to stimulate general mission interest. So we started to give more information not only about our opportunities but also about the funds required to meet them.

MAF is a complex and unique organization: a mix of professional aviation and Christian mission. It needs a board aware of mission principles and practice, able

to promote the strict disciplines essential to aviation,
possessing the financial acumen of business, understanding difficult overseas situations and, above all,
strong in Christian faith.

Our board included chartered accountants like Herbert Adams and Ken Taylor. Peter Clarke, a solicitor,
put in a tremendous amount of legal work for us,
playing a vital role in this and in other ways for
many years. He visited the work in Africa with me a
number of times, as did other board members. Some
members, like Mr Adams, were church leaders.

From the start our experienced senior managers
were key members of the board, bringing to it essential information on the overseas work, national
churches, missions, management, field and flying
operations. Our legal constitution also required me,
as chief executive, to act as chairman.

More recently Charity Commission rules have
excluded full-time staff from membership of boards
of Registered Charities. (Such members are considered to have too much of a vested interest.) Even
though our senior managers can no longer vote at the
meetings, they can still attend and contribute their
experience and knowledge.

I sought to bring everything of importance to the
board who constitutionally had the ultimate decision
in policy matters. No major decisions were made
without its approval. At this time our financial situation came under especially careful scrutiny at every
meeting. But however desperate it appeared, as a
board we never said, "Should we continue?" We
asked rather, "How do we continue?"

Because the financial situation made it so difficult
to plan, we issued a special "Statement of Intent" at

the end of 1976. It would have been hard to continue without it:

> God has called MAF into being in the first place. God is continuing to bless and use the work overseas. If we lose faith and draw back we will fall short of His call. We must monitor the financial situation closely, prayerfully seeking God to guide us. We believe MAF will become more, not less, effective than in the past.

The statement went on to set out a wide-ranging series of overseas objectives, including those in which we were already involved.

We went ahead with renewed confidence.

PART V

HOPE HAS WINGS

(1980–1993)

29

Samaritans and Lions

Briefcase in hand, I pushed through the large glass rotating doors and walked into the foyer of the Charing Cross Hotel. It was one of the classic central London hotels: deep carpets, ornate furnishings and graceful chandeliers. This was December 1980, four years after we had issued our Statement of Intent. We were still flying low financially.

A slight, dark-haired man in a grey suit greeted me with a pleasant Scots accent.

"Stuart King? I'm David Cormack."

It was my first meeting with Dr Cormack. Ron Collard, our full-time MAF representative in the UK, who knew I was looking for a good Christian management adviser, had met David at one of his meetings and found him interested in MAF. He also discovered he was in charge of training and organization development at the headquarters of Shell International in London.

We moved through into one of the lounges, settled in a quiet corner and David ordered tea. But we hadn't met for a pleasant tête-à-tête. I had burdens I wanted to share. David was soon asking me about the background of MAF, my hopes and visions for it and what problems we were facing. It took several hours to give him an overview of our organization. I explained something of the pressures and tensions of this par-

ticularly difficult period. I wondered whether I was
the man for the job any longer. Perhaps someone
more capable should take over as chief executive? I
was interested in his opinion – it could be more objective than mine. What did David think from his own
experience?

"Do you feel your work with MAF is finished,
Stuart?"

I looked at him with surprise. There was much I
still wanted to see achieved.

"No, there's so much more I'd like to see done," I
answered.

"Then you should stay and see it done. Let's work
on a plan to see how the necessary goals can be
accomplished."

Within a couple of weeks he was in our Folkestone
headquarters. Through the next year he gave time
and advice without stint. Some things that worked
for Shell International wouldn't work for us, but
many of the basic principles would. Our management
structure was improved. We redefined goals for each
department of MAF: field operations, finance, administration, public relations, recruiting and training. A
recovery plan was made to keep running expenses to
a minimum and at the same time generate new support and income. Weeks were spent in working out,
budgeting and applying the plan.

For ten years we'd been seeking to improve our
management skills. I had attended excellent seminars
in Nairobi. We had used management consultants in
our work there. We fully realized that developing
these skills was no substitute for the work of God's
Spirit in our hearts, but we recognized that they could
be God-given tools. We had experience in flying and

maintaining aircraft and a good understanding of mission pioneering and of the growth of the Church overseas. But we had still lacked sufficient management experience to handle what MAF had now become. It was because of this that I was grateful to God for David Cormack.

"How can you plan ten years ahead?" people asked.

But that's just what we did. We carefully worked out what we believed should happen over the next decade: right into the early 1990s. With David's help this was translated into a long-term Strategic Plan.

I'd done a great deal of research into the future needs of the churches and missions we served overseas, visiting our different fields to collect data. It had been a challenging and revealing exercise. MAF was wanted. Its services needed to increase to meet the demands. We looked at trends and opportunities worldwide; we considered the position of supporting churches in the homelands.

The Strategic Plan was drawn up in faith and much prayer. The first years could obviously be worked out in much greater detail than the later ones. Nevertheless, we envisaged increasing impetus throughout, based on our belief that God wanted us to respond to the many opportunities before us.

How were we to get to the point where we could do this? We looked first at our current position. We were in touch with ten thousand people who prayed for us regularly, many of whom were able to contribute to our support as well. But it was amazing how many churches, how many Christians in the UK, still knew nothing about MAF. One thing we needed to do was to improve our publicity and increase the circle of those concerned and involved. We particularly wanted support from people not already committed to other missions. We wanted to see interest in overseas missions and churches increased, not just reshuffled.

We also looked to stronger links with other European countries, a few of which had already set up MAF groups.

"A man was going down from Jerusalem to Jericho, when he fell into the hands of robbers . . . but a Samaritan, as he travelled, came where the man was . . . took pity on him . . . bandaged his wounds . . . brought him to an inn and took care of him."

The future position we believed God wanted for MAF we named "The Good Samaritan Scenario". Like the Good Samaritan, we longed to be able to respond effectively to those in need.

Wishful thinking? A futile vision? No. MAF had been founded on the call of God and the belief that He was able to supply our needs. The call and the belief were as valid as ever. We believed God intended that within ten years we should have adequate staff and finances to carry on our task. The Strategic Plan set us clear aims and priorities. We knew which way we had to go, which things were important.

I met with our MAF managers regularly at headquarters to clarify our goals and try to ensure that we were keeping to the plan God had given us. We defined the key activities of each department, listed the expected results and decided how we would assess their achievements. We monitored progress, seeking to avert diversion from the main aims.

The task of making MAF known in the UK had been energetically carried out by Steve Stevens as part of his work as Home Director. Five years after Tom Frank had taken over that role, Ron Collard came in to be responsible full-time for key church meetings, visiting schools and encouraging local MAF representatives. He also fostered the growth of many prayer groups. But he still had to refuse many invitations.

Eventually we were able to appoint several full-time regional managers under Ron. By then the different MAF groups around the world were serving nearly four hundred mission and relief agencies. This enabled representatives to present a panoramic view of God's work: a view to stir the imagination, encourage faith and commitment.

Publicity was improved, better filmstrips and films, and later high quality videos, were produced. Our existing supporters played an active part in bringing in others: the circle of those seriously interested was increased by twenty per cent. The work of every department was geared towards the Good Samaritan Scenario.

Recovery was slow at first – we had expected that. But even during this early period there were gaps in the clouds through which the sun shone brightly. Some supporters responded continuously and tremendously to our needs. One man wrote to say that he believed God wanted him to give a large part of his savings to MAF. But for his gift we would not have been able to keep going that particular year. Surely a Good Samaritan.

The Royal Air Force Chaplains' Department, which designated its church collections to some Christian organization each year, chose MAF. Its target was to buy us a Cessna. By the end of the year it had raised more than enough to buy our first Cessna 210. This newer type was similar in size to the 206, but its cleaner design and a retractable undercarriage made it faster and cheaper to fly. Money left over from the purchase of the 210 went towards yet another aircraft. People, too, continued to come from the RAF, and from other Air Forces as well.

Trusts and funding agencies helped with capital items such as hangars, aeroplanes and housing. Some of the missions who used us were generous donors too.

"How many aeroplanes could you use for your work in Africa?"

The question came from an aristocratic Swedish gentleman, Ture Nydren. He was sitting in my office with an equally dignified compatriot, Lars Braw. They had arrived at short notice on a Saturday when our headquarters were normally closed. A phone call had told me simply that they were from Lions International and wished to talk about getting us aircraft.

I didn't know what to think. What did they want to propose? What restrictions would be attached to any gift they might make. What was their motive? What was it all about? I called in two MAF managers who were available at the time, together with one of our board members who lived locally to help assess the situation.

Ture Nydren told us that he was chairman of Lions

International Air Relief in Sweden; Lars Braw was founder of the von Rosen Foundation.

"For a number of years we have been supporting the humanitarian work of the Swedish Count Carl Gustaf von Rosen in Ethiopia." Ture explained. "We have supplied him with aircraft for relief operations. He is now dead, but we want to continue to help in a similar way."

"What do you know about our work?" I asked.

"We learned of it while assisting in Ethiopia. We know that you help people at grass-roots level. We'd like to try and get some aircraft for you."

I thanked them, but asked if they knew we weren't just a philanthropic organization, but a Christian one, albeit involved in medical, humanitarian and development work as part of our call to serve God and show His love to those in need.

Yes, they were aware of this.

"Would there be strings attached?" I asked them. "Would you want the planes located in specific places or just serving Swedish missionaries or flown only by Swedish pilots?"

"No, there would be no such conditions," was the reply.

Ture came back to his point: "How many aeroplanes could you use at present?"

Rarely before had we been approached by a donor agency asking what it could give. Normally we'd had to take the initiative in approaching trusts and foundations. They'd naturally required that we substantiate in great detail what we were doing and why we wanted support. This was so different. There must surely be a catch. But it was good to meet such an eagerness to help us.

I mentally ran over our different field situations and their great opportunities.

"We could use six aircraft," I said.

I think I surprised myself when I realized what I'd asked. But it was true. It would take six aircraft to meet our immediate needs.

"All right," said Ture. "We'll see what we can do about getting them for you."

There was no catch. Our Swedish friends were genuine. I must admit, though, I was still uncertain what would come of it. But even one plane would help.

Four years later I visited Sweden for the dedication of the fourth plane we'd received. Ture and Lars had worked hard, travelling, speaking and writing to arouse interest and funding. At first the response had been small.

"After two years I was ready to give up," confessed Ture, "but my wife urged me on and typed all the correspondence."

Through Swedish Rotary, a Cessna 206 was purchased for use in a tuberculosis eradication programme among the Somalis in northern Kenya. The popular Swedish family magazine *Hemmets-Journal* raised funds for another plane for Tanzania.

All the promised six aircraft came. In fact, eventually seven, for another one has just arrived in Tanzania as I write. The Lions and the von Rosen Foundation were Good Samaritans too.

Our board and finance committee were joined by a prominent Christian businessman, Bill Cross. His background suited our needs: he was an ex-Navy pilot, a chartered accountant and had worked in government service in Dar es Salaam in Tanzania.

He'd followed the progress of MAF for many years. As an experienced businessman who'd been director and then chairman of an international company, he was well aware of the disciplines and pressures of finance.

Bill helped us tremendously. He kept us in line, asked the awkward questions, insisted we made the difficult decisions, yet at the same time he encouraged us. For he had a heart for the aims of MAF. As with our other board members, I was grateful to God for him. He became Chairman of our board for the next eight years.

When the terrible famines in Ethiopia hit the headlines and television screens in 1982, the concern of the Christian public for Africa revived. When we were twice involved in famine relief the response from our supporters was almost overwhelming. Our accounts and secretarial staff could hardly keep up with the inflow of desperately needed funds and we praised God we could begin to fulfil the tasks He'd given us.

By 1985 our finances were showing a very strong upturn. In His own time God had lifted the clouds and we'd learned further lessons of trust and gratitude.

Meanwhile we had been strengthening our links with the rest of Europe and I was visiting different countries there. Other MAF managers from our Folkestone headquarters were also making contacts. A MAF Council had been formed in Finland in 1976, the first on the Continent. Two years later the MAF Holland board was constituted. By 1982 pilots, engineers and avionics experts were beginning to come from a

rapidly increasing number of Continental European
countries.

"Shouldn't we have a conference of the European
MAF groups?" asked KLM Airline Captain Hans
Rijke, President of MAF Holland.

I appreciated his initiative. I'd often wondered
about something like this, but hadn't wanted to push
for anything other European groups didn't really
desire.

From 1982 on, European MAF conferences were
held annually and a European coordinating committee was formed to explore ways we could all work
together more closely.

Meanwhile we were also having increasing contacts with Canada. The MAF group there had helped
us pay for the Sudan hangar and the Becks had been
with us for years. Other Canadian pilots and
resources had been linked with MAF USA. At this
stage, however, MAF USA didn't need pilots from
Canada and the Canadians asked if we had vacancies.
We had.

We altered our constitution so that the newer European groups and Canada could join our MAF UK
board and become more closely involved in directing
the work. Which they did.

Four years later we all became part of a new MAF
board. MAF Europe was born.

We had moved to a much more effectual, well-
supported position. God's grace had led us into the
Good Samaritan Scenario.

30

More Than We Imagined

"Mark, we need someone to develop village airstrips in Tanzania. You have the experience. Would you be willing to do it?"

Mark Knight, one of our pilots, had been making landing strips and helping the AIM among the Turkana in Kenya's Northern Frontier District. I knew he worked well with national church leaders and was deeply concerned to get into needy areas. If he could encourage Tanzanians, in even a few villages, to start clearing airstrips, others would probably follow their example and the idea could snowball.

Things were difficult financially. This was 1977, four years before our Good Samaritan Scenario had been developed, let alone become a reality. But the work in Tanzania had grown. After the closure of Ethiopia, the Finnish family, the Kurkolas, had started to establish a more permanent base at Dodoma. Within two years we had five pilots and an engineer in the country.

Bishop Madinda had caught the vision of village airstrips. Mark spent much time with national leaders visiting villages to find landing areas. Local people proved enthusiastic and very willing to clear the ground. Other churches and missions had become interested when they saw how planes could help church growth.

We soon realized that in a territory as large as
Tanzania, one major base was not enough. Sub-bases
were needed to reach such a widespread population.

The Kurkolas moved on again to open our first sub-
base at Moshi in 1979 and over the next three years
another three were established at strategic points
around the country. They included one with the
German Brethren in the extreme south who had now
become enthusiastic about using the plane for village
outreach. It proved very effective for them.

More and more ways were found of using our
services. Soon after arriving in Moshi the Kurkolas
were called upon to provide regular flights taking
Bible teachers to the Sukumas around Lake Victoria.
These teachers trained local evangelists to spread the
gospel in neighbouring villages, which they did with
such success that within a few months three thousand had become Christians and fifty-six new
churches had been established. Later follow-up
showed that almost all remained committed.

Another call for MAF's help came from a German
anaesthetist, Georg Kamm. He had learned of a secret
formula developed by the US Space Agency for con-
verting impure water to a pure intravenous fluid. He
wrote direct to the President and obtained permissin
to use it. Hospitals in Tanzania, as in many African
countries, could not afford the vital but costly intravenous fluids imported from Europe. Georg adapted
this technique to produce units which could trans-
form water even from dirty African boreholes into
pure intravenous infusions at only five per cent of
the imported cost.

There was one snag: Georg's units were shattered
by rough road journeys. He called in MAF. We trans-

ported the delicate apparatus safely by air and helped
to install it in distant bush hospitals. Altogether fifty
units were installed and treatment for patients
throughout Tanzania was transformed. It was an
unusual and important contribution by MAF to the
medical needs of the country. Other countries took
up the idea.

We were able to help in Tanzania in other ways
too. Medical staff, flown in our planes, developed
mobile clinics in a country too short of funds and
medical personnel to provide anything like enough
permanent fixed clinics. Thousands with no other
hope of treatment were helped in this way. Similarly
eye diseases, so prevalent in that dusty atmosphere,
were tackled by MAF "eye safaris" carrying ophthal-
mic surgeons.

The Tanganyika Christian Refugee Service administrators also relied on MAF to speed them over long
distances to areas of urgent need. Finally, major
church leaders were enabled, for the first time, to
coordinate and encourage the work of believers scattered throughout the country.

Bishop Madinda saw with delight real spiritual
revival among the semi-nomadic Masai. They presented him with the "Ebony Stick", which entitled
him to authority and a hearing throughout the tribe.
Asked how he would use it he replied simply, "What
else have I to tell them about but the love and sal-
vation of Jesus?"

At one stage the very speed of growth brought its
own problems. Staff were overloaded and over-
strained. Three accidents in a single year put planes
out of action at a time when all our five planes could
barely keep up with demand. Trust in our services

was undermined by our inability to meet all the
needs. Fortunately this proved only a temporary setback.

Eventually a sixth plane was provided, repairs were
completed and activity increased yet again. Swede
Tom Nyquist opened a much needed aircraft radio
servicing workshop at Dodoma. Before long a fifth
sub-base was opened too. Flying in Tanzania went up
a further twenty per cent.

Many of our hopes for Tanzania had now been
realized. There was more effective penetration at village level; Christian workers were more ready to live
in remote places because the plane was available;
MAF was able to maintain a "bird's-eye view" of
what was happening throughout the country and
improve the coordination of Christian work. Perhaps
most significantly of all, as in Ethiopia and elsewhere,
the indigenous churches rather than expatriate
missionaries had now become MAF's major "cus-
tomers".

Twenty years before, our three children, Becky, John
and Priscilla, had looked down with fascination as
our Cessna circled over the volcanic rim of a 10000-
foot mountain. It was one of the rare Cessna flights
we were able to do together as a family. We were on
our way from Nairobi to Dodoma. Slight wisps of
smoke came up from the glowing red centre of the
crater. The dark sides of the mountain fell away
sharply to the Masai "steppe" below. The people
living on those dusty scrubland plains called the
mountain Ol Doinyo Lengai, Mountain of God.

Now, in 1985, another MAF Cessna flew over Ol
Doinyo Lengai. Its two passengers were Masai elders,

one of them a wizened chief called Kuraru. He peered intently through the plane's window, his deep-set eyes scanning every detail of the mountain from this unusual viewpoint.

The month before, the pilot, Peter Empson, now back in MAF, had been sitting in the dusty sand of the Masai village of Monik talking to the people crowded around. Further back were herds of lean cattle and goats. Bush flies were everywhere. Twenty miles away to the south rose the sombre outline of Ol Doinyo Lengai.

Peter had landed at Monik with Pastor Lemashon, himself a Masai. But outsiders were not welcome to these independent semi-nomadic people.

Kuraru had pointed to the distant volcano, "Our god Khambageu lives on the top of that mountain. He is angry with the plane's coming. He will cause it to crash."

An idea suddenly struck Peter. "Would any of you like to fly over the mountain with me?"

No one moved. The offer of a car trip would probably have been refused, let alone a flight in a plane.

But the following month Kuraru and another elder agreed to go. Peter went to get the plane ready, radioed the MAF base at Dodoma and told them: "I'm going now. Pray for us."

"The air is likely to be turbulent around the crater", he thought rather anxiously as the Cessna neared the lip of the crater. "If it is, the chief may say their god is showing his anger by shaking the plane." Praying hard, he gently eased the aircraft over the mountaintop and started to circle it.

Below was the crater, sunlit and calm. Kuraru could see it clearly. That day there was not even a wisp of smoke, let alone a gleam of red, only some blackened vegetation. There was no turbulence.

The plane landed back at Monik. As the people crowded round, the old chief got out and turned to them:

"No god lives there in the mountain. The top looks just like scorched grass."

He told Peter on a later visit: "All I saw was just a mountain, not a goat, cow, sheep or anything else alive there. I knew then that no god lived there. I now believe in your God." He went further: "I was sick and I prayed in the evening that God would make me well. I woke in the night and found myself talking to God and I felt God healing me. We need the teachers and the medical help you bring."

The plane was always welcome at Monik after that. The change in Kuraru made it possible to reach other Masai villages too. More airstrips were made and Tanzanian pastors and evangelists spent weeks patiently sharing the harsh way of life of these nomadic people.

MAF flew a young German nurse into another remote area among the Masai. She lived among them, won their confidence and esteem and has been greatly used by God. Hers is an epic story of its own.

A real hunger for teaching arose as Masai turned to God. With eager smiles they learned Christian songs. It would have been unthinkable before. The hard work to reach them had all been worthwhile.

Throughout Tanzania the Church continued to grow, though there still remained much to do. There was an openness to the gospel. People were healed and freed from the influence of evil spirits.

"It's often just simple faith," one of our pilots said.

"A pastor or evangelist will pray for a sick person and healing comes."

Evangelism was a part of every day church life. People didn't need urging to witness to their faith: it just came naturally.

The churches were also deeply involved with the community projects. They saw them as a practical way of sharing God's love. They helped in water schemes, farm improvement plans, schools, clinics and hospitals. MAF was a partner with them, flying them to places of need and opportunity. The plane attracted people. They took special notice of the witness of those it brought: "People who come by plane," they reasoned, "must have a real concern for us."

When Jack Hemmings and I had made our slow dispirited way back to Nairobi across those dusty plains of Tanzania after the Gemini crash we could not have foreseen such a future. When, as a family, we'd flown over Ol Doinyo Lengai, I had no inkling of how God was going to use MAF there. Even when we had first resurveyed Tanzania in 1976 and our initial staff had arrived, we still hadn't realized the full potential. He "is able to do immeasurably more than all we ask or imagine," says St Paul.

31

Famine

Safe and fed in comfy chair,
Now confronted with despair.

Swollen bodies, pleading eyes,
Fragile limbs and feasting flies.

Tiny wasted children they,
Grieving parents with no say.

Walking slowly, stony roads,
Few possessions, heavy loads.

Dusty, ragged, many ill,
Day time heat, then night time chill.

Unmarked graves, so sad to see,
What if it were you or me?

Could we bear with dignity,
Hunger, sorrow, misery?

Brought about by Mankind's greed,
Lord, please help them in their need.

Can we show them that we care?
How our hearts ache bowed in prayer.

Governments just muddling through,
Needing vision, purpose too.

Needs so great and wants so few.

It's up to me, and you, and you.

Perhaps at home we have to stay,
But help we can, in our own way.

Have we given? Yes, indeed.
May our prayers now back the deed.

Have we given? Give again!
Pray God send the needed rain.

A sensitive MAF supporter wrote that.

We had seen famine in Tanzania and often in Sudan.
One of Don McClure's early contacts with the Anuak
people in the 1950s had been to relieve a desperate
famine around Akobo. We had been similarly
involved in the '70s. Famine, together with war, had
worsened and widened in Sudan in the '80s.

In 1982 a World Vision Twin Otter aircraft crewed
by American and Canadian MAF pilots had been
ceaselessly flying famine relief in Ethiopia. They flew
a BBC team to Korem where they filmed the horrific
pictures of piles of dying babies, rows of fly-covered
corpses in the largest famine camp in Ethiopia.

The BBC film clip lasted only five minutes, but it
shook millions of people out of their complacency all
round the world. Overnight, individuals, international charities and governments began pouring in
money and supplies at an unprecedented rate.

From mid-1984 to early 1985, hundreds of thousands of Ethiopians died of starvation. The United
Nations warned that, throughout Africa, 150 million
were threatened with starvation and diseases if
nothing was done. Five million children would die in
the continent's worst ever drought and famine.

The period saw us incredibly busy assisting famine relief organizations. Over 10000 miles were flown taking administrators from World Vision into remote areas of northern Kenya, close to the Ethiopian and Somalia borders, to enable them to assess needs and check on food distribution. Hundreds of thousands of families were in urgent want.

In July 1985, our MAF News reported: "Some countries in Africa have had no rain for the last fifteen years. Countries which used to export grain are now having to import it. Armed conflict in Ethiopia, Sudan, Somalia, Mozambique, Angola and Chad are making the food crisis greater. Men are leaving their land to fight. Women and children leave farming to become refugees. The farmlands become battle-grounds. Food reserves dwindle to nothing."

The same year a hundred thousand Chadians made a thousand-mile long, weary journey in search of food and water, fleeing across the border into Darfur in the Sudan. Many didn't make it: they died in the desert on the way. Six hundred Chadian children a day were dying in Darfur alone – that was one every three minutes.

Back in November 1980, Dr David Seymour, large as ever, had visited us in Folkestone, asking us to re-establish our air service in Chad as soon as possible.

In spite of the turmoil of fighting between north and south, rebel group against rebel group, his medical and evangelistic work in the bush dispensaries had continued to grow. These centres were now serving over seventy thousand sick people a year. New dispensaries were still under construction and the

Chadian church had already selected men to run them. Our plane was needed to make the project really effective. David was spending too much of his time driving, yet was still unable to get around enough by road.

We were glad to respond. It was impossible to return to the north because of the fighting, but in March 1981, Ernie Addicott and Maurice Houriet went back to survey the south. The authorities there were desperate to see medical services re-established and were unstinting in their welcome. So were the national churches and the missions. The church leaders at Koumra said: "Your return is in answer to our prayers."

Funds came in. Tear Fund helped. A famine relief agency, working in the sub-Sahara regions, promised funds for a Cessna 206. A Dutch inter-Church development organization paid for an initial fuel stock. The southern Chadian authorities granted immediate permission to import the aircraft and reopen MAF airstrips and operations, including a radio network. All was cleared with amazing speed.

By June, the Houriet family were establishing themselves at Bebalem in the south. It was far from easy amid the continuing instability, but we saw the programme restarted two years after our enforced departure.

A year later, the Arnlunds, the first Swedish family to have joined us, arrived in Chad. The roads were in a lamentable state, the whole country set back by the civil unrest and fighting. But the church was alive and eager to evangelise. The missions in the south had all resumed work. Flight requests and enthusiasm were high. The Arnlunds' arrival relieved some of the burden on the Houriets. For a while there was a level of stability in the south.

Power struggles between the northern Muslim groups continued. Then one of these gained the upper hand. President Hissein Habré took over, attacked the south, overthrew its administration and reduced it to chaos. At the same time the north returned to relatively unified government, enabling missions to resume work there.

The new government insisted that MAF re-establish its headquarters at N'djamena, where they could keep an eye on our operations. People who used radio transmitters and flew around in small aeroplanes could be a threat to security. We'd hoped to go back to the capital in due course anyway; this accelerated the process.

In the south, thirty-two dispensaries were still being visited monthly, involving half of MAF's flying. But problems mutiplied. Many different fighting factions sprang up. Armed bands of young Chadians roamed everywhere. Poor rains and poor harvests aggravated the plight of the people.

So it was, that early in 1985, word came to us from Chad: thirty thousand would die of starvation in the Bebalem district if nothing was done. The most vulnerable were the children. Three thousand had already died since the meagre harvest of the previous year.

Four hundred thousand tons of food were urgently needed. One of the Cessnas from the Lions was ready and we immediately flew it to Chad. We started a programme of ferrying food to Bebalem from places further south where it could be grown. Other forms of transport were no longer feasible. Only planes could carry the grain over the dangerous bandit-ridden areas.

At first Maurice Houriet and Kea Arnlund did all the flying. Then we were able to bring in other pilots, using the concept of a Mobile Task Force, consisting mainly of ex-MAF pilots who could give short periods of service in emergencies. Over the following months eighteen pilots and engineers, some with their wives, were at Bebalem involved in the relief programme. Though this put heavy demands on the permanent families looking after them, their help was essential.

A few of the Mobile Task Force pilots were borrowed from our other MAF programmes. American MAF provided several short-term pilots, including those for the larger turbo-prop Cessna Caravan which they loaned to the programme for two months. A MAF USA pilot from the Central Africa Republic to the south also came up several times with his own aircraft.

Oxfam provided £60000 for food. Further large gifts came from Tear Fund and the Dutch inter-Church coordinating organization. Our own MAF supporters gave £86000 to help the desperate Chadian people.

One of the mission houses at Bebalem was converted into a grain store and filled with tons of millet, rice, beans and wheat. Chadians were kept fully occupied preparing sacks for distribution to forty starving villages. A mission doctor supervised the project. Parallel to the food distribution was a vaccination and health education programme designed to help the badly malnourished people.

The distribution of the food was administered by the Chadian Christians and local village pastors.

They ensured that everyone received supplies. Fifty-five thousand were fed. Because MAF was able to fly in grain, people were able to stay in their own villages. There was none of the usual displacement in search of food. Such displacement invariably causes further hardship, deprivation and loss of life.

It wasn't a large operation by international standards, but every ton of grain reached its rightful destination. A visitor to the country commented, "You don't have to ask what the Church is doing in Chad. It's self-evident."

During the famine months our regular flying programme also increased by thirty per cent to meet new opportunities opening up in the north and east of the country. The famine flying added more than 1100 hours on top of that. Again the effort was worth it. Thousands of lives were saved. We heard that only ten adults died during this period.

The concept of going into needy areas, sometimes at short notice, had now become part and parcel of our operations. Fast changing political, economic and environmental situations demanded it. We'd use the idea of the mobile task force to supplement a programme's resources and meet an emergency. The whole of MAF could, perhaps, be classed as a mobile task force. I've sometimes thought that the initials should really stand for "Mobile Action Force". Our work, our planning and our people have to have that mobility.

The famine in Chad was followed by the highest rainfall for thirty years; there were good harvests. At the end of the year I visited again. The church was now growing at the rate of eighteen thousand a year.

I watched a three-hour service as ninety people were baptized in the river Chari at N'djamena. It was wonderful to see the rejoicing over each person.

I realized how much they needed teaching to consolidate their faith, and what a shortage there was of trained pastors and teachers. One mission also told me that they'd had no new male missionaries for ten years. It seemed that the difficulties were more than today's average missionary candidate could face. Whatever that said, it emphasized the importance of MAF's ministry to save time and multiply the effectiveness of the Chadian church leaders and the comparatively few missionaries who were there.

A dozen different fighting factions were still roaming the country. "MAF is our only way to travel — the roads are too dangerous," I was told repeatedly. I met missionaries who'd been ambushed, harassed and robbed. Famine relief and development work needed the plane for communications. Important church work was hindered without it.

Revisiting David Seymour and his wife at Koumra helped me realize, in a personal and startling way, how insecure the country had become. As we talked in their house in the familiar hospital compound, a Land Rover roared up and stopped in a cloud of dust. Camouflaged soldiers bundled out and made for the door. We rapidly put away the maps we'd been studying. The soldiers might accuse us of being involved with one of the other warring groups. Fortunately they'd only come for medicine. David gave it to them.

That was just a tiny glimpse of the unrest. Medical and evangelistic outreach, even by air, was restricted. David now dared visit only five dispensaries. Many had been pillaged, Chadian evangelists and medical

staff robbed. Difficult and dangerous situations could
face pilot, passengers and plane when they landed.
All around were sorrow and suffering, fighting and
killing.

I thought back again to the time when some suggested that the need for air travel would diminish in
Africa, that roads would improve and movement by
car become increasingly easy. The reverse had happened. Chad had gone backwards more than fifty
years. Further south, Zaire had annually lost 1500
miles of the roads that had existed when we surveyed
it in 1948. Less than twenty per cent remained. Many
other countries were in the same plight. What few
roads they had could not be maintained. Political
upheaval and war made surface travel incredibly
dangerous.

In MAF we were privileged to help people who
were prepared to go on working in such grim conditions. Our call was to support them: to give them
wings of help, encouragement and hope.

32

Changes and Challenges

"Without the logistics service from Kenya our medical work would be impossible, we cannot obtain our supplies by any other means."

The doctor who was speaking worked at a large inter-mission medical centre in eastern Zaire, serving five million people. All the medical equipment and medicines they needed, as well as any staff from abroad, came in through Nairobi. Roads from there into Zaire ran the gauntlet of countless armed bands as they crossed war-torn Uganda.

When the emergence of AIM-AIR lessened the need for some of our internal air services in Kenya we were able to give attention to developing the logistics programme from Nairobi, not only into Zaire but into other adjacent countries too.

It was soon in full use. We were carrying many passengers and much freight into Zaire: books and Bibles, drugs and medical supplies, building materials of all sorts (from roofing nails to kitchen sinks) and spare parts for many kinds of vehicles.

All this called for something larger than our single-engined Cessnas. MAF USA lent us an eight-seat Aero-Commander together with an experienced pilot. Though still too small, it provided a vital stopgap.

American MAF had their own well-developed programme throughout Zaire, their bases across the

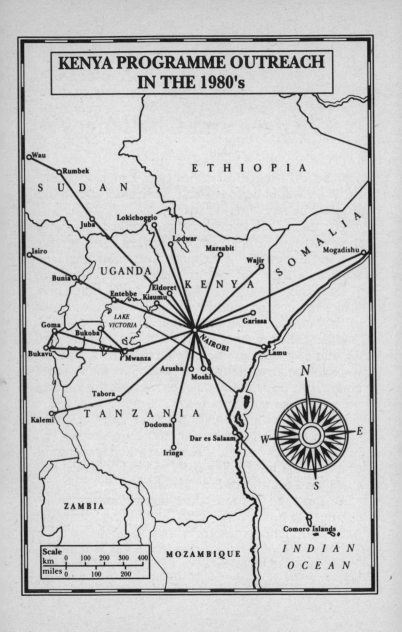

KENYA PROGRAMME OUTREACH IN THE 1980's

border from East Africa serving many outposts. They were being obliged to divert aircraft from their own programmes in Zaire for regular trips to Nairobi to pick up passengers and supplies. So they were keen to be involved in plans for the new supply line. This led our two MAF groups to decide to share in the management of the Kenya programme.

Joint ventures are not easy, even among Christian groups. For the Nairobi operation, not only staff, but costs, equipment and spares had to be shared. Who would control the finance? How would decisions be made? How would the management be appointed? To whom would it be responsible? It all took a lot of working out. Our two boards met and agreed on a plan, with a joint steering committee to oversee the new venture.

Teething troubles were inevitable. But the manager, appointed from MAF USA, came from a business background and our own staff were able to learn much from him. At the same time they shared with him their experience and understanding of national churches and missions.

The Beech 99 turbo-prop aircraft eventually purchased by American MAF for the logistics programme was a miniature airliner: an efficient, sophisticated two-crew commuter plane, tough enough for work in Africa. It could operate from short airstrips carrying fifteen passengers or a ton of freight. It cruised at 220 miles an hour – fifty per cent faster than our single-engined planes: more work could be done each day. Wide loading doors, easily removable seats and an underside pod made it a good cargo carrier. With full instrument-flying facilities and radar, it could maintain a regular schedule rela-

tively unhampered by bad weather which could
hinder our smaller planes. It fully met the need
of the logistics operations for capacity, range and
speed.

Peter de Bourcier came to Nairobi to set up the
flying operations for the Beech. He was the epitome
of an RAF Transport Command squadron leader, tall,
precise and always impeccably dressed, one of the
continuing number of our staff with Air Force background.

He brought the experience and professionalism
vital to the introduction of this sophisticated aircraft,
so different from anything MAF had operated before.
American MAF sent turbine-experienced engineers to
ensure the mechanical maintenance of the aircraft
was of a similar high standard.

At that time the Beech was supported by two fast,
single-engine Cessna 210s, much smaller, but ideal
for long-range flights when fewer passengers needed
to be carried. AIM-AIR planes helped in the link to
Zaire too.

Max Gove had now acquired twelve years' experience
and he'd held responsible positions first in Ethiopia
and later in Kenya. After the Joint Venture had been
running for a couple of years he and his family
returned to the UK where he took over as Director of
Overseas Operations at our Folkestone headquarters.

Max worked well with his MAF USA counterpart.
After four years of the Kenya Joint Venture, the two
of them proposed that it should revert to the total
management of MAF UK. They felt the cooperation
had served its purpose in establishing a new service

which neither of our groups could have achieved so well alone.

Their proposal came before our two boards, was thoroughly discussed and then accepted. MAF Europe later purchased the Beech from the Americans. The logistics programme grew, bringing Christian workers, health care and relief to the countries around. We had been given a new resource to meet a growing need.

Others in MAF were finding new ways of meeting new challenges and opportunities. From the earliest days we had been dedicated primarily to providing flights which helped others in their endeavours to spread the knowledge of God's love. That, however, had never prevented our staff – without any reduction of or distraction from their central MAF work – from seizing any opportunities to share the good news themselves. Some examples, among many, stand out in my mind.

It's sunset in the African bush. Scrub, thornbushes and trees have merged into the night. Crickets chirrup, bats swoop through the still, warm air. The local village has gathered: old and young, men and women, mothers and children. Before them two bamboo uprights support a large white cloth tied somewhat precariously with strings. It's a cinema screen.

To show a full-length sound colour movie at a remote village in Africa is quite a struggle. Everything has to be flown in: projector and film, large speakers for the sound and a heavy petrol-driven generator to supply the electricity. Is it worth the hassle?

The MAF pilot, having carefully brushed all the travel dust out of the precision machinery and set it

going, monitors it closely. To the African audience
the projector matters little. What holds them is the
film it projects. They've never seen a film before.
Many have never known the story this one tells. They
watch with rapt attention.

The "Jesus" film has been brought to this remote
spot so that people familiar with the powers of darkness can learn of the God of love and light. It follows
accurately the Gospel of Luke. Five years of research
and filming in Israel went into its making by the
Agape organization. Scenes come vividly to life,
much in them familiar to this audience: shepherds,
sheep and goats.

The languages of the film versions used by our
people in East Africa are Swahili and Masai. Words
and pictures bring a clear understanding of who Jesus
Christ is. Many realize, for the first time, the meaning of the crucifixion: that He died to take the punish-
ment of their own wrongdoing; to free them from the
power of evil; to bring them into the family of God.

Christians find their faith informed and strengthened, their desire to witness to their friends and neigh-
bours increased. MAF staff gladly take it to distant
places by plane or by Land Rover, seizing any chances
to show it. To them it's well worth the hassle.

John Halls, a building worker, had been a drunk. He'd
contemplated suicide at the age of nineteen. Then a
Gideon Bible led him, in the words of the flyleaf, to
"a knowledge of Jesus Christ, hope for the future,
peace of mind and an assurance of eternal life." He
eventually became one of the specialist builders we
had brought in to help MAF and the missions with
construction work in Tanzania.

Remembering what the Bible had meant to him, he used his spare time, together with two Christian Tanzanian members of our engineering staff in Dodoma, to make Bibles and Scripture portions available to people in the surrounding villages. He bought them from the local branch of the Bible Society and sold them at prices the people could afford. At first he subsidized the sales himself, later some UK supporters shared in this.

Fifty thousand Bibles were distributed in two years. Pastors living in outlying villages could seldom otherwise have afforded a Bible or Christian literature. Some received them with tears of joy. Now they had the means to learn and teach much more about their faith. People came in to buy from all around. Many went away singing, the new Bibles on their heads. John had responded to the challenge he'd seen.

Marcos Habtetsion was an Eritrean Christian pilot; he came to us in Nairobi three years after Peter de Bourcier. Marcos had served with distinction in the Ethiopian Air Force for eleven years. When the Communists came to power he was imprisoned; he was never told why. It was probably because of two things: his nationality – the Ethiopian Government was at war with Eritrea – and the fact that he was a Christian.

Nothing daunted, he had managed to obtain a Bible and share his faith with his fellow prisoners. At this time he became aware that, in his own phrase, "God wanted me to be involved in His work." He and his wife, Zufan, eventually escaped to Germany where they heard about MAF. In Nairobi he played a full part in MAF operations. "I am here to serve," he said.

When not directly occupied in flying, he worked in a church he had established in Nairobi among Tigreans and Eritreans who, like himself, had had to flee their own country.

"We have church for them in the town," he told me on one of my visits. "They come home here too for Bible studies, especially the young people. There are tremendous needs."

Marcos and Zufan made their home a spiritual haven and oasis for many.

Stephen King'ori, an electrical and instrument fitter in the Kenyan Air Force in Nairobi, wandered into a Christian rally in the camp's cinema.

An old man put a question to the crowd: "If Jesus Christ came now and asked for an account of your life, what kind of account would you give?"

The words went home to Stephen. When Christ came back he would be found empty, with nothing to give or to say.

"Tell me what I'm to do, Lord," he asked. Once he determined to follow Jesus Christ he immediately experienced a deep peace and joy. He'd previously been notorious as a hard, rebellious person.

Three weeks later at a large students meeting the expected speaker failed to appear and Stephen was suddenly called upon to preach. He could only get up and say how his life had been changed.

"How many of you would like the peace of mind that I've got?" he asked. So many hands went up that he thought they had misunderstood, so he asked again. The same hands went up. After that God opened many opportunities to him in churches, schools, colleges, in open-air markets and on the streets, to tell people about Jesus Christ.

Later, he joined MAF in Kenya at the beginning of the Joint Venture, and took an increasingly responsible part in aircraft maintenance. But at weekends he and his wife, Irene, travelled long distances to speak at Christian meetings where time and time again large numbers of people committed themselves to follow Christ.

There were many other examples. Pilots, administrators and engineers were taking opportunities to show the Jesus film, distribute Bibles, or both. In one month a Dutch pilot showed the film and sold books in ten different areas to several thousand people: all this in addition to his flying.

Our Tanzanian mechanics, Henry Kambenga and Dickson Chussi, were often out preaching at weekends. A Canadian couple started a MAF evangelistic team in Dodoma, using puppets as a means of communication. Presentations were made in Swahili in schools, the market, the hospital and out in prisons and villages. They proved very effective.

Away in Mali, one of our families loaned to MAF USA was closely involved in sharing God's love with the local people in many ways, including Bible teaching and the provision of greatly needed village wells.

MAF ladies were involved in running clinics, helping in women's work, teaching and other church activities. Some men became elders in local churches. Our pilots were more than just pilots; our engineers more than engineers; our administrators and specialists more than good planners and workers.

Now big changes and new challenges lay ahead for Phyllis and me, too.

"How are you going to cope with stepping out of the chief executive job after all these years?" I was asked.

And, "The change is going to mean a lot of adjustments for you, isn't it?"

By 1985 I'd been in MAF UK for thirty-eight years. For thirty-five of those I'd been – with the help of colleagues – co-ordinating and leading the work.

The idea of handing on leadership was not new to me. I'd have been happy to have done so earlier. Twelve years before, I'd asked Tom Frank to think of taking over. He'd considered it, but eventually felt called elsewhere. But now, as part of our Strategic Plan, I'd devised a succession of target dates to phase myself out. First, "Identify successor for chief executive"; second, six months later, "Work alongside new chief executive-designate"; third, "New chief executive takes over."

Time moved on. The major factors of the Plan worked out almost exactly within the anticipated time frame – except for one thing. The identification of my replacement seemed to be delayed. Together with the board I explored various possibilities without success. Finally I presented a memo to the board, stating simply: "I would like to be replaced, at the latest, in twelve months." They set up a search committee. I wrote to other missions, enquiring if they had any suitable candidates. One or two suggestions came from our field staff. I also contacted Charles Wilson who was retiring as chief executive for ACROSS, the Christian relief agency working in the Sudan.

As a founder member and vice chairman of ACROSS, I had worked closely with Charles. I was

clear that MAF needed a man of deep Christian commitment, able to oversee its increasing management
and financial needs. The world's economic picture
had changed vastly since our early days. Our recent
years of financial crisis had further impressed on me
the need for someone who combined sound business
experience with a deep understanding of mission.

Before coming into mission work, Charles had
extensive business and financial experience. His
work with ACROSS had furthered his knowledge of
Africa and brought him close to the African church
as well as to missions and missionaries of all nationalities. An excellent administrator, he had already
developed much experience of fund raising and was
highly respected among funding agencies. He knew a
lot about development projects in Africa. Where he
worked, things happened.

He was familiar with MAF and the use of aviation
overseas. Our planes had played an important part in
the operations of ACROSS. David Cormack, as an
adviser to the ACROSS board and now vice chairman
of our own MAF board, also knew Charles well. So
did our own senior management, who felt happy
about the possibility of his appointment.

In March 1986 the board's search committee agreed
unanimously that Charles should be offered the job.
He took over from me at the beginning of June.

Everyone warned me that I'd find the change trau-
matic. It wasn't. I was enthusiastic about what was
happening.

Though Charles was only slightly younger than I
was and would be Chief Executive for only a few
years, he had much to give us, much that we needed.
I believed this was the right moment and a God-sent

opportunity. For ourselves, Phyllis and I felt we'd be entering a new phase in our lives.

Max Gove arranged a special party for us. It was more of a celebration than a farewell. Many of those involved at the very beginning of MAF were there, others sent messages, taking us back forty years. They remembered the good things we had done and forgot the failures. We felt overwhelmed, but grateful to God for their love and affection.

We still had involvement with MAF. Charles and others always made us welcome in the office. So did those who succeeded him. Life remained exciting both within MAF and with new challenges outside. God had been good to us in every way.

The organization took a leap forward under Charles's leadership, meeting greater challenges than ever before.

33

The Needs Never End

It was with amazingly light hearts we were able to take a six-month sabbatical after Charles took over. We visited our daughter and family in Canada; saw many relatives and friends in southern California. There were lots of reunions, including a very happy time with American MAF. There was no need for the mini-office that had dogged our steps on every other leave. We were entirely free to visit and spend time seeking God's leading and blessing on the days ahead.

By 1987 I had completed forty years with MAF and it felt good to see God's hand as others carried on the work so ably. What were the future years to hold for MAF Europe? Would its main task be to consolidate and extend the services it was already developing in countries like Tanzania? Would we continue to watch and wait for opportunities to return to countries we had served in the past like the Sudan and Ethiopia? Might we be called upon to enter new areas in Africa, or even beyond?

That very year, 1987, a new MAF programme started in Uganda.

Uganda was once called the "pearl of Africa". When we first knew it, with its well-ordered towns, its quiet villages, neat farmsteads, beautiful trees and banana plantations, it had seemed a delightful land. In those earlier days it had some of the best roads in Africa.

Moreover God had blessed its people with a sustained spiritual revival. It had little need of our services.

Since then what horrors had swept across that beautiful country and its people. Its beauties had been drenched with blood, its tranquillity turned to terror. The pearl of Africa had become a pit of atrocities. Few families were left unscathed during the fifteen years of Amin's dictatorship. One in ten Ugandans, princes and paupers alike, met a violent death at the hands of government agents. The economy was devastated, education deteriorated, medical care suffered and the country was reduced to total chaos.

Not until Yoweri Museveni became president in 1986 did the nation edge back towards recovery and stability. But there was still a long way to go. The previously beautiful roads were ruined. Churches, missions, hospitals and aid projects were isolated. Across the north of the country bandit ambushes were leaving many dead. Vehicles and equipment were being hijacked. Without a plane much of the badly needed relief and development work was impossible.

At this point church leaders in Uganda asked MAF to become partners in the huge task of rehabilitation.

Gad Gasaatura, a Ugandan pilot, had been flying with MAF USA in Zaire. They lent him to us to establish an office in Uganda's capital, Kampala, and he was soon flying from the international airport at Entebbe. The base there became a hub of communications for churches, Christian work and aid projects.

Two years later Gad, already co-pastor in a vibrant Kampala church, also became a member of the Ugandan Parliament and left MAF. But the work continued

to grow, carried on by other MAF pilots, engineers,
administrators and their families.

The flight routes radiating from Entebbe reached
the peripheries of the country and beyond. Thousands
of southern Sudanese refugees, fleeing from the
famine and civil war in their own country, crossed
the border into neighbouring Zaire. They were in a
pitiful condition, dulled by misery and sickness. Our
Uganda-based MAF pilots flew emergency medical
teams and urgently needed vaccines to halt epidemics
amongst them. Housing, water supplies and dispensaries followed. Now they could start growing food for
themselves. Their eyes, instead of showing despair,
shone with hope. We were even able to fly doctors
over the usually closed borders into southwest Sudan
itself to care for those still there.

Within Uganda, pastors and evangelists used
MAF's services to keep in touch with large and otherwise inaccessible areas. Church-based agricultural
programmes were made possible. Desperately needed
AIDS care and control programmes were taken much
further afield than would otherwise have been feasible. Hospitals were reopened, eye-treatment safaris
inaugurated, epidemics checked.

"We would be hard pressed to stay if MAF did
not come," said one community health doctor. "We
would have either to risk our lives trying to make
trips to the capital, or stay without supplies and
achieve very little."

Nowhere, up to now, had MAF been so used in
rehabilitating a whole country as it had in Uganda.

In 1989 Seppo Kurkola attended a mission conference
in his home country of Finland. There he met an

African, Bishop Dumeni, leader of the Evangelical Lutheran Church in Namibia. The bishop was interested to hear of MAF and later wrote to Charles Wilson asking whether he would be prepared to start work in his country. Charles promptly replied that he'd gladly arrange a further survey as soon as possible.

Namibia had been on our minds since the early 1970s and Gordon Marshall, soon after his return to South Africa, had carried out our first survey there. For years the tense struggle for independence had inhibited any service, but at last guerrilla warfare had ended and self-government had come. Forty-two thousand refugee Namibians had returned to their country. In the aftermath of the fighting thousands of displaced people, many of them Christians, needed spiritual and physical assistance. There was both the need for help and the opportunity to give it.

Max Gove and Seppo Kurkola made a fresh survey. They found the country largely desert except in the north where seventy per cent of the people lived. Development had been held back during the many years of fighting. Now, with the area open, new schools, clinics and farming projects were being planned. Their construction and supervision required extensive travel.

Every contact confirmed that this was exactly the right time to start a MAF operation. Though there were commercial air services, they couldn't reach the wide variety of remote places where churches, missions and development agencies wanted to go.

Andy Stratton was a pilot and engineer who'd already had wide experience with MAF in Africa. Early in 1991 he and his wife, Margaret, established

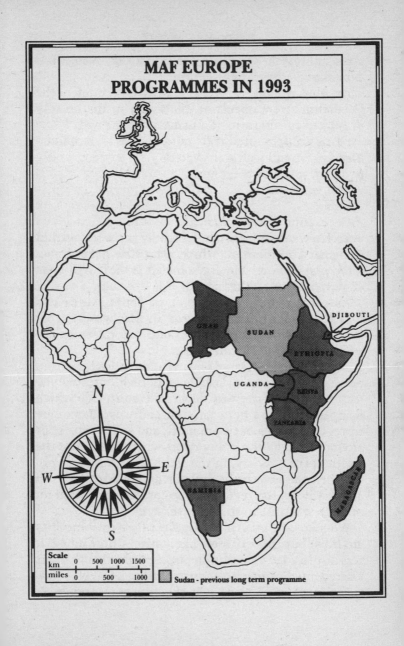

MAF EUROPE
PROGRAMMES IN 1993

N

W   E

S

DJIBOUTI

CHAD   SUDAN   ETHIOPIA

UGANDA   KENYA

TANZANIA

NAMIBIA   MADAGASCAR

Scale
km   0   500   1000   1500
miles   0   500   1000

Sudan - previous long term programme

a programme headquarters at Windhoek, Namibia's capital and government centre.

By the middle of 1991, a Swiss couple, the Diethelms, were operating effectively in the heavily populated northern region using a Cessna 210.

"This couple are real missionaries," remarked Bishop Dumeni's church secretary. "They don't only fly, they speak of their faith."

The work grows.

An operation outside Africa?

So far we'd concentrated entirely on work within the great continent to which we'd first been drawn forty years before. But for some time there had been enquiries from further afield.

As early as 1974 our people in South Africa had told us about the travel needs in Madagascar, that large and beautiful tropical island 300 miles to the southeast, in the Indian Ocean.

Madagascar is an island nearly 1000 miles long from north to south, with a backbone of high, forested plateau running all the way down its eastern side which hampers journeys between east and west. There are travel difficulties between north and south too. They are increased by the many rivers which cut across the width of the country. In the south there are some all-weather routes. But the few northern roads that exist are very poor; the region can be completely cut off for months at a time in the rainy season.

We learned that Air Madagascar flew to some fifty airstrips, but this still left many places unreached. It was also hard to get seats on planes. Christian workers wasted much time and energy in tedious travel.

For more than a decade the rise of Marxism in

Madagascar prevented us from going in to help. By 1988, however, that influence had waned and, with the backing of the churches there, we were permitted to launch an air service.

With characteristic speed, the Houriet family arrived within a few weeks of permission being granted. The aircraft chosen for Madagascar was an Italian Partenavia, particularly suited to the long-distance needs of the country. Its twin engines were calculated to give additional safety over the extremely rugged mountain and river terrain. But, once again, a new venture was to start with disaster.

During the plane's very first flight over the mountainous east coast both engines failed. Maurice crash-landed in a bamboo swamp on a hillside. He was injured, so was one of his missionary passengers, even more seriously. Much worse, the injured missionary's five-year-old daughter was killed. Our subsequent investigation showed there'd been fuel starvation to both engines.

Church leaders in Madagascar, far from being deterred, encouraged Maurice not to give up. The bereaved missionary family faced their loss with great courage, confident that God would still bring good out of this tragedy.

Our supporters were not deterred either. Within a month their gifts enabled a new Partenavia to be purchased. After some weeks Maurice recovered sufficiently to resume the service.

Since then the work in Madagascar has grown, though the potential has still to be fully realized. Church rural outreach, medical work, agricultural schemes and water projects are all candidates for help. Many remote villages, still accessible only on foot, need medical help and the chance to hear and see God's love. We believe that this programme, having started with tragedy, will go on to see the triumph of all its hopes, to the glory of God.

From the time he'd first found his way to our London office, Max Gove had believed God was calling him into MAF. He'd followed that call with enthusiasm and determination. He had now gained twenty years' extensive flying and leadership experience.

In 1991 Max was appointed Chief Executive of MAF Europe. Charles Wilson became Executive Vice Chairman of the board. Max's former post of Director of Overseas Operations went to David Marfleet, our ex-Army Air Corps helicopter pilot, who'd just completed eight years on loan to MAF USA in Indonesia.*

Others who'd worked with MAF for many years had also now been in management positions for some time. God had continued to provide and prepare the next generation to carry on the work He had started. The future wouldn't always be easy, any more than the past had been, but I was sure that the One who had called and led us through all our own time in MAF would just as surely lead them – and enable them to meet the challenges ahead.

> In Xanadu did Kubla Khan
> A stately pleasure-dome decree:
> Where Alph, the sacred river, ran
> Through caverns measureless to man
> Down to a sunless sea.

*See *Wings Like Eagles*, Clive Langmead, Lion Publishing, Oxford, 1991

I had to learn Coleridge's fantasy poem as a schoolboy. Tales of Kubla Khan and the great Mongolian
empire stretching from China to Hungary always fascinated me.

Nowadays Mongolia's mountains and deserts have
few roads and only one railway line to serve their
sparse populations. To get to hospital many still have
to ride horses. It can take a week. A British
missionary, John Gibbens, with his wife, Altaa (one
of the first Mongolian Christians), were requested by
the Mongolian Ministry of Health to get help for the
country's medical needs. John knew that any effective medical programme would need aircraft. He contacted Charles and Max.

To fly out to Mongolia was one of Max's first challenges as Chief Executive. Seppo and David Cormack
went with him to Ulan Bator to meet John and visit
officials of the Ministry of Health and Civil Aviation.
They also wanted to see something of the country
itself.

It was clear that if MAF established a service there,
other missions and organizations planning to come
would be encouraged, knowing there would be air
transport for their needs. The Mongolian Government and the Ministries of Industry, Mining and Agriculture were also potential users. The Minister of
Health said he hoped MAF could come into the
country and support his work. MAF plans to do just
that.

The Madagascar programme had been our first step
outside Africa. The Mongolian venture would take
us 6000 miles away. MAF Europe's new strategic plan
had already envisaged such possibilities.

All over the world the different MAF groups have reached the remotest places. They've given wings to those who bring help and hope. But let's ask again: what happens when missions and MAF leave? When there's war or repression? When pain and persecution strike? When help cannot come?

What will happen to those whose lives have been transformed? To those given new hope by God? Will they survive? Will what's been done be worthwhile? Will anything be left?

That's what my next and final chapter is all about.

34

Hope Has Wings

It was mid-January 1993. I was at Lydd airfield in Kent on a wet and windy day. I'd joined our MAF headquarters staff for the dedication of our latest plane. Jack Hemmings, still a keen pilot, had come over from his home nearby to view it too. It was good to see him again. The aircraft was a turbine-engined de Havilland Beaver – ready to be flown by a ferry pilot to Ethiopia.

Ethiopia? Yes, MAF was going back to Ethiopia. Conditions there had begun to change. The world-wide backlash against Communism, the demands for democracy and the unwinnable civil war with Eritrea had all forced the Mengistu regime to declare that the country was no longer Marxist. By 1991 freedom of religion was proclaimed. A few months later the Ethiopian People's Revolutionary Democratic Front took control. Mengistu fled. Churches and missions asked us to return.

At Max Gove's request the Sikkemas, and later the Kurkolas, went back to explore the situation. They were met with a universal welcome from the churches and missions: very different from the mixed reception Bob and Betty Hutchins had faced in Addis Ababa when they first went there in 1960. They brought back encouraging reports. They confirmed beyond question that all the earlier efforts had been worthwhile.

In the highland regions north of Addis Ababa, we'd previously helped the Southern Baptist mission start new work. Along with many other missions, they'd been obliged to leave in 1977. At that time there were only twelve believers in the area. Thirteen years of persecution and problems followed. But during the severe famine of 1984, the mission had been invited to return and help in relief work. They found the number of believers had risen to a hundred. The work was still developing and they looked forward to MAF's help again.

In the southwest, where the American Mission had worked among the Ethiopian Anuak, there were now fifty congregations, with Christians in all the major Anuak villages. Church leaders had grown in knowledge of the scriptures left for them in their own language. One senior Anuak pastor claimed: "There is a great harvest now coming as the Spirit of God moves among the Anuak people." The new freedom of religion enabled some of the missionaries to give them the further Bible and leadership training they hungered for.

In other tribal areas, where the American Mission had also worked with MAF's help, the church had continued to grow in numbers and spiritual depth. Among the Nuers one "small" congregation now numbered over nine hundred. Any group with fewer than two hundred to two hundred and fifty members was counted only as a "beginning church".

And what about the Majang? Harvey Hoekstra's work among them in the remote rain forest had depended greatly on the MAF air service. The church was still small when he was forced to leave. But, as one of his fellow missionaries put it, "This work out in the middle of nowhere grew and took off." Now there were three thousand Majang believers in more than thirty villages throughout the region. The church was full of enthusiasm. It had reached out to another nearby tribe and already there were several hundred new Christians.

"What is happening to these Majang people?" the merchants in the Teppi area had been asking. "They're no longer drinking themselves to death. They no longer kill each other. And when they're sick, they go off into the forest and pray to their God, and when they come out they're no longer sick."

Harvey's fellow missionary summed up: "We are thankful for all MAF did in the past. We are grateful it is now coming back again."

In 1965 we'd supported the Christian Missionary Fellowship when they began their work in remote areas 150 miles northwest of Addis Ababa. They'd also had satellite airstrips for outreach and when they left there were some three thousand Christians. During the troubles that followed, the numbers, far from declining, rose to ten thousand. As elsewhere, church leaders now wanted missionaries to start Bible teaching to strengthen the church further.

Under the Communist regime many church buildings had been closed in places familiar to us all over Ethiopia. There had been much suffering and persecution. Nevertheless, the Christians had continued to meet, sometimes in the bush or forest, sometimes in houses. Thousands of small church groups had been formed. Now church buildings had reopened in

Addis Ababa and throughout the country. At one place in the south when a church opened again, over ten thousand people arrived and the first service lasted four days.

As we planned for re-entry, we saw we'd need a bigger plane for Ethiopia than in the past. It would need to have a turbine engine since fuel supplies were now hard to get for piston-engined planes. When the turbine version of the Beaver was chosen Max wrote to our prayer partners: "It's almost as if the plane had been especially designed for the rugged flying in Ethiopia." Its strong construction meant that it could survive the rough airstrips; its simple design made it cheap to maintain. It could carry ten people or a ton of urgent freight.

The news that MAF was returning to Ethiopia brought an enthusiastic response from our supporters. Planes like the Beaver are not cheap, yet within a few weeks the money to buy it was there. Donors gave with generosity and sacrifice. One sent part of his redundancy payment, another the money set aside for a new carpet. A housewife sent the savings intended to buy a cooker. Many promised to pray for the new work.

I soon learned more about the long-term results of the work in other areas where we'd been – areas where there were still pain and persecution. Some of the information came on the radio. At home on Easter Monday 1992, I turned on the BBC news:

This is *The World at One* . . . At the little town of Akobo, in south Sudan, fifty thousand people are starving to death. They are refugees in the civil war in that country. United Nations planes had been providing food and medical aid to Akobi and the surrounding area. But permission for these flights was withdrawn by the Sudan Government three weeks ago.

Eight thouand Christians at Akobo gathered to pray for help yesterday evening. Their prayers were answered. The government has now agreed that flights can be resumed. The first United Nations plane will go in again tomorrow.

What had brought Akobo, that remote village, to the centre of world news, even for a few moments? Why were fifty thousand people gathered there? Where had those eight thousand Christians come from?

Almost exactly forty-two years had passed since Jack Hemmings and I had first flown through cloud and rain from Malakal to Akobo, to be welcomed by Don McClure and his fellow missionaries. Jack and I, and later the Stevens, had seen the beginnings of the church there: the early river baptisms, the way the American Mission had pioneered amongst the Nuer and Anuak, bringing medical, agricultural, educational and spiritual help. We'd seen how those early missionaries had served, loved, laughed and identified with these remote Nilotic people.

But MAF and missionaries alike had been forced to leave southern Sudan. Apart from the brief years of the Peace Accord, conflict between north and south Sudan had continued without remission ever since. Many of the Anuak, Nuer and other tribes had fled across the border into Ethiopia to escape the fighting.

The Ethiopian Government allowed the United Nations to establish a camp for them at Itang, a tiny

isolated spot in the hot lowland plains of southwestern Ethiopia. By 1990 it had become one of the
world's largest refugee camps. More than two
hundred and sixty thousand who had fled war, starvation and even slavery in Sudan found some sort of
security there. More kept arriving.

Even this situation was soon to be disturbed. In
May 1991, when the Marxist regime in Ethiopia was
overthrown, the new administration decided to expel
Sudanese anti-Khartoum rebels and, along with them,
many innocent refugees at Itang. The already war-
shocked Sudanese, now numbering four hundred
thousand, abandoned their settlement and fled back
into their own still troubled country. Of those who
survived travel through many miles of wet-season
swamp (many didn't), fifty thousand poured into
Akobo.

As the BBC had announced, the United Nations
and also the Red Cross were permitted to give some
help at this point. Tons of food were flown in from
Kenya to the starving populations at Akobo and
Nasir. ACROSS was involved and our own MAF
planes were able to take part.

Tuberculosis, hepatitis, kala-azar and the ever present malaria were rampant. Medical care and feeding
centres were set up together with orphanages for the
many children who had lost their parents in fighting
and famine.

Nigel Reilly was one of our pilots helping the relief
operations. He met Nuer Christians at Akobo whom
he'd known when based in Malakal nine years previously. Though they'd been refugees in Ethiopia and
Sudan, Nigel found that the number of Christians
had grown greatly and their churches now gathered

with large congregations. They took a lead in organiz-
ing the distressed communities, arranging the distribution of relief supplies with care and fairness.

Nasir had been bombed almost to extinction by the
northern government. Only one building in the town
had been left with more than two walls standing. But,
whereas when the missionaries had been expelled
from there the church attendance was less than a
hundred, it had now grown to almost three thousand.
In the wider surrounding area it had expanded to
nearly *ten times* that number. Rather than being
halted, the work of God had accelerated.

Remember the Uduk? Mal and Enid Forsberg, Mary
Beam and Betty Cridland and other early missionaries
had worked painstakingly to translate the Bible for
them and to bring them basic education and modern
medicine. A small church had been established with
its first Uduk pastor. I still recall the original airstrip
we sited among them, at Chali-el-fil, and many subsequent flights in support of the missionaries and
the church. Before the first expulsions we'd flown
in quantitites of the newly printed Uduk scriptures.
There were already hundreds of Christians when the
mission departed and their numbers continued to
grow. Thirty years later there were seventeen thriving
churches.

But Sudan's civil war reached the Uduk in 1987.
Some were killed. Their villages, homes and churches
were burned and pillaged. Together with some
Mabaan and a few Dinka, they fled across the border
to Asosa in Ethiopia.

They arrived there destitute, with only what they
could carry on their backs. But they hastened to

re-establish their life and traditional structures.
Teachers amongst them organized crude classrooms
under grass roofs. They established churches for themselves and the Mabaan. The United Nations found
their camp at Asosa a model of orderliness and gave
the Uduk community the credit.

They were attacked again and their camp looted by
Sudanese militia. Survivors had to flee once more
into the bush. Many escaped southwards through
Ethiopia's western mountains and reached Itang. As
the newest arrivals at the already overloaded camp,
they had to make do with the barest of benefits. But
soon their churches were functioning again. They
baptized more than six hundred new Christians.

When, like the rest of the refugees in Itang, they
had to flee back to Sudan, thirty thousand of them
settled close to Nasir. The country was at its wettest.
They crowded into a small dry area a few feet above
the floods, surrounded by swamps. With scarcely
room to walk between their little grass huts, they
still left a number of empty circles, twenty yards in
diameter. These were "churches": clearings in the
dirt amid the heat and humidity under the open sky.
There were six for the Uduk, one for the Mabaan.
They called them "places of prayer". Yet these
churches were continuing to grow. There were over
a hundred and sixty Uduk attending baptismal classes
with others waiting to join future groups.

They still had over a hundred copies of the scriptures. This in spite of being driven from their homes
three times and walking hundreds of miles. The fact
that any Bibles survived at all testified to the Uduk's
respect and love for them, for each time they fled they

had had to carry their most cherished possessions on their backs, including their children.

Still further south in the Sudan, other churches also were continuing to live through the horrors of civil war. In some regions the situation, sadly, was aggravated by factional fighting within and among different tribes. Yet, even in these circumstances, the churches experienced unprecedented growth. Hundreds of new worship songs were written amid the sorrows; thousands became Christians.

The spectres of famine and war in the Sudan continued and became blacker than ever. The suffering went on. There were reports of tens of thousands still fleeing or being killed and starved, of leaders being eliminated, villages destroyed, tribes and families broken up and forcibly moved in a determined drive to eradicate them.

On 8th September 1992, the BBC World Service referred to the horrors again:

> A complete tribe in Sudan is in danger of extinction. The Uduk became Christians as a result of the teaching of missionaries. But they have been driven from their villages by militia. They now face starvation and extinction.

It was a brief, lonely cry, mentioning only one of the Sudan's many suffering tribes. The Uduk were being forced to move and flee again. Many had died.

A week later our MAF board was meeting in Denmark. David Cormack had now become Chairman. When evening came we left our intensive discussions to join together with the Karlslunde Strand

church for a time of worship, prayer and Bible study.
I had been asked to be the preacher.

As I sat at the front, the young people in the music
group were leading us in the opening worship. Some
of the songs were in Danish, some in English.

Suddenly the young musicians started a song I'd
not heard for many years:

> I have decided to follow Jesus
> No turning back, no turning back.
> The Cross before me, the world behind me,
> No turning back, no turning back.

In a flash my mind went back to that fateful day
when the missionaries had to leave the early Uduk
church at Chali-el-fil. The deep implications of those
same words the Uduk had sung swept over me. I was
almost overcome as I thought of all they had been
through since. They had not wavered in their
decision. Through all the horror, they'd held to their
hope more strongly than ever. They had never turned
back.

I realized again, where men and women have
accepted God's Word, how much their lives have
been changed. A living hope has been given them. A
hope that, even in hostile environments, continues
to grow.

As Jack and I watched the Beaver taxi out on its way
to Africa, we thought of another scene: that January
day in 1948, almost exactly forty-five years previously, when our little Gemini had taken off on our
first long journey for MAF. The buffeting winds and
drenching rain had symbolized the difficulties we
were to face in the months and years ahead. Yet in

spite of the problems, God had established and used the work of MAF.

The Beaver took off and quickly disappeared into the low misty clouds. It was going to a world of continuing and increasing needs; a world in which the Church still faces enormous challenges, but one in which, under God, hope still has wings.

"There must be a beginning of any great matter," said Sir Francis Drake, "but the continuing unto the end, until it be thoroughly finished, yields the true glory." It is God who will see the work of MAF "thoroughly finished", and the true glory belongs to Him.

Milestones

1944   Murray Kendon proposes MAF concept.

1945   MAF office opened in London, UK.

1947   First aircraft dedicated (Miles Gemini)

1948   Gemini survey of Africa.

1949   De Havilland Rapide purchased for Sudan.

1950   Sudan: First MAF regular flight operations commenced.

1953   First flights from Sudan into Ethiopia.

1957   Sudan: Single-engined Cessna 180 aircraft introduced.

1958   Survey of Southwestern Ethiopia.

1959   Kenya: MAF programme started.

1960   Ethiopia: MAF programme started.

1964   Sudan: Expulsion of missions and closure of MAF operations there after fourteen years.

1965   Chad survey.

1966   Chad: MAF programme starts.

1974   Ethiopia: six MAF aircraft now operating.

1975   In Chad: Bitter persecution of the church.

1976   Finnish council of MAF formed.

1977   Tanzania: New MAF Programme started.

       Ethiopia: Marxist government restrictions force closure of MAF's operations. Programme ends after seventeen years.

       Sudan: A respite in the civil war. MAF programme restarted.

1978   MAF Holland formed.

1979   Chad: Fierce fighting and civil war in Chad
       forces MAF to fly its planes out of the
       country after thirteen years.

1981   Chad: Programme reopened.

1982   FFM, later MAF Sweden, formed.

       First European MAF conference. Representa-
       tives from Finland, Holland, Germany,
       Norway, Sweden, Switzerland and UK.

       Tanzania now has six aircraft operating all
       over the vast country from five bases.

1983   Sudan: After seven years of further operations
       (twenty-one years in all in the Sudan) pro-
       gramme is closed due to government restric-
       tions.

1985   Chad Famine.

1986   MAF Norway formed.

1987   Uganda programme starts.

1988   Madagascar programme starts.

1989   MAF Denmark formed.

       MAF EUROPE Board officially constituted
       with representatives from Canada, Holland,
       Sweden, Switzerland and UK.

1990   Finland, Denmark and Norway join MAF
       Europe.

1991   Namibia: MAF service initiated.

       Mongolia surveyed.

1992   Ethiopia: programme restarted.

       MAF France and MAF Germany established.

1993   MAF Europe now operating thirty aircraft and
       has over eighty family units overseas.